A DICTIONARY OF NOVEL

Sunil Kumar Sarker

ATLANTIC
PUBLISHERS & DISTRIBUTORS (P) LTD

Published by
ATLANTIC
PUBLISHERS & DISTRIBUTORS (P) LTD
7/22, Ansari Road, Darya Ganj,
New Delhi-110002
Phones : +91-11-40775252, 23273880, 23275880, 23280451
Fax : +91-11-23285873
Web : www.atlanticbooks.com
E-mail : orders@atlanticbooks.com

Branch Office
5, Nallathambi Street, Wallajah Road,
Chennai-600002
Phones : +91-44-64611085, 32413319
E-mail : chennai@atlanticbooks.com

Printed in India at Nice Printing Press, A-33/3A, Site-IV, Industrial Area, Sahibabad, Ghaziabad, U.P.

For

My sons

Dr. Suman Sarker and Dr. Sutanu Sarker

PREFACE

A Dictionary of Novel comprises 972 terms (entries) which are frequently used in criticisms and discussions about novels. Perhaps the most difficult task of the lexicographer of a special subject (such as novel, poetry, drama, etc.) is selection of terms to be included in his dictionary, for the inclusion of certain terms in it may lead it to be judged by some critics as unwisely too inclusive while exclusion thereof may make it seem to be indiscreetly too exclusive to others. Therefore, to strike a balance, I have decided to be rather moderately inclusive.

Following the lead of Jeremy Hawthorn's *A Glossary of Contemporary Literary Theory*, I have selected and included in this *Dictionary* a good number of critical terms from the following Schools and Approaches (but taking only some of the terms in that book): Anthropology and Cultural Studies, Bakhtin Group, Deconstruction, Discourse Analysis, Electronic Media/Science Fiction, Feminism, Linguistics, Marxism, Modernism and Postmodernism, Narratology, New Criticism, New Historicism and Cultural Materialism, Phenomenology and Geneva School, Postcolonialism, Pragmatics, Prague School/ Prague Linguistic Circle, Psychology and Psychoanalysis, Reader-response Criticism, Russian Formalism, Semiotics and Information Theory, Sexual Politics/Queer Theory, Sociology of Literature, Structuralism and Post-structuralism, and Style and Stylistics.

Before using this *Dictionary*, the following points should be noted:

(i) countries (e.g. England, U.S.A., etc.) to which writers (novelists, poets and playwrights) belong have not been mentioned in this *Dictionary*;

(ii) dates of births and deaths of all the novelists (and sometimes of a few poets, playwrights, critics, etc.)

have been provided in all the entries where their names have been mentioned (ignoring the fault of repetition, in order to facilitate prompt identification of their times of creative works);

(iii) foreign terms/words (e.g. French, German, Russian, etc.) that have already been anglicised have not been italicized;

(iv) terms/entries having cross-references have been asterisked, but terms having cross-references but occurring in quotations have not been asterisked;

(v) when a single entry is to contain two or more identical terms (one of them may be beginning with a capital letter) or similar or closely related term, only the first term of it has been asterisked for cross-references (e.g. *horror novel, horror story or *purple passage, purple patch);

(vi) when a single entry is to contain two or more similar or closely related terms, the terms have been arranged either alphabetically or in the order of their more to less frequent usages;

(vii) all the insertions in quotations, within brackets, are mine;

(viii) diacritical marks have not been used in non-English terms/words;

(ix) the terms 'novel' and 'fiction' in many places have been used in the same sense;

(x) more important, complex or difficult entries have been given relatively more space than those which are not so; and

(xi) entries directly relevant to criticisms of, and discussions about, novels are given relatively more space than those which are tangentially so.

In the preparation of this *Dictionary*, I have frequently sought help especially from the following works (see Bibliography): (i) Abrams, M.H., *A Glossary of Literary Terms*; (ii) Baldick, Chris, *The Concise Oxford Dictionary of*

Literary Terms; (iii) Cuddon, J.A., *The Penguin Dictionary of Literary Terms and Literary Theory*; (iv) Fowler, Roger, *A Dictionary of Modern Critical Terms*; and (v) Hawthorn, Jeremy, *A Glossary of Contemporary Literary Terms*. Besides, I have used the other books, mentioned in the Bibliography, either for clarifying my knowledge of many of the entries or for helping me in explaining them.

My wife, Manju, has very carefully typed the manuscript, like she did earlier ones, sometimes bringing to my notice 'slips of my pen' and other faults in my writing that I had overlooked. So she certainly deserves my loving thanks. Lastly, Dr. K.R. Gupta, Honorary Adviser, Atlantic Publishers and Distributors (P) Ltd., New Delhi, deserves my thanks for promptly and beautifully publishing this *Dictionary*.

It will prove extremely useful to the students and teachers of English literature, particularly fiction, and researchers in this field.

Sunil Kumar Sarker

CONTENTS

A

Abenteuerroman [from German *Abenteuer*, adventure, and *Roman*, novel]. A form of adventure novel or fiction, analogous to the *picaresque novel, which was in moderate vogue in Europe in the 16th, 17th and 18th centuries and was primarily intended for entertainment. Thomas Dekker's (c. 1570-1632) *Old Fortunatus* is an English example.

ab ovo [from Latin *ab*, from, and *ovo*, egg]. The term means 'from the beginning' and alludes to a story that is related from the very beginning events or episodes of it, as opposed to the story that is narrated from the middle of it, which story is said to be **in media res*.

absence. A critical term coined by the French philosopher Jacques Derrida (b. 1930). Derrida distinguished between speech and writing saying that in speech the speaker remains present but in writing the writer remains absent, i.e. in speech there is the *presence of the speaker or the originator of the words while in writing there is the absence of the writer or the originator of words.

absolutism. The doctrine that in literature there are certain values or standards which are fundamental, inviolable, unconditional and perennial. It is opposed to *relativism.

absurd, the [from Latin *ab*, from, and *surdus*, deaf, i.e. deaf to reason]. The absurd is that which is irrational, inharmonious, incongruent, and ridiculous. The notion of the absurd especially pertains to the modern and post-modern human condition, and in this sense it was given currency particularly by the existentialist philosopher Jean-Paul Sartre (1905-80), as is revealed in his novels *Being and Nothingness* and *Nausea*; by Albert Camus (1913-60), as may be found in his novels *The Outsider*, *The Myth of Sisyphus* and *The Fall*; and by Jean Genet (b. 1910), as is revealed in his novels and plays, such as *Our Lady of the Flowers*, *Miracle of the Rose* and *The Balcony*. The absurd refers to the bewildering human condition in a scabrous and abject world sans meaning, value or purpose. The notion of the absurd came into being particularly in the post-World War II inhumane human condition marked by man's sense of alienation, sterility of life, helplessness, hopelessness, purposelessness, mental paralysis, spiritual vacuity, incomprehensibility of life, nihilism and rootlessness, coupled with a free-floating fear of alarming predicaments. In the modern hostile world man, as the propounders of the absurd believed, felt to be an *outré*, exile, to be *de trop*, superfluous. In his *The Myth of Sisyphus*, Camus writes about the absurdity of the modern man: "In a universe that is suddenly deprived of illusions and of light, man feels a stranger. He is an irremediable exile.... This divorce between man and his life, the actor and his setting, truly constitutes the feeling of Absurdity." The absurd is also present in most of the plays of Harold Pinter (b. 1930), Edward Albee (b. 1928) and Arthur Adamov (b. 1908) as well as in the novels of Franz Kafka (1883-1924).

action. The term has two basic meanings: (a) the main series of events that constitute the *plot of a *novel or play; and (b) the essential *story of a novel, play or *short story. Action unfurls the plot and reveals the characters.

actual reader. This term and the other, *implied reader, were invented by Wolfgang Isar as critical terms and were discussed by him in his *The Implied Reader* (1974) and *The Act of Reading: A Theory of Aesthetic Response* (1978). The implied reader is the 'model' reader—"the reader which the text (or the author through the text) suggests that it expects" (Hawthorn, 289). The implied reader "is active as well as passive; the text structures his or her response, but he or she also produces meaning and has the task of 'consistency building' (the expression used by Iser). The 'actual reader', by contrast, receives mental images while reading; but these images are, inevitably perhaps, modified by the experience and knowledge (and thus other images) which the reader brings to the text. The hypothetical implied and actual reader co-exist, are one and the same person responding to a text in different ways and at different levels of consciousness" (Cuddon, 416). See *ideal reader.

aesopic language. As a critical term, it was introduced by Mikhail Saltykov (1826-89) to describe the disguised, misty, confabulatory language that the Russian dissident political writers used to evade censorship. Now it denotes that kind of writing or language which is periphrastic, confabulatory and laden with hints, kennings and allusions, such that no superficial reading of it would reveal its true meaning—that sort of writing or language that pertains to the fables of the Greek fabulist Aesop (6th c. B.C.).

aesthetic distance ['aesthetic' from Greek *aistheta*]. The term—its alternative term is *psychological or psychic distance—refers to the degree or extent of emotional involvement of one who is enjoying a work of art (novel, painting, motion picture, music, etc.) in that work of art itself. His extent of aesthetic distance is inversely correlated with the degree of his involvement: the less he is involved, the greater is his distance, and the other way round. Aesthetic distance, on the other hand, is positively correlated with detachment: the greater the detachment, the greater the aesthetic distance, and, likewise, the less the detachment, the less the aesthetic distance. Some critics believe that the ideal aesthetic distance is that distance where one can enough involve oneself in an art object with maximum enjoyment while, too, he can well keep himself maximally detached from the art object so as to be able to contemplate the values or qualities of the artistic properties of the art object quite serenely, tranquilly.

aestheticism [from Greek *aistheta*, 'things perceptible by the senses', and *aesthetes*, 'one who perceives']. It is the belief that beauty is the most fundamental value of human life and that beauty underlines all the other human considerations—moral, social, political and otherwise. It denotes a great love of beauty, and so of objects and works of beauty. Aestheticism upholds the belief that art is for art's sake (*'l'art pour l'art'*). The root of the concept of aestheticism may be found in the German philosopher Immanuel Kant's (1724-1804) *Critique of Judgement*, where he has strived to propound that true aesthetic contemplation or enjoyment is absolutely disinterested (i.e. devoid of all extra-aesthetic considerations) and that aesthetic contemplation or enjoyment is independent of any consideration of reality or utility of the object of beauty. Proponents of aestheticism include Edgar Allan Poe (1809-49), Theophile Gautier, Charles Baudlaire, Gustave Flaubert (1821-80), Stephane Mallarme, Walter Pater, Oscar Wilde, etc. Aestheticism also denotes the aesthetic movement of the late 19th century, which some view as 'the further phase of Romanticism'. The aesthetic movement was a European phenomenon having its epicentre in France. Also see *Romanticism.

affectation. A style or mode of writing which involves assumed elegance, pretension and artificiality, and is incongruous with the subject it treats, in violation of the principle of *decorum.

akhyana [from Sanskrit *akhyaṇa*, folk tale]. It is an Indian beast epic or *folk tale, often with a moral. It is always in prose, the climactic middle part being in verse.

Alazon, *alazon*. A stock cowardly and mean character in ancient Greek comedy who is distinguished for his boasting of his attributes in bombastic terms. The vacuity of his swagger is ultimately betrayed by the **eiron*, another *stock character of ancient Greek comedy, who achieves his end through pretending to be a dull person of modest speech and simple manners. Shakespeare's Falstaff and Moliere's Tartuffe are examples of the *alazon*. See also *braggadochio, **miles gloriosus* and *rodomontade.

aleatory writing, aleatoric writing [from Latin *aleator, alea,* dice]. In a game of dice, what numbers the dice will show, after being cast, is unpredictable, for it depends on chance, contingency, fortuity. Likewise, the elements of an aleatory writing are not consciously or pre-meditatedly chosen, selected and arranged but are left to haphazard, randomness or luck. A writer may, for instance, jot down a multitude of words, randomly picked up, on pieces of paper and then throw them up in the air. When they will descend he will collect them randomly and then write the words in the sequence in which they are collected. The result may be a short piece of creative writing. Curiously, the mode or technique of aleatory writing has been successfully adopted by some creative writers. Two such creative writers are: the British novelist Brian Stanley Johnson (1933-73) and the American novelist William Seward Burroughs (b. 1914). Johnson's famously curious novel *The Unfortunates* is actually a box of 27 loose sheaf sections. The reader may shuffle the sections in any way he chooses and read the whole novel, but his knowledge or experience will be the same—the knowledge or experience of the recollections of the narrator. Burroughs, on the other hand, used his cut-up technique in some of his novels. He would snip up pages of his earlier written novels, shuffle at random the cut segments, and then write down the segments in the order in which they appeared to create the finished novel. His novel *The Ticket That Exploded* is a classic example of his already cut-up technique. Tom Phillips adopted another aleatory technique. He just randomly erased a great multiple of letters and words in W.H. Mallock's (1849-1923) novel *A Human Document* by blacking them out and thus created his new novel *Humument*. Further, De Chirico's novel *Hebdomeros* is but a collection of dreams deliberately randomised [Cuddon, 18].

allegory [from Greek *allos*, other and *agoreuein*, to speak]. A story that has two levels of meaning: on the surface of it, it is simply a narrative (its first or literal meaning), but on the deep level it is a hidden moral or satire (its second or symbolic meaning). Aesop's *Fables*, Langland's *Piers Plowman*, the anonymous *Everyman*, Spenser's *Faerie Queene*, Bunyan's *The Pilgrim's Progress* and Milton's *Paradise Lost* are all moralistic and didactic allegories. *The Pilgrim's Progress*, for instance, narrates the physical progression or journey of a man named Christian along with his wife Christiana and their children through distresses and their ultimately reaching their goal in the house of the Interpreter. This is the literal or surface meaning of the book. But, symbolically, the journey of Christian and his family signifies spiritual progression towards Christian salvation, as the sub-title of the book well suggests—'(Progress) From This World to That Which Is to Come'. George Orwell's (pseudonym of Eric Arthur Blair: 1903-50) novel *Animal Farm*, on the other hand, is a satirical allegory in so far as the farm in it is a national state and the pigs are Marxist revolutionaries. See also *fable, *parable.

allonym [from Greek *allos*, other, and *onoma*, name]. The name of another person that a writer sometimes assumes for his work, i. e. publishes his work under the name of another real person. See also *pseudonym, *pen-name, **nom de plume*.

allusion [from Latin *ad*, towards, and *ludere* or *lusum*, to play]. Unlike the quotation, it is an indirect reference to some character, episode, point, idea, etc. of another well-known work, usually of another author, to throw light on an author's work. In the case of quotation, the source of it is usually acknowledged, but in the case of allusion the source is not stated. When Wordsworth, for example, writes in a sonnet, 'Milton! Thou should be living at this hour, / England hath need of thee', he uses an allusion. Newspaper headlines are often allusive: *The Laser's Edge* [an allusion to Somerset Maugham's (1874-1965) novel *The Razor's Edge*], *Comedy of Terrors* (an allusion to Shakespeare's *Comedy of Errors*), etc. Though generally employed particularly in poetry, as figures of speech, allusions are also used in novels, though sparingly.

als ob [from German *als*, as, and *ob*, if]. It is a German phrase which in English may be translated as 'as if '. It originated in the German philosopher Hans Vaihinger's (1852-1933) philosophy of 'as if', according to which we have a willingness to believe in the fiction that the world is an ordered phenomenon, and is not chaotic, because our idealism demands it. In literature, the phrase suggests that a pre-requisite of our ideal enjoyment of an art object is our *willing suspension of disbelief in the reality of an art object, i.e. we must believe the art object to be as it appears to be, and not as a fiction.

alternative literature. A rather vague and loose term, it denotes the sort of literature that does not follow the commonly accepted rules and tradition of literature. In this sense, it is anti-tradition and off-beat. Such things as *anti-novel and *aleatory writing may be brought under the rubric of alternative literature. Alternative literature is generally supposed to be the product of so-called alternative society and its *sub-culture.

American Renaissance. A romantic and transcendentalist movement that surged across America since about 1835 till the breaking out of the Civil War (1861-65) being reinforced by the writings of Ralph Waldo Emerson (1803-82), Henry David Thoreau (1817-62), Walt Whitman (1819-92) and the two novelists, Nathaniel Hawthorn (1804-64) and Herman Melville (1819-91). The spirit of the movement was distinctively American, as F.O. Mathiessen has demonstrated in his *The American Renaissance*.

anabasis [from Greek *ana*, up, and *basis*, going]. The state of the *action of a dramatic literature while it is rising up to a climax.

anachronism [from Greek *ana*, backwards, and *chronos*, time]. It is a thing, person, behaviour, etc. which is incongruous with the time in which it appears. In Shakespeare's *Julius Caesar*, for instance, a clock strikes the time. But during the emperor's time there was no clock in Rome. So the clock is an anachronism, or it is anachronistic.

anagnorisis. [from Greek *anagnorisis*, recognition or discovery].The term is found in Aristotle's *Poetics*, where it denotes recognition of truth, just at the moment when the curtain of ignorance is lifted up. Oedipus in Sophocle's *Oedipus Rex*, for instance,experiences anagnorisis when he dumbfoundedly realises that he has actually killed his own father Laius *incognito*. In anagnorisis, that is, a character moves from ignorance to cognition of truth. Likewise, Pip in Charles Dickens's (1812-70)* novel *Great Expectations* has an anagnorisis when he discovers that Magwitch, and not Miss Havisham, is his real benefactor. Anagnorisis leads to *denouement. Also see *turning point.

anagoge, anagogy [pronounced *an-a-go-je, an-a-go-ji*; from Greek *anagoge*, leading up, elevation]. Mystical interpretation. In anagogic drive, the unconscious strives towards the morally and spiritually high ideals. Anagogical meaning of a text is the text's spiritual, hidden, allegorical or mystical meaning. Anagoge or anagogy is, in fact, a sort of allegorical interpretation. See also *allegory.

analepsis [from Greek *ana*, back, and *lambanein*, to take]. Same as *cutback, *flashback, *switchback. See also *prolepsis.

analogue [from Greek *ana*, according to, and *logos*, ratio].The meaning of the term derives from 'analogy' which means agreement or resemblance between two things. When one thing is like another, the second thing is said to be an analogue of the first. In literature, a work (a *novel, *short story, play, etc.) is an analogue of another work when it resembles the second work as regards some basic elements, such as *theme, *story, *plot, etc. For instance, the tale in Chaucer's *The Pardoner's Tale* is said to have an analogue in a third century Buddhist *Jataka* or in the Italian *Libro di Novelle e di Bel Parlar Gentile* (1572). The story of 'pound of flesh' in *The Merchant of Venice* has also an analogue in an Italian story in *Gesta Romanorum*.

anamnesis [from *ana*, back, and *mimneskein*, to recall to memory]. The term denotes recalling to memory things (notion, concept, idea, etc.) forgotten. It also refers to poets' and novelists' technique of recalling past experiences and utilizing them in their works. In his novel *A la recherché du temps perdu*, Marcel Proust (1871-1922) has utilised the anamnesic technique very successfully.

anatomy [from Greek *ana*, up, and *tome*, a cutting]. Originally a medical term for dissection, it also means an exhaustive analysis of a subject. Examples are to be found in: Lyly's *Euphues or the Anatomy of Wit* (1589) and Burton's *Anatomy of Melancholy* (1621). "A humorous display of extensive and detailed knowledge as in Melville's account of whaling in *Moby-Dick* (1851) or Thomas Pynchon's rocket-lore in

Gravity's Rainbow (1973) is characteristic of this genre" (Baldick, 10).

androcentrism [from Greek *andros*, male, and *kentron*, a sharp point]. As a critical term, it was introduced by feminist theorists. It refers to a set of attitudes of some males which ignore or reject or do not respect the general feminine feelings, attitudes and interests. Androcentrism or androcentricity involves a belief in male superiority and rests on male perspective. See also *gynocentrism.

anecdote. A short narrative or 'story' of a single incident of the private life of a person, it occupies an important place in literature and is very popular. Examples of collections of anecdotes are: Isaac Disraeli's (father of Benjamin Disraeli) *Curiosities of Literature* (3 vols) and *Calamities of Authors* (2 vols); John Nichols's *Literary Anecdotes of the 18th c.* (9 vols); and *The Oxford Book of Literary Anecdotes*.

Angry Young Men. The term was coined by some contemporary journalists, taking the words from John Osborne's play *Look Back in Anger*, to designate some novelists and playwrights of the late 1950s and early 1960s who were themselves disillusioned of the British middle class or bourgeois social and spiritual values and protested against them through their works with a vengeance. The Angry Young Men writers betrayed in their works the angry bewilderment of their contemporary young people who had once internalised the bourgeois values but soon realised the hollowness of all these in the face of the hard social reality that they now entered into. The angry young people, who were now bereft of the comfortable but futile ideological values of the bourgeoisie, violently protested against them with hopelessness and glum in their hearts. Some of the more radical works of the Angry Young Men writers were: John Osborne's (b. 1929) play *Look Back in Anger* ; John Wain's (b. 1925) novel *Hurry on Down*; Kingley Amis's (b. 1922) novel *Lucky Jim*; John Braine's (1922-86) novel *Room at the Top*; and Alan Sillitoe's (b. 1928) novel *The Loneliness of the Long-Distance Runner* (the novelists outnumbered the playwrights, indeed). The protests of the Angry Young Men later somehow and somewhat influenced the literature of the *absurd, as John Russell Taylor has shown in *Anger and After* (1962).

antagonist [from Greek *anti*, against, and *agon*, contest]. The most prominent character in a drama or narrative work who opposes, hinders, obstructs and thereby endeavours to frustrate the *protagonist's or *hero's (or heroine's) intention, and thereby sets out the conflict and complication. For example, king Claudius is the antagonist in *Hamlet* in so far as he opposes Hamlet in achieving his objectives. The antagonist is generally evil, but where the protagonist himself or herself is evil, the antagonist is good or virtuous. In *Macbeth*, the protagonist Macbeth himself is wicked and so, naturally, the antagonist Macduff is of a virtuous and sympathetic character. The term 'antagonist' is not synonymous with the term *'anti-hero'.

anti-art. A term of *postmodernism which does not recognise any *centre, *form, or *structure, and advocates creation in painting, music and literature by chance. Also see *aleatory writing.

anticlimax. A term antonymous with *climax. In the dramatic or narrative writing, it refers to the relatively fast-falling action or descent, or to the rapid reduction in the intensity of the emotion earlier aroused, deflating the suspense. If the descent is unintentional and ridiculous, the anticlimax is called *bathos, but if it is deliberate and funny, the anticlimax is called *comic. Anticlimax immediately follows the climactic moment.

anti-hero, anti-heroine. A term antonymous with *hero or heroine. The anti-hero or anti-heroine is a central*character in a drama or *novel, like the hero or heroine, but lacks in the cardinal qualities of the hero or heroine, such as bravery, nobility, magnanimity, honesty, etc. The anti-hero or heroine is a non-hero or heroine, the antithesis of the traditional hero or heroine—weak, defeatist, bloodless and muddle-headed. Instances of anti-hero in the domain of drama are: Willy Loman in Arthur Miller's (b. 1915) play *Death of a Salesman* and Jimmy Porter in John Osborne's (b. 1920) *Look Back in Anger*. And instances of anti-hero in the field of novel are: Tristram Shandy in Laurence Sterne's (1713-68) *Tristram Shandy*; Leopold Bloom in James Joyce's (1882-1941) *Ulysses*; Jim Dixon in Kingsley Amis's (b. 1922) *Lucky Jim*; Herzog in Saul Bellow's (b. 1915) *Herzog* and Captain John Yossarian in Joseph Heller's (b. 1923) *Catch-22*. The anti-hero or heroine should not be confused with the *antagonist and the *villain.

anti-literature. A term invented in 1935 by David Gascoyne (b. 1916), an upholder of *surrealism. It denotes the sort of literature which spurns away the control of the traditional rules and conventions of literature and emphasises the importance of the Unconscious and the surrealistic techniques in literary creations. See also *alternative literature, *anti-novel, *surrealism.

anti-novel. A mid-twentieth century type of experimental and innovative *novel which quite ignores the traditional rules and conventions about novel, such as unfolding a *plot, developing *characters, conjuring up an illusion of *realism or *naturalism. However the anti-novel has its own sorts of rules and conventions, some of which are:

i. it creates its own kind of realism;

ii. it tries to debar the reader from identifying with characters;

iii. it does not develop any recognizable plot;

iv. it does not strive to develop characters;

v. its episodes are not organized but are diffusive;

vi. it comprises repetitions of some of its elements;

vii. it engages in detailed analysis of objects;

viii. it frequently varies its time sequences;

ix. it often experiments with various linguistic elements, such as vocabulary, syntax, punctuation, etc.;

x. sometimes, it resorts to even some very queer novelistic techniques, such as interpolation of some blank or coloured pages or drawings or some detachable printed pages which can be shuffled like cards within the body of the text, employment of *collage effect, and use of hieroglyphics;

xi. it 'concerns itself with tiny inner dreams on the border of consciousness'.

Traces of some of the features of the anti-novel may be found as early as in Laurence Sterne's (1713-68) *The Life and Opinions of Tristram Shandy* (1759-67) in which there are some blank pages and unconnected comic *Obiter dicta*. However, some of the fairly recognised anti-novels are: James Joyce's (1882-1941) *Ulysses*; Virginia Woolf's (1882-1941) *Mrs Dalloway*, *To the Lighthouse* and *The Waves*; Samuel Beckett's (b. 1906) *Molloy* and *Murphy*; Jean-Paul Sartre's

(b. 1905) *La Nausee* (*Nausea*); Nathalie Sarraute's (n. d.) *Tropismes* (*Tropisms and the Age of Suspicion*); Albert Camus's (1913-60) *L' Etranger* (*The Outsider*); Alain Robbe-Grillet's (b. 1922) *La Jalousie* (*Jealousy*); Michel Butor's (b. 1926) *L'emploi du temps* (*Passing Time*) and *La modification* (*Second Thoughts*); Christine Brook-Rose's (b. 1926) *Out*, *Such* and *Between*; and Vladimir Nabokov's (b. 1899) *Pale Fire*. However, anti-novel is a misnomer in that it is not a fact that the anti-novel is in any sense antonymous with, or contradictory to, the novel, but it is really a different type of novel that may be favourably compared with**nouveau roman*. See also **anti-roman*.

anti-roman [from French *anti*, against, and *roman*, novel]. Same as *anti-novel, **nouveau roman*.

apercu [French *apercu* (pronounced ap-air-soo), perception, glimpse]. The term is used in three different senses: (a) unanalyzed and unexamined perception, or insight; (b) an outline, summary, or brief exposition; (c) a writer's sudden discovery of some truth.

apocalyptic literature [from Greek *apo*, from, and *kalyptein*, to cover]. The term derives its meaning from Apocalypse (or the Revelation of St John), the last book of the New Testament, which speaks of the last things or happenings of the world or of the end of the world, or of the coming great holocaust. Apocalyptic literature is concerned with such things as eschatology or the coming world-consuming holocaust, and is prophetic, minatory and somber, like sermons. In the field of poetry, some of William Blake's (1757-1827) poems and W.B. Yeats's (1865-1939) poem 'The Second Coming' are apocalyptic. And in the field of novel, for example, the following works are apocalyptic or apocalyptical: George Orwell's (1903-50) *Nineteen Eighty-Four*, Doris Lessing's (b. 1919) *The Four-Gated City*, Norman Mailer's (b. 1923) *Armies of the Night*, and J.G. Ballard's (b. 1930) *The Drowned World*.

apocrypha [from Greek *apo*, from, and *kryptein*, to hide]. Litarally, the term means 'hidden or secret things' and originally it applied to some books or parts of Septuagint and Vulgate translation of the Old Testament not accepted as canonical by Jews and Protestants. The adjectival form of the word (apocryphal) connotes, generally, things of doubtful authority. In literature, apocrypha denotes writings ascribed to authors on insufficient or doubtful grounds or evidences. For instance, such plays as *Pericles, Prince of Tyre* (in part), *The Troublesome Reign of King John*, *The Birth of Merlin* and *Arden of Feversham* are ascribed to William Shakespeare on insufficient evidences, and so these plays are apocrypha (or apocryphal).

Apollonian. The word is derived from the Greek god Apollo, sometimes identified with the sun. He was the messenger of all the other gods and was the presiding deity of prophecy, medicine, music and poetry. He symbolized or represented reason, restraint, abstraction, youth, light, serenity, culture, form, beauty, symmetry, etc.—things that are mostly prevalent in the type of literature we call Apollonian. The novels of Stendhal (1783-1842) and Jane Austen (1775-1817), for instance, are, generally, said to be Apollonian. See also *Dionysian.

apologue [from Greek *apo*, from, and *logos*, speech]. The term is synonymous with *fable, especially that about beasts (and, of course, with a moral lesson). In this sense, all Aesop's fables are apologues. The French fabulist Jean de la Fontaine (1621-95) has left a great number of apologues (or fables) where 'animals speak like men and men are described like animals.' He and Aesop are the world's greatest masters of apologues (or fables).

aporia [from Greek *aporia*, impasse, puzzle, or difficulty in passing]. Basically, a rhetorical term, meaning uncertainty, doubt or hesitation as to what to say (such as *'I hardly knew where to start, it's really all so confusing'*), it, by extension, also denotes a 'gap', or a lacuna, or a difficult or insoluble conflict between what a text means to say and what it actually says.

aposiopesis [from Greek *apo*, off, and *siope*, silence]. A rhetorical device in which one suddenly breaks off in the middle of a sentence, to create a special effect, such as to show extreme exasperation, heightened emotion, threat, wonder, etc. or the speaker's unwillingness or inability (due to circumstantial constraints) to continue. For instance, 'Behave, or else—' (the special effect here is the direness of the consequence of not behaving). Another example from James Joyce's (1882-1941) short story 'Grace' (in *Dubliners*): ' There's not much difference between us,' said Mr. M'Coy. 'We both believe in—'.

apparatus. A collective term for an ensemble of appendices, footnotes, glossaries, emendations, introductory explanations, variant readings, conventions, etc. of a literary text provided in a scholarly edition of it as aids to its proper (critical) study. Alternative terms are: *apparatus criticus* and scholarly apparatus.

aptronym [from Latin *aptus*, apt, fit or suitable, and *onym*, name, the 'r' being interpolated as an epenthesis]. The word denotes a name that has been chosen because it matches or reveals some cardinal trait or traits of a person to whom it belongs. For instance, the name 'William *Rum*hole' (*Rum*, intoxicating liquor) is aptronymic, because the person, so named, is addicted to rum. Many fictional names, particularly in allegories and morality plays, are aptronymic, such as Worthy, Sin, Hunter, Draper, Mason, etc. Aptronyms are also to be found in novels, such as those of Henry Fielding (1707-54), Charles Dickens (1812-70) and W.M. Thackeray (1811-63). William Archer, the drama critic, called aptronyms 'label names'.

Arcadia, Arcady, Arcadian. A mountainous pleateau and administrative district in ancient Greece away from the rather urban area, with calm pastoral, bucolic and idyllic features, its inhabitants—mostly shepherds—being simple, innocent, primitive in manners, and given to music and dancing. Virgil in his *Eclogues* (42-37 B.C.) imagined it to be a model of the ideal world. The adjective 'Arcadian' refers to the legendary Golden Age of shepherds and shepherdresses, far removed from the 'real life' and their idyllic habitation.

archetype. [from Greek *arche*, primitive, and *typos*, model or type]. Archetype is the 'original pattern'. According to the analytical or depth psychologist C.G. Jung, archetype denotes the contents of the racial or collective Unconscious, or the innate or genetically inherited ideas, or the inborn tendency to organise experiences in innately predetermined patterns. In literary criticism, an archetyle denotes a universal character (called archetypal character), image or *theme that recurs frequently in all the literatures of the world of all ages, as well as in the myths, dreams and social rituals of all the peoples the world over. Some of the archetypal characters are: the Promethean rebel-hero, the scapegoat, the womanizer Don Juan, the all-conquering hero, the braggadocio, the country bumpkin, the Robinhood, the social climber, the traitor and the *femme fatale*. Some of the archetypal images are those of the lion, the eagle, the snake, the rose, the paradisal garden, the Paradise-Hades dimension, and the earth goddess. And some of the archetypal themes are: the journey underground, the heavenly ascent, the search for the father, the pursuit of vengeance, symbolic fertility rites, etc. Archetypal literary criticism emphasizes the importance of the archetypes in the creation and interpretation of literary works. C.G. Jung ('On the Relation of Analytical Psychology to Poetic Art'), Northrop Frye (*Anatomy of Criticism*), G. Wilson Knight (*The Starlit Dome*), Robert Graves (*The White Goddess*) and Richard Chase (*The Quest for Myth*) are some of the critics who have been prominent practitioners of archetypal criticism.

architectonic novel ['architectonic' from Greek *archi*, chief, and *tekton*, a builder]. The word architectonics was introduced into literary criticism from the science of architecture or the science of systematic arrangement of knowledge by Ezra Pound (1885-1972) to denote the art or skill of moulding or arranging some disparate elements of some literary matter into a neatly shaped organic whole. Consequently, in literary criticism the term architectonic pertains to the qualities of the structural proportions, quantity, priority, arrangement, etc. of the parts of a whole literary work. The novels of Sir Walter Scott (1771-1832) and Thomas Hardy (1840-1928), for instance, said to be architectonic novels.

argot [from French *argot*, a beggars' guild, criminal cant, slang]. A pejorative term and synonymous with *jargon and nearly synonymous with *slang. Argot is the jargon or slang of a restricted lower or far lower class of a society; for instance, that of sailors, thieves, social outcasts, prostitutes, etc. Some argot words are: bimble, yomp, bop, etc. [McArthur, 81-82].

ars est celare artem [a Latin expression, meaning 'art is to conceal art']. It is a sort of theory about art that the best art should seem 'artless', though, in fact, it is not; and that it should seem spontaneous and unpremeditated, and also that it should diligently avoid being *arty.

art. A term with varied meanings, for none has yet been able to define it satisfactorily. We cannot, therefore, say what art is, but can definitely say what it is not. It is not life or nature, on the one hand, and craft, entertainment and propaganda, on the other. However, art may be explained as application of skill or adroitness in creating beauty or aesthetic quality in perceptible objects as well as in imaginatively rendered literary works. Roger Fowler has stipulatively defined art thus: "*any work characterized by an obvious aesthetic element is to be deemed a work of art*" [Fowter, 13].

art for art's sake. This slogan-like phrase, or, simply, slogan, is the motto of some writers who believe that art has nothing else to serve but itself, and that art has its intrinsic value, i.e. the value of art is not determined by anything outside itself, say morality, politics, economics, etc. and also that creation and enjoyment of beauty is the only single objective of art. Those who believe in the spirit of this motto insist that art has no reference to life and subscribe to Oscar Wilde's flippant dictum that one should cultivate art, not life, or life as art, art being artificial and the better alternative to life: "'The first duty in life is to be as artificial as possible. What the second duty is no one has yet discovered'" [Cuddon, 12]. The philosophy of 'art for art's sake' was first emphatically argued for by the German writer G.F. Lessing (1729-81) in his *Laokoon*. Those who believed in the slogan included Oscar Wilde, James Joyce (1882-1941), Konstantinovich Tolstoy and

E.M. Forster (1879-1970); and those who did not comprised Wordsworth, Shelley, Edgar Allan Poe and Leo Tolstoy (1828-1910). See also *aestheticism.

art nouveau [French *nouveau*, new]. Art nouveau literally means 'new art'. It refers to the particular elaborate, florid, garnished, ornamental and fantastic style of architecture and decoration that prevailed in America and the European countries from c. 1890 to c. 1914, and exerted considerable influence on German *expressionism and the literary atmosphere of France and Belgium of the same period.

arty. A pejorative term, it refers to a literary work that deliberately, and not indifferently, aspires to be artistic. In an arty literary piece, the writer consciously over-emphasises the artistic aspects of his creation rather than the signifying or meaning aspects of it.

aspect of a story. Literally, aspect means look, glace, view, appearance, face, way of viewing, etc. The title of E.M. Forster's (1879-1970) *Aspects of the Novel* suggests an application of the term in this sense. As a critical term, the word is borrowed from linguistics, where it means "a grammatical category which deals with how the event described by a verb is viewed, such as whether it is in progress, habitual, repeated, momentary, etc." [Richards, *et al*, 18]. However, the aspect of a story may denote one of the following three things: (1) "those traits which are specific to it and which distinguish it from other stories"; (2) "the *vision*, or point of view in terms of which a story is presented"; and (3) "'the way in which the story is perceived by the narrator'" [Hawthorn, 21].

atmosphere. It is the mood or emotional tone prevailing in the *setting or *scene of a play or *novel, in which an episode occurs. It is the intangible, psychological quality of a setting that affects our sensory as well as extrasensory perception of what happens in that setting. The atmosphere of the opening scene of *Hamlet*, for example, is significantly somber and ominous and that of G.B. Shaw's *Arms and the Man* is highly romantic. Again, the atmosphere of the opening chapter of E.M. Forster's (1879-1970) novel *A Passage to India* is manifestly portentious as that of Thomas Hardy's (1840-1928) novel *The Return of the Native* betrays a threateningly brooding presence through the description of the Egdon Heath. Atmosphere is different from setting in that setting is basically objective, physical and geographical while atmosphere is fundamentally subjective or emotional. Setting comprises such things as geographical location, scenery (such as positions of windows, doors, etc.) and time (such as season, hour, etc.). Atmosphere, on the other hand, comprises the emotive or subjective qualities of the setting, such as mood, passion, feeling, temper, etc. of the characters as well as the tenor of the play or novel. In short, atmosphere "is the emotional tone pervading a section or the whole of a literary work, which fosters in the reader expectations as to the course of events, whether happy or (more commonly) terrifying or disastrous" [Abrams, 14].

atmosphere of the mind. The phrase was coined by Henry James (1843-1916). It denotes the 'atmosphere' of the mind of the novelist, or, better, the thought and emotion of the novelist that are there in his mind and that he strives to convey into the mind of the reader.

Atticism, Attic style. The term derives from Attica, the ancient Greek state and centre of urbane refinement in all spheres of taste. Hence Atticism is contradistinguished from *Doric rusticity. In the sphere of literature, Atticism or Attic style refers to a predilection, during the 5th and 4th centuries B.C., for directness, sharpness, witticism, purity and simplicity as opposed to the 'Asiatic' (from Asia Minor) style of excessive artifice and ornamentation. An example of Atticism or Attic style is the following sentence of Samuel Johnson (1709-84): "A man is generally better pleased when he has a good dinner upon his table, than when his wife talks Greek." [McArthur, 87].

Augustan age. The age or period during which Emperor Augustus reigned in Rome, i.e. from 27 B.C. to 14 A.D. Some historians of literature, though, deem the age to have began not since 27 B.C. but since 44 B.C., the year in which Julius Caesar died. It was the age in which such great masters of Latin literature as Virgil, Ovid, Horace and Sextus Propertius flourished. In English literary history, of course, Augustan age denotes the period from 1702, the year of the accession of Queen Anne, to 1745, the year in which Swift (1667-1745) died. During this period, the great poet Pope, the great dramatist George Farquhar, and the great novelists—Defoe (1660-1731), Swift, Richardson (1689-1761: only *Pamela* part I) and Fielding (1707-54: only *Joseph Andrews*)—either flourished or showed definite signs of flourishing. This particular period of the history of English literature is called Augustan age because the writers of that period consciously emulated the sophisticated urban style of the great Latin masters mentioned above, and also adopted those masters' literary forms, especially the epistle (Richardson's *Pamela*, for instance) and *satire (Swift's *Gulliver's Travels*, for example). The English Augustan age is noted for its literary refinement and excellence. In the history of French literature, however, the Augustan age refers to the age of the great dramatists Pierre Corneille (1606-84), Moliere (1622-73), Jean Racine (1639-99) and such other great poets and writers. Thus the French Augustan age is obviously earlier than the English.

aura. The critical term was introduced by the German Marxist critic and essayist Walter Benjamin (1892-1940) to express "the mystical sense that surrounds artistic or ritual objects like a halo" [Hawthorn, 22], i.e. to express the uniqueness and the organic unity of a work of art, which, for instance, are absent in the postmodernist artistic works that deliberately lay emphasis on *pastiche, *collage and *aleatory elements.

aureate language, aureate style [aureate from Latin *aureatus*, gilded]. An excessively or superfluously decorated or ornate, florid or overdone language or style of writing, like those of the 15th century poets William Dunbar (c. 1465-1530) and John Lydgate (c. 1370-1449). Such a language or style is laden with Latinism, periphrases, decorative words and phrases, etc.

author, death of. The phrase simply means the non-recognition of the existence of the author as the originator of a *text. The traditionally and commonly accepted idea of an author is that he is a person who intellectually and imaginatively remoulds his experiences in a particular way and thus creates a unique literary work. The work is the 'product' of the author and the author is the 'originator' of the product. But since the 1960s, some structuralists and poststructuralists, notably Roland Barthes (1915-80) and Michel Foucault (1926-84), challenged the authenticity of the idea of the author as the originator of the text.

The idea or notion of the death of the author was first spoken of by Barthes in his essay 'The Death of the Author' (1968) and then by Foucault in his essay 'What is an Author?' (1969). Barthes argues that the author is rather an hypothesis of the reader than a real being. The reader confronts a text, interprets it at liberty, and then assumes that there is an author who created the text. The author is, therefore, so to say, dead, while the reader is very much alive and kicking. The author is dead, Barthes contends, because he is extremely unreliable. There is a great discrepancy between what the author intends to express and what he actually expresses through language. The reader, on the other hand, is solid and reliable: he interprets the text at liberty, and what he understands is the actual text (and not the printed book). But, then, the reader is not the only interpreter of the text; there are many readers, each of whom may interpret the same text in his own way. Therefore, the text may mean various things, though the author intended but only one thing. It is for this reason that Barthes says that the author is dead, or, which is the same thing, the idea or notion of the author is nullified, demolished.

autobiographical novel. A *novel that overtly or covertly deals with the biography of the author. Joyce's (1882-1941) *A Portrait of the Artist as a Young Man* and Maugham's (1874-1965) *Of Human Bondage* are clear instances of the autobiographical novel. All the novels of Louisa Alcott (1832-88) and most of the novels of Sherwood Anderson (1876-1941) are also autobiographical.

automatisation. See *defamiliarisation.

autotelic. See *didacticism.

avant-garde [from French *avant*, before or in front of, and *garde*, guard or watchman]. A French military term for the vanguard of an army convoy, but since the late 19th century the term has come to mean "that body of artists and writers who are dedicated to the idea of art as experiment and revolt against tradition" [Baldick, 20]. *Avant-garde* literature demands exploration, innovation and invention, and it is always ahead of the time of its composition, and is revolutionary in nature. The poems of Vertaine, Rimbaud and Mallarme; the plays of Adamov, Beckett, Genet, Ionesco, Pinter and Gunter Grass; and the novels of Alain Robbe-Grillet (b. 1922), Michel Butor (b. 1926) and Nathalic Sarraute, (n. a.) for instances, are *avant-garde*.

B

background. A term taken from plastic art, where it denotes the part of a painting which shows itself from behind the picture of the principal object. In literature, it signifies two things: (i) the physical setting, or the geographical and atmospheric features, and social, cultural, religious and political conditions of the people, of a locale against which a literary work is presented; and (ii) the philosophy, convictions, attitude, objective, point of view, etc. of the writer from which he produces a particular literary work. For instance, the geographical, atmospheric, social, cultural features or conditions of 'Chandrapore' as well as E.M. Forster's homosexuality, concern for human relationship, love of the down-trodden, etc. collectively constitute the background of his novel *A Passage to India*. Also see *atmosphere, *setting.

baroque, barock, barocco [from Portuguese *barroco*, 'a large rough pearl of the kind used in florid jewelry']. Herbert Read, in his *The Meaning of Art*, writes about the derivation of the term as it is used in literature: "coming from the Portuguese *barroco*, meaning a large rough pearl of the kind used in florid jewelry of the period [late 16th c. to early 18th c.]—but how the word came into general use of the art of the period is (again) a mystery" [Read, 150]. The baroque art is opposed to the classical; while the latter is rational and idealistic, the former is fanciful and whimsical; and while the latter is measured, restrained, the former is ornate, superfluous. The baroque style is 'heavy, swollen, over-nourished' and it stresses movement and energy. The baroque art avoids repose, passivity, insouciance and complacency; it seeks to impinge upon our consciousness by startling us with the unusual and the unexpected. The broken rhymes of John Donne's (c. 1572-1631) verse and the prose of Sir Thomas Browne (1605-82), John Cleveland (1613-58) and Richard Crashaw (1612-49) are full of baroque extravagance. See also *rococo.

bathos [from Greek *bathos*, depth]. A sudden *unintentional* (of the writer or speaker) ridiculous descent from the elevated or the *sublime to the mean in writing or speech is called bathos, in the pejorative sense. But when such a descent is *intentional* (of the writer or speaker) it is called bathos, in the non-pejorative sense. Bathos in the non-pejorative sense is also called *anticlimax. Bathos is the consequence of unskillful straining after achieving over seriousness, dignity, deep pathos or elevation of style and failing to keep it up. An example of bathos in the non-pejorative sense is the following two lines from Lord Byron's (1788-1824) *Don Juan* (I. ix): 'A better cavalier ne'er mounted horse, / Or, being mounted, e'er got down again.' And yet another from Alexander Pope (1688-1744): 'Ye Gods! annihilate but Space and Time / And make two lovers happy.'

beast fable. A fable in which animals and birds (but not inanimate things) behave like human beings. It is distinguished from the *fable in that in the fable inanimate objects also may behave like human beings. However, the beast fable, like the fable, concludes with a moral.

Beats, Beat generation, Beat writers. The term 'beat', as here used in this entry, was first used by the novelist Jack Kerouac (1922-69), and then it was employed by the novelist John Clellon Holmes (1926-88) in an article published in *New York Times* in 1952. In the same year, Holmes in his novel *Go* used the term to describe the particular group of writers (mostly poets) who in the 1950s developed a highly idiosyncratic style of poetic and prose language, and were significantly unconventional, anti-intellectual and anti-hierarchical in attitude. This group of writers who launched their movement—the Beat movement—from Greenwich Village (New York), North Beach (San Francisco) and Venice West (Los Angeles) are known as Beat writers. Those who subscribed to their views and adopted their peculiar life-style are called Beats and their generation is known as Beat generation. "The word 'beat' has a range of meanings including depressed (to the point of wild escape from conventional living); exhausted; holy in poverty and beatific in joy and mystic illumination (with literary references back to Whitman, Blake and Rimbaud, and jazz associations with Lester Young and Charlie Parker), and to catching the note of spontaneous living (with reference to Zen Buddhism, [American] Indian peyote cults and visionary experience)" [Mottram, 30]. Some also thought that 'beat' meant 'beaten down' (the Beats were, as if, beaten down by the mainstream society). The life-style of the Beats was bohemian and associated with such things as 'free sex', boozes, drugs and deeply pessimistic philosophy. The Beats were antagonistic towards the middle-class values, commercialism, materialism, militarism and the ethics of conformity, and were viscerally anti-modern. Later on, most of the Beats converted themselves into 'hips' or into the 'beatniks'. The life-style and attitudes of the Beat writers are reflected in their literary productions. However, some of the noted Beat poets are Lawrence Ferlinghetti (*Pictures from the Gone World*), Allen Ginsberg (*Howl*), Gregory Corso (*Gasoline*), etc. and some of the distinguished Beat novelists are Jack Kerouac (1922-69: *On the Road*), Seward William Burroughs (b. 1914: *Junkie*, *The Naked Lunch*, *Minutes to Go*), John Clellon Holmes (b. 1926: *Go*, *The Horn*) and such others.

beau ideal [from French *beau*, beauty or beautiful, and *ideal*, ideal, perfect, model]. The term means the most perfect beauty ever imaginable or the "'perfect model' of a particular quality, kind of person, etc.'" [Ayto, 37].

beau monde [from French *beau,* beautiful, and *monde*, world, people, society]. Fashionable society or "the sort of people who are hounded by paparazzi and whose most trivial doings are lovingly recorded by newspaper gossip columnists" [Ayto, 38].

belles-lettres. [from French *belle*, fine, noble, good, and *lettres*, literature, writing]. The term signifies 'fine writing or a piece of fine, artistic, or elegant literature'. Max Beerbohm's (1872-1956) essays, Aldous Huxley's (1894-1965) essays (such as *Themes and Variations*, *Vulgarity in Literature* and *Music at Night*) and Lewis Carroll's (1832-98) *Alice in Wonderland*, for instance, are generally considered as *belles-lettres*.

ben trovato [from Italian *ben*, well or good, and *trovato*, found]. "The Italians have a saying, *Se non e vero, e (molto) ben trovato* 'If it is not true, it is (very) well found'—that is to say, even if a particular story is not true, it is a very appropriate invention, which captures the spirit of the truth.... English began to use the abbreviated form *ben trovato* [since the end of the 19th century] to encapsulate its sense of apt fabrication: '*Trovato* though the story no doubt is, it is very *ben*, and thus, by means of fiction, conveys fact'" [Ayto, 40].

bestiary [from Low Latin *bestia*, beast]. A form of prose or verse description of lives of real or imaginary beasts (like the phoenix or the unicorn) with a moral at the end of it, to be learned from the lives of those beasts. Bestiary was very popular in the Middle Ages.

best-seller. A term that got currency in the 1920s. It denotes the book that sells the most during a particular period of time (generally 10 years) in a certain country. Time, space (country) and number of copies sold—these are the three parameters of the best-selling book. Examples of best-sellers are: Voltaire's *Candide* (1759), Lord Byron's *Don Juan* (1819), Margaret Mitchell's (1900-49) *Gone with the Wind* (1936: it sold more than 25 million copies and was translated into more than 27 languages), Erich Maria Remarque's (b. 1898) *Im Western nichts Neues* (tr. *All Quiet on the Western Front*: 1929: it sold 2.5 million copies in 25 languages in just 18 months), etc. The principal religious books, such as the *Gita*, the *Bible*, the *Koran*, the *Tripitaka* and the *Granth Saheb* are perennial best-sellers.

bienseance [from French *bienseance*, propriety, decorum]. The term is akin to **vraisemblance* which means *verisimilitude or the *decorum or appropriateness of *characters of a *novel or play. Decorum or appropriateness is of two kinds—external and internal. The external appropriateness requires that a character behave in consonance with his or her station in the society, profession, education, sex, etc. and the internal appropriateness demands that the same character behave as the novelist or the playwright conceived him or her as a concrete personality within the space of the novel or play.

Bildungsroman [from German *Bildung*, formation, growth, and *Roman*, novel]. A novel that describes how its central character develops, matures, or becomes experienced, informed, educated, generally from childhood to adulthood, through a series of hurdles, external and internal (psychological). The central character, or the hero or heroine, of the *Bildungsroman* learns through the course of the novel the ways of the world through his or her encounters with the hard reality. It is for this reason that it is also called *education novel. Many *Bildungsromans* are autobiographical, for instance, Goethe's (1749-1832) *Wilhelm Meister* and *Die Leiden des jungen Werthers*, James Joyce's (1882-1941) *Portrait of the Artist as a Young Man* and Dickens's (1812-70) *David Copperfield*. Some of the non-autobiographical *Bildungsromans* are Daniel Defoe's (1660-1731) *Moll Flanders*, Dickens's *Great Expectations*, George Eliot's (1819-90) *The Mill on the Floss*, Samuel Butler's (1835-1902) *The Way of All Flesh*, Fielding's (1707-54) *Tom Jones*, Jane Austen's (1775-1817) *Emma* and E.M. Forster's (1879-1970) *Where Angels Fear to Tread*.

biographical fallacy. The error or mistake of supposing that the writer's life is somehow and somewhat blended, commingled with his work, and, therefore, a knowledge of the writer's biography will help in understanding his work better. The term biographical fallacy "is also used to cover what is often distinguished as the

Romantic fallacy: the assumption that a work is valuable in the degree to which it gives insight into the heart of the writer" [Rodway, 172].

block characterisation. The process of introducing the nature and particular qualities of a *character of a *novel, to the reader, not by *'showing', i.e. not by presenting him through his conversations with other characters or through his other activities, as narrated by the novelist, but by overt, explicit description by the novelist of his nature and particular qualities, i.e. by *'telling'. Briefly, block characterisation is "An explicit, introductory characterisation of a literary character by overt description rather than 'showing' through action or dialogue" [Hawthorn, 30]. For instance, Jane Austen (1775-1817) in *Emma*, introduces to the reader the heroine or protagonist Emma Woodhouse in the very beginning sentence of the novel not by 'showing' but by 'telling' about, or describing, her at some length, without any break (*block*): 'Emma Woodhouse, handsome, clever, and rich, with a comfortable home and happy disposition, seemed to unite some of the best blessings of existence; and had lived nearly twenty-one years in the world with very little to distress or vex her.'

Bloomsbury Group. The term refers to a group of writers and intellectuals who stressed the importance of art in life and were much impressed and informed by George Edward Moore's (1873-1958) anti-idealistic and pragmatic philosophy of life that he propounded in *Principia Ethica*: man's prime objects in life should be to love and to be loved, to create and enjoy art, and to acquire knowledge. This Group was censorious but tolerant about the social and artistic sanctions of the Victorian society and professed freedom of the individual regarding moral and social principles. The Bloomsbury Group is so named because its members used to meet regularly on Thursdays since 1905 at the house of Virginia Woolf (*nee* Stephen: 1882-1941) and Vanessa Bell (*nee* Stephen) at 46 Gordon Square, *Bloomsbury*, London. Some of the most prominent members of the Group were Virginia Woolf (1882-1941), the novelist; her husband Leonard Woolf, the author and social reformer; Vanessa Bell, the painter; her husband Clive Bell, the critic of art and literature; Sir Leslie Stephen, the father of Virginia Woolf and Vanessa Bell and the critic and scholar; E.M. Forster (1879-1970), the novelist; Lytton Strachey, the biographer and essayist; and Maynard Keynes, the economist. The Group was elitist and sceptical, *avant garde* and intellectual. It was liquidated in 1941 when Virginia Woolf committed suicide. The Group left an indelible influence on the contemporary literary field.

blue book. A kind of cheap and third-rate *novel (*thriller, shocker, etc.), *horror story or *romance, bound within *blue* covers, that was very popular in the closing decades of the 18th century and the beginning decades of the 19th. Blue books were crassly crude and sensational. See also *penny dreadful, *dime novel, *pulp novel.

blue-eyed English. English without its Latinate elements.

Blue Stocking, Bluestocking, blue stocking, bluestocking. Since the early 1750s till the end of the 18th century, such intellectual and intelligent ladies of taste, of London, such as Mrs Vesey (perhaps the first hostess), Elizabeth Montagu (conversationalist and defender of Shakespeare against the attack of Voltaire), Mary Delany (letter-writer), Elizabeth Carter (translator, linguist and poet), Mrs Boscawen, Hester Chapone (moralist and author), etc. arranged consecutively and regularly in their homes assemblages of leading poets, writers, artists and philosophers for conversations *a la* the French salon. These assemblages were known as the Blue Stocking Society, the title apparently being invented by Admiral Boscawen from the fact that the poor Bishop Benjamin Stillingfleet could not afford to wear the required evening clothes for those assemblages and so used to come to the gatherings wearing ordinary *blue stockings*. The literary, fashionable, and aristocratic members of the Society included such famous persons as: Hannah More (dramatist), Fanny Burney (1752-1840: novelist), Horace Walpole (letter-writer and aesthetician), Joshua Reynolds (portraitist), David Garrick (actor and dramatist), James Boswell (the biographer of Samuel Johnson), Samuel Richardson (1689-1761: novelist) and (Dr) Samuel Johnson (lexicographer, poet, critic and man of letters). When the epithet 'bluestocking' is applied to a woman well-meaningly it signifies that the woman is of pronounced literary and intellectual interests, but when it is used pejoratively of a woman, it signifies that the woman is pedantic, affects literary taste and behaves in a dilettante manner.

Bobadil. A swaggering boaster. The term was taken from the name of the soldier in Ben Jonson's *Every Man in his Humour*. See also *braggadochio, *rodomontade.

bodice-ripper. A raw and popular variety of *romance that capitalises on sexual adventures (slashing or tearing open the close-fitting woman's gown covering the body, particularly the waist). The *setting of the bodice-ripper is appropriately colourful and lush and the *characters are modeled on pirates, highwaymen, burghlers, low-class wenches, etc. The bodice-ripper, like the *S & F, is low *fiction. A classic instance of bodice-ripper is Kathlin Winsor's best-selling *romance *Forever Amber* (1944) [Baldick, 25].

Boerde. A tale which tends to be bawdy or satirical and is akin to **fabliau* or **novelle*. Chaucer and Boccaccio wrote a good number of Boerdes.

bombast [from Low Latin *bombax*, cotton, or from Greek *bombyx*, silk]. Originally, the word meant cotton-wool or horse-hair used for padding. Later on it came to mean insincere inflated or exaggerated speech, ranting or writing, or, simply, grandiloquent or extravagant language, such as the Tudor dramatists had an inclination to employ. See also *fustian, *hyperbole.

bon mot [from French *bon* (pronounced *bo*), and *mot* (pronounced *mo*), word]. The French term literally means 'good word'. As a critical term it signifies a clever comment, statement or repartee, or, simply, witticism.

book. [from German *buche*, beech (tree), and *buch*, book (beechen boards were once used to make books)]. Ordinarily, a book is a single collection of printed and sewn pages. It also means a sub-division of a single literary work, such as *Paradise Lost* is divided into 12 books and *Tom Jones* into 18.

bovarysme. The term signifies a drive or propensity towards escapist daydreaming. Emma Bovary, the protagonist of Gustave Flaubert's (1821-81) celebrated novel *Madame Bovary*, used, in her youth, to romantically dream herself to be a real heroine. But, as ill-luck would have it, in fact she became the wife of a roughshod, rude, thick-skinned country doctor. To escape from this unhappy situation of her married life, she habitually continued to day-dream romantically as earlier and thus imaginatively exist in a romantic world.

Such a habitual tendency to day-dream is called *bovarysme*.

bowdlerisation. The term derived from the name of Dr. Thomas Bowdler, M.D., (1754-1825), who drastically expurgated the plays of Shakespeare of anything whatsoever that he thought to be offensive to decency or good taste or 'unfit to be read by a gentleman in the company of ladies', and then published them under the title *The Family Shakespeare* (1818). Dr. Bowdler also published an expurgated edition of Gibbon's *Decline and Fall of the Roman Empire*. The term now means cleansing or purging a literary work of indecent, indelicate or offensive portions of it. An expurgated version of D.H. Lawrence's *Lady Chatterley's Lover* was published in 1932 (the first unexpurgated edition of it was published in England long afterwards—in 1960). Bowdlerisation has a slightly pejorative sense, because it signifies unnecessary cleansing or purging; when the cleansing or purging is imperative as per law or taste, it is called expurgation.

braggadochio. A *stock character who is cowardly, idle and swaggering, and is akin to the **alazon* and the **miles gloriosus*. Edmund Spenser (1552-99) in his *The Faerie Queene* created a *character, called Braggadochio, who is a veritable braggadochio; but Shakespeare's Falstaff is perhaps the best exemplar of a braggadochio.

bricolage [from French *bricolage*, tinkering]. The term signifies a makeshift or improvised handiwork or artifice. In literature, it denotes a work that is the result of an improvised assemblage or collection of materials earlier done and ready to hand; or it denotes incorporation of 'found' materials in a new work. *Bricolage* is akin to **collage*.

bridge. The term denotes a passage or a group of passages intended to fill up the time lapse that separates two consecutive incidents of a novel. Somerset Maugham (1874-1965) in his *Ten Novels and Their Authors* writes about bridges: "Events often require to be separated by a lapse of time, and the author for the balance of his work has to insert, as best he can, matter that will fill up this lapse. These passages [i.e., the matter] are known as bridges" [Maugham, 14-15].

Briefroman [from German *Brief*, epistle, letter, and *Roman*, novel]. The term means 'epistolary novel' or 'letter novel'. The German *Briefroman* is identical with the English *epistolary novel. Examples of German *Briefromans* are: Goethe's (1749-1832) *Die Leiden des jungen Werthers* and Holderlin's (1770-1843) *Hyperion*. In English, Samuel Richardson's (1689-1761) *Pamela* may be called *Briefroman*.

brut. The term derived from the name of *Brutus*, "the legendary and eponymous founder of Britain and the reputed grandson of Aeneas" [Cuddon, 98], as it is narrated in Layamon's alliterative verse *Brut* (late 12th century) which presents an account of the history of England that goes back to Brutes. The term has now come to denote a *chronicle.

bucolic. When used as a noun, the term denotes a *pastoral poem, like that of the Greek poet Theocritus (c. 310-250 B.C.) or that of the Roman poet Virgil (70-19 B.C.) or it denotes a pastoral poet. But when the term is used as an adjective, it means pastoral, rustic, 'countrified'.

bull. A *cock-and-bull story or a *tall story.

bunkum. An effectual or inconsequential bombastic speech or writing that may be considered as rubbish.

burlesque [from Italian *burlesco*, which is from Low Latin *burra*, a flock of wool, a trifle]. A ludicrous imitation or a literary piece that mocks its original for entertainment. Burlesque is akin to *parody, but it exceeds parody in poignancy. Further, whereas parody has an association with the stage, burlesque has none; and whereas parody's ultimate aim is correction through laughing entertainment, burlesque aims just at entertainment. "In fiction [Thomas Love] Peacock [1785-1866] came close to burlesque of the Gothic novel (...) with his *Nightmare Abbey* (1818)" [Cuddon, 100]. Also see *caricature.

by-plot. A subsidiary *plot. Also see *sub-plot.

Byronic hero. The term denotes the type of hero (or protagonist) that we encounter in Lord Byron's (1788-1824) autobiographical poem *Childe Harold's Pilgrimage*, in his unfinished 'epic satire' *Don Juan* and in his verse drama *Manfred*—a hero who is brave, intrepid, recalcitrant, contumacious of social norms, 'bitterly self-tormenting outcast', proud, aloof but worldly, egoistic, extremely passionate, and one who suffers from some unspeakable guilt or unnamed sin and is subject to tantrums and fits of melancholy. Heathcliff, in Emily Brontë's (1818-48) novel *Wuthering Heights*, appears with many of the traits of the Byronic hero.

C

cadence. It is the melodic pattern of recurrent emphases in a sentence, when pronounced. Different prose writers generally have different cadences, which betray their respective identifying *voices. Thus, for example, the cadence of Sir Thomas Browne's (1605-82) prose is different from that of Thomas de Quincey's (1785-1859).

camera-eye narrative. A critical term, it denotes a *narrative in which there is zero *focalisation, i.e. in which there is no particular perspective, or in which the narrator or *voice speaks from an *omniscient point of view. Camera-eye narrative "is generally taken to imply some sort of neutrality [as to the *point of view] in the narrative determinations—as if a camera were left in a room to record anything that took place in front of it" [Hawthorn, 258].

campus novel. A novel with a university as its setting, and generally written by one who had been, or is, an academic. Examples are: Randall Jarrell's (1914-65) *Pictures from an Institution* and Kingley Amis's (b. 1922) *Lucky Jim*. Some other examples are: Mary McCarthy's *The Groves of Acadame* (1952), John Barth's *Giles Goat-boy* (1966), Alison Lurie's *The War between the Tates* (1974), David Lodge's *Changing Places* (1975), Malcolm Bradbury's *The History of Man* (1975) and Robertson Davies's *The Rebel Angels* (1982) [Cuddon, 107].

cancelled character. A critical term coined by Brian McHale in his *Postmodernist Fiction* (1987). A cancelled character is a highly marginalized character with zero or extremely minimal self-identity. Such a character is "exposed as textual function [or narrative function] and no longer seen as 'integral creature' possessed of self-identity" [Hawthorn, 34]. Such a character is merely 'a congeries of letters, mere words'. Tyrone Slothrop, in Thomas Pynchon's (b. 1937) *novel *Gravity's Rainbow*, is an example of cancelled character.

canon. The term denotes either (i) all the recognised works of an author taken together or (ii) "a list of works set apart from other literature by virtue of their literary quality and importance" [Hawthorn, 34], such as 'Biblican canon', 'literary canon', etc.

cant. The term has three imports or significances: (i) it means a hackneyed language or a "language whose meaning has evaporated from continued repetition" [Macdonald, 191]; (ii) it denotes the *jargon or *slang of a particular class, trade, calling, profession or group, generally of low social standing or of reprobates, such as pedlars, tinkers, vagabonds, thieves and prostitutes; and (iii) it signifies use of affected or hypocritical language with a view to impress honesty, magnanimity, piety, etc.

caricature. A kind of writing that satirises or ridicules a person or a thing through excessively distorting or exaggerating certain aspects of that person or thing, and thus induces laughter. Caricature is akin to *burlesque, and like burlesque it can be both derisive and benign. Caricature is more associated with cartooning than with literature.

carnivalisation [from Latin *carnem*, flesh, and *levare*, to put away]. Originally, carnival was a ritual of riotous feasting and indulgences of all sorts, observed by the Roman Catholics just before the Lenten fasting used to begin. Eating meat (or 'flesh') was prohibited (or was required to be 'put away') during the Lenten, and so the revelry of riotous feasting and indulgences before it was so named—carnivalisation. In course of time, 'carnival' began to mean all sorts of uproarious feasting or merriment any time anywhere. In the further course of time, 'carnival' signified throwing away all authoritarian controls and subverting hierarchical scales of all sorts. Taking a cue from this fact, Mikhail Bakhtin (1895-1975) coined the word 'carnivalisation' in his book *The Dialogic Imagination* "to describe the penetration or incorporation of carnival into everyday life, and its shaping effect on language and literature" [Cuddon, 111]. According to Bakhtin's *Problems of Dostoevsky's Poetics*, carnivalisation is "the liberating and subversive influence of popular humour on the literary tradition" [Baldick, 30]. "Early examples of literary 'carnival' are the Socratic dialogues (in which what appears to be logic is stood on its head and shown to be illogical) and Menippean satire [admixture of the comic and the serious]" [Cuddon, 111]. Francois Rabelais's (?1494-1553?) *Pantagruel* and *Gargantua* are examples of carnivalisation, or of carnivals, as is also Fyodor Dostoyevsky's (1821-1881) tale *Bobok*, in which the dead, unencumbered of the natural laws of this world, freely reveals the truth about it's previous existence for pure fun.

Caroline Age [from Latin *Carolus*, Charles]. The period of time from 1625 to 1649 during which Charles I ruled England.

carpe diem [from Latin *carpe*, snatch, seize, *diem*, day]. The term, a Latin expression, comes from Horace's (65-8 B.C.) *Odes* (I. xi), and means 'seize the day', i.e. 'enjoy yourself while you can' or 'make the best of the present moment'. The *carpe diem* *theme or *motif or attitude is frequently met with in lyric poems; for instance, in Robert Herrick's (1591-1674) famous poem 'To the Virgins, to make much of the time' from which the following lines are taken:

> Gather ye rose-buds while ye may,
> Old time is still a-flying:
> And this same flower that smiles to-day,
> To-morrow will be dying.

The same theme or attitude also occurs in Edmund Spenser's (1552-99) *Faerie Queene* (II. Xii. 74-75): 'Gather, therefore, / The Rose, while yet is prime'. The same theme or attitude will also be found in many poems of Omar Khayyam and in Andrew Marvell's (1621-78) celebrated poem 'To His Coy Mistress'. Interestingly, "In some Christian poems and sermons, the *carpe diem* motif warns us to prepare our souls for death, rather than our bodies for bed" [Baldick, 31]. See also **ubi sunt*.

catastrophe [from Greek *kata*, down, and *strophe*, a turning]. Originally, the term refers to the final *resolution or unknotting of the entanglements of the *plot of a play, usually in some revelation of identity or in the death of the protagonist. Also called *denouement. By analogy, the term is sometimes used to denote the similar resolution of the plot of a *novel or *fiction as well. The final parting of Aziz and Fielding with an uncertain sense of re-union in future at the fag end of E.M. Forster's (1879-1970) *A Passage to India* may be called catastrophe.

catharsis, *katharsis* [from Greek *katharos*, clean]. Literally, the term means 'evacuation of the bowels'. Aristotle (384-322 B.C.) first used the term, in his *Poetics* (ch. VI), in the sense of purification of the emotions by a tragic drama through giving a vent or outlet to some pent-up emotions or repressed thoughts. Like after a storm a calm prevails, after the most heightened tension aroused by a tragic drama, during the climax, a happy feeling of therapeutic release descends upon the spectator or the audience as well as upon the suffering protagonist. This is catharsis. The term may be used in the case of *drama novel, dramatic novel.

causerie [from French *causerie*, chat, light talk]. A chat, gossip or talk of no consequence. The term also applies to any short, informal essay about literature or art in a newspaper or magazine in a light, non-serious manner and in a conversational tone.

Celtic Revival, Keltic Revival. 'Celtic' is the adjectival form of 'Celt' that denotes a branch of the Indo-Germanic people, originally of Gaul or France, but latterly of Ireland, or the language of such people. The term Celtic Revival or Keltic Revival is synonymous with such other terms as Irish Literary Renaissance, Celtic Renaissance, Celtic Dawn and Celtic Twilight. The term denotes the remarkable creative period in the history of Irish literature from 1880 or 1885 to 1939 (death of W.B. Yeats) when Celticism dominated the Irish literary scenario. "Celticism involves an idea of Irishness based on fanciful notions of innate racial character outlined by the English critic Mathew Arnold in *On the Study of Celtic Literature* (1866), in which Celtic traits are said to include delicacy, charm, spirituality, and intellectual sentimentality" [Baldick, 32]. Celtic Revival was a movement "to create a distinctively national literature by going back to Irish history, legend, and folklore, as well as to native literary models" [Abrams, 32]. Prominent leaders of the movement included the poet and dramatist W.B. Yeats (1865-1939) and the dramatist Lady Gregory. Other notable poets of the movement were A E (George Russell) and Oliver St. John Gogarty, and other important dramatists were John Millington Synge (1871-1909) and Sean O'Casey (1880-1964). And among the notable novelists of the period were George Moore (1852-1933), James Stephens (1882-1950) and James Joyce (1882-1941), who, of course, spurned the extreme nationalism of the movement.

cenacle [from French *cenacle* (pronounced: say-nahkl), upper room, coterie, group]. A coterie or group of writers that assembled around a leading literary personality during the Romantic movement in France. The first *cenacle* is believed to have been formed around the French writer Charles Nodier (1780-1844) in his *salon*. The second *cenacle* gathered around the celebrated French poet and novelist Victor Hugo (1802-85) at his house, and the third around the noted French critic and novelist Charles Sainte-Beuve (1804-69). The *cenacles* were a characteristic of the hero-worshipping cult of the French Romantics.

centre. The term is Jacques Derrida's (b. 1930). According to Derrida, the propounder of deconstruction, each and every culture has a centre which bestows meaning, significance or import, elements or aspects of a particular culture. Derrida says that the centre is the Origin, the Truth, the Ideal Form, the Fixed Point, the Immovable Mover, the Essence, the God or the Presence (all to be conceived of metaphorically), and that the significance of everything of the culture is determined by this all-important centre or central symbol(s). For instance, says Derrida, for around 2000 years the centre (or the central symbol) of the Western culture has been the idea of Christianity and Christ. The centre is "'an image, an event, or even a theoretical construct functioning as a nucleus or point of concentration that holds together a particular verbal sequence. That centre gives coherence, a semblance of order at least, to what would otherwise appear to be a random, meaningless sequence of expressions'" [Hawthorn, 38]. Therefore the province of language is also ruled by the centre.

The concept of centre necessarily entails another concept—that of the *Other. If the centre of a certain culture is Christianity, then only Christians will be central to that culture, and, consequently, Hindus, Buddhists, Muslims, Jews, etc. will be pushed away from the centre—will be marginalised—and will be collectively conceived of as the Other. "To characterize a person, group, or institution as 'other' is to place them outside the system of normality or convention to which one belongs oneself. Such an activity is referred to by some theorists by means of a verb form: *othering*. Processes of exclusion by categorization are central to certain ideological mechanisms. If a woman is other, then that which is particular to the experience of being a woman is irrelevant to 'how things are', to the defining conventions by which one lives. If members of a given racial group are collectively seen as other, then how they are treated is irrelevant to what humanity demands—because they are other and not human" [*op. cit.*, 249]. This fact leads to a centre spawning binary opposites, with one term of the opposition being central and the other term being marginal (the marginalised Other), and the central term being the privileged one. Examples of binary opposites are: man/woman, spirit/matter, nature/culture, Christian/pagan, etc. It was one of the principal objectives of Michel Foucault (b. 1926), in his influential *The Archaeology of Knowledge*, to burst out the myth of the centre or to decentre us, and thus to deconstruct our knowledge.

chanson de geste. See *chivalric romance.

chapbook. A type of popular and cheap book or pamphlet, containing short *fairy tales in verse, ballads, rhymed verses, etc. sometimes illustrated with wood-blocks, hawked by a chapman or pedlar during the period from the 16th century to the early 19th century.

character. The term denotes two widely different things. (1) A minor literary *genre introduced by Theophrastus (371-287 B.C.) in his *Characters*. In this sense, a character is a composition that contains a short humorous sketch of a good or bad person betraying in some details his good or bad qualities just for entertainment only. The person so sketched is generally living. Theophrastus used to read out his characters before his students at their monthly dinners at school of which he was the president. The vogue of the character melted away soon after the death of Theophrastus, but was revived in the 17th century chiefly by Sir Thomas Overbury (1581-1613), who wrote some 82 characters. (2) A person in a *novel or a play, or the particular personality of that person. Hamlet in *Hamlet* and Desdemona in *Othello*, or Ishmael in Herman Melville's (1819-91) *Moby-Dick* and Aziz in E.M. Forster's (1879-1970) *A Passage to India* are, for instance, characters.

"Characters are the persons represented in a dramatic or narrative work, who are interpreted by the reader as being endowed with particular moral, intellectual, and emotional qualities by inferences from what the persons say and their distinctive ways of saying it—the dialogue—and from what they do—the action" [Abrams, 32-33]. E.M. Forster, in his *Aspects of the Novel*, calls characters just 'people'. According to the great novelist and critic Henry James (1843-1916), in a *fiction or *narrative some *characters are major and belong to the centre of the narrative and thus determine the course or trajectory of it, while others are minor and constitute what Roger Fowler [Fowler, 28] has very aptly called 'a contextual society'. "More recently the concept of 'character' has come under attack for methodological and ideological reasons in structuralist and post-structuralist theories (see *structuralism and *post-structuralism). In the work of Roland Barthes (1915-80), for example, we find 'character' dispersed into constitutive 'indices' or 'semes' of narrative discourse" [*loc. Cit.*]. Character is now seen more as a *site of striving, struggle, division, than as a source or cause of those things; more as a puppet than as a puppet-master. In this regard, the noted critical theorist Jean-Francois Lyotard (1924-98), in his *The Postmodern Condition: A Report on Knowledge*, writes: "A *self* [which may be compared with a character of a narrative discourse] does not amount to much, but no self is an island; each exists in a fabric of relations that is now more complex and mobile than ever before. Young or old, man or woman, rich or poor, a person [or a character of a narrative discourse] is always located at "nodal points" of specific communication circuits, however tiny these may be. Or better: one is always located at a post through which various kinds of message pass" [Hawthorn, 41]. Also see *flat character, *round character, *static character, *dynamic character, *stock character, *stereotype character, *type character, *Theophrastian character, *chorus character, *character tags and *characterisation.

characterisation. It is the depiction, delineation, portrayal, description or representation of the *characters, *dramatis personae* (particularly in a drama), 'persons' or 'people' in a 'narrative or dramatic work. There are two principal methods of portraying or representing a character: *telling, which is the direct method of speaking to the reader by the author about the attributes, traits, features, dispositions, aspects or marks of a character; and *showing, which is the indirect, dramatic or mimetic method in which a person or character in a narrative is shown by the author to the reader through that person's appearance, speech and actions.

character tags. These are "specific physical features, turns of expression, or mannerisms that identify flat characters" [Lemon, 48]. See also *flat character.

character zone. The critical term was coined by Mikhail Bakhtin (1895-1975). According to Bakhtin, the reader of a *novel generally forms an idea or conception of a character from the narrator's *telling or description about that character, from the narrator's *showing that character's actions, reactions, thoughts, etc. and also from 'transcriptions' of the character's speeches. But beyond all these, lies the character zone which the reader can recognise from the character's semi-discourses and the discourses of other characters. According to Bakhtin, character zones are formed "'from the characters' semi-discourses, from various forms of hidden transmission for the discourse of the other, by the words and expressions scattered in this discourse, and from the irruption of alien expressive elements into authorial discourse (ellipsis, questions, exclamations). Such a zone is the range of action of the character's voice, intermingling in one way or another with the author's voice" [Hawthorn, 42]. "In other words, the reader of a novel builds up a picture of the character's identity not just from direct descriptions of his or her actions or from 'transcriptions' of his or her speech, but from a wider zone of verbal implication" [*loc. Cit.*].

chef d'oeuvre [from French *chef*, chief; *d'* (*de*), of; and *oeuvre*, work, opus]. The masterpiece or best piece of work of a particular artist, author or writer.

chimerat. A *form of *folk-tale or *story of the Indo-European culture which lacks *verisimilitude, but possesses universality, for which reason it widely differs from **novellat*.

China-Box narrative. A *narrative within another narrative. Synonymous with *framed narrative, *nested narrative, *embedded narrative.

chivalric romance [from French *cheval*, horse, and *romance*, love-song, sentimental ballad]. A sort of **romance* prevalent during the medieval period (hence also called 'medieval romance'), especially in the 12th century, in France. Chivalry signified such qualities as bravery, faith in God, truthfulness or fidelity to lady-love, readiness to rescue maidens in distress and people under duress of tyrants, and courtly manners. The heroes of the chivalric *romances* or ballads possessed these ideal qualities, which used to inspire the reader. The emphasis on love and courtliness distinguished the chivalric romance from *chanson de geste* [from French *chanson*, song; *de*, of; and *geste*, gesture] in which masculinity and military heroism were adulated.

chorus, choral character [from Greek *choros*, dance]. The ancient Greek chorus was a group of persons (in comedy upto about 12 and in tragedy upto about 28, and all male who, wearing masks, performed dance-like manoeuvres along with singing or chanting verses during annual festivals of Dionysus, the god of drinking and merriment. Thespis (6th c. B.C.), the Greek inventor of the tragedy, first used a member of the chorus as a dramatic character (the 'answerer') who talked with the leader of the chorus—another dramatic character—and thus projected the enaction of a *plot. The Roman tragic playwrights took the idea of the chorus from the Greeks. The chorus was used in England for the first time, in the Elizabethan period, in the tragedy *Gorbuduc*, written by Norton and Sackville. During the same period, the nature of the Greek or Latin chorus changed phenomenally; the English dramatists applied the term 'chorus' not to a group of persons but to a single person who spoke the prologue and the epilogue; commented upon the *characters and the course of the play; informed the audience of the off-stage events; and did *foreshadowing and *flash-backing through song or speech. Christopher Marlowe's (1564-93) *Dr. Faustus*, William Shakespeare's (1564-1616) *Henry V*, John Milton's (1608-74) *Samson Agonistes* and T.S. Eliot's (1888-1965) *Murder in the Cathedral* are some of the English plays each of which presents a chorus.

In course of time the chorus invaded the *novel where it was, in most cases, a group of persons and not a single person, as in most dramas. Examples of such a chorus are the rustics in George Eliot's (1819-80) *Silas Marner*, the Mellstock musicians in Thomas Hardy's (1840-1928) *Under the Greenwood Tree* and the rustics in his *The Return of the Native*. William Faulkner's (1897-1962) novels, *The Hamlet*, *The Mansion* and *The Rivers*, also utilize the tool of the chorus. The persons who constitute the chorus of a novel are each an individual choral character, but there are 'group choruses' in some novels as well, where a number of persons, so to say, unitedly behave like a single character. Examples of individual 'chorus' characters in Thomas Hardy's novels are: the turf-cutters in *The Return of the Native*—Fairway, Christian, Grandfer Cantle and others; the cottagers of Little Hintock—Wood, Cawtree, Upjohn and Crendon; Bathsheba's labourers in *Far from the Madding Crowd*—Joseph Poorgrass, Henry Fray, Bill Smallbury and Jan Coggan; the grave-diggers in *A Pair of Blue Eyes*; and Haymoss, Blore and others of Lady Constantine's tenantry in *Two on a Tower*. The choir in Hardy's *Under the Greenwood Tree* is an instance of the 'group chorus'. The persons—the individual 'chorus' characters—always appear in a group, like a 'group chorus', never separately, and they are never full-length portraits, as in the novels of Hardy [Cecil, 91-92].

chosism [from French *chose* (pronounced *shoz*), thing, matter, affair]. Literally, the term means 'thinginess', but as a literary and critical term it denotes a highly detailed description of objects (animate and inanimate)—their shape, colour, texture, weight, parts, etc. Some French novelists, particularly those associated with the **nouveau roman* movement, have shown a penchant for *chosism* in their works. Chosism sometimes has had some attraction but when overdone, it proves boring and counter-productive. The French novelists Alain Robbe-Grillet (b. 1922) and Michel Butor (b. 1926) have shown mastery in *chosism*.

chronicle. The term denotes a register of sequential events. In this sense, it is synonymous with annal. Chronicle is to be differentiated from history in that while chronicle records every incident, history records selected incidents with the purpose of showing some trend, the cause-effect relationship between incidents, etc. Chronicles tend to mix facts with legend and rumour. Bede's *Ecclesiastical History* (c. 731), King Alfred's (871-99) *Anglo-Saxon Chronicle*, Holinshed's *Chronicles* (1577) and Camden's *Britannia* (1586) are examples of chronicles. *The Tale of Bygone years*, *The Novgorod First Chronicle*, *Rogozh Chronicle*, *The Laurentian Chronicle*, etc. are some of the popular Russian chronicles [Raduga, 178, 266].

chronicle novel. The **Bildungsroman*, *roman cycle, **roman-fleuve* and *saga novel fall within the category of chronicle novel. The chronicle novel deals with its historical subject-matter chronologically unlike, say, the **nouveau roman* or the *stream-of-consciousness novel.

cinema-verite [from French *cinema*, cinema, and *verite*, verity, truth]. Literally, the term means 'cinema-truth', but as a critical term it "denotes a style of film-making which sets out to capture as closely as possible the appearance of real life" [Ayto, 64]. An alternative term is *cine-verite*.

circular plot. In whatever way it is conceived, generally, a *plot has a 'beginning', a 'middle' and an 'end'. But when the plot is constructed in such a way that at the end of a novel the 'beginning' once again appears as the 'end', it is called a circular plot. "A circular plot is one that, after taking the protagonist through a series of experiences, leaves him with the problems he began with; it can either be a trick to give the work a kind of specious unity by bringing the reader back to the work's starting point, or it can be a thematically effective device for indicating that despite the experience of the protagonist, there has been no real change" [Lemon, 42-43].

classic, classical, classicism. The term 'classic' has at least three meanings: (i) it means "a work suitable for study in school classes" [Baldick, 36]; (ii) it denotes a piece of literature of the highest class or excellence, such as *Paradise Lost*, *Hamlet*, etc.; and (iii) it refers to a piece of literature that may be thought to be a parallel to a piece of literature of the ancient Greece (5th and 4th centuries B.C.) or of the ancient Rome (1st century), as regards excellences of style, form, and content. The term 'classical' is used in two senses: (i) as an adjectival form of the term 'classic' in the above-mentioned second sense; and in this, we may say that the 17th century was the classical age of French literature as 'the 19th century was the classical period of the Western novel'; and (ii) as an antonym to the term *'romantic', because while being romantic (in art) signifies being highly imaginative and emotional, being classical means especially cold, ordered, rational and formal. Classicism is "an attitude to literature that is guided by admiration of the qualities of formal balance, proportion, decorum and restraint attributed to the major works of [ancient] Greek and Roman literature ('the classics') in preference to the irregularities of later vernacular literatures, and especially (since about 1800) to the artistic liberties proclaimed by Romanticism" [Baldick, 36].

climax. [from Greek *klimax*, ladder, which is from *klinein*, slope]. The two terms climax and *crisis pertain to the *story, drama or *narrative and are naturally complementary. Climax is the fourth stage in the six-stage pyramid or triangle of *Freytag. It is the point or moment at which the action or narrative becomes the most intense and takes a turn and inclines towards the 'slope'—towards resolution. At the same point or moment also the crisis [from Greek *krisis* or *krinein*, to decide] occurs, when the *protagonist's fortune faces a reversal or **peripeteia* due to **anagnorisis* and he has to take a decision.

cloak-and-dagger novel. A *novel which involves espionage and disguised adventure, sabotage, subversive activities, etc. It is also called *spy novel.

cloak-and-sword romance. A kind of Spanish, French or Italian *novel or play distinguished for its proud, gallant, courtly and gracious hero who is a skilled swashbuckler and is in love with a fair lady, its plot being full of intrigues.

closed novel. This term and its contrasting term 'open novel' were introduced by Alan Friedman as two critical terms in his *The Turn of the Novel* (1966). Friedman says that the closed novel is one in which the *storyline, or rather the novel itself, ends in a solution of the crisis, or in a clarification of the complexity, it previously built up; or the closed novel is one that simply has a beginning, a middle and an end. Traditional novels generally are closed, for they conclude or close in marriages, deaths, ensconcings in limbo, etc. as envisioned by the authors. For instance, Henry Fielding's (1707-54) *Tom Jones* ends in the marriage of Tom with Sophia and Jane Austen's (1775-1817) *Emma* closes on Harriet's marriage with Robert Martin and George Knightley's proposal to Emma. Friedman maintains that in the closed novel as the storyline progresses, various events come into play to make the plot complex, and the central *character's experience or his *'stream of conscience' expands and expands. But, in the end, the author bridles or checks the process of expansion by bringing in a 'delimiting moral synthesis', which, further, he causes to happen by arranging for a resolution of the climactic complexities or crisis. The *open novel, on the other hand, does not aim at any check or delimitation on the ever expanding course of the storyline, i.e. it does not aim at any resolution of the crisis or at any moral 'synthesis'—it just leaves the storyline at a convenient point. Or, in other words, the open novel does not aim at an integration of the conflicting experiences of the central character but only shows the ever growing piles of various heterogeneous fragments of life.

Friedman's categorisation of novels into the two groups—closed novels and open novels—ultimately depends on his conception of 'moral synthesis' in the novel. He understands the novel as a continuum of events which ceaselessly and ever influence and mould and remould the selves of the central characters, or, which is the same thing, mould and remould the consciences of the characters, while all through the characters (or their selves) happen to be, as if, in a serious dialogue with the world—with 'other selves, social institutions, conventions, values, sometimes nature itself.' It is for this reason that Friedman very rightly says that "with respect to structure, the fundamental form of fiction is the stream of events. With respect to meaning, it seems reasonable to suggest that the fundamental form of the novel is its stream of conscience" [Friedman, 13]. In the close novel, 'the stream of conscience', or 'the stream of morality', we may perhaps say, is restrained, checked at some convenient point; in the open novel it is not. Friedman says: "By a closed novel, then, I mean a novel in which ... the stream of conscience, is finally contained. By an open novel I mean a novel in which the stream of conscience is finally not contained" [*op. cit.*, 16].

closed text. The term and its antonym 'open text' must be carefully distinguished from the paired terms *closed novel and *open novel, introduced by Alan Friedman in 1966 in his book *The Turn of the Novel*. Thirteen years after Friedman's book the Italian novelist and linguist Umberto Eco introduced another pair of critical terms—*closed text and *open text—in his book *The Role of the Reader*. Eco's definitions of the terms are initially disarmingly confusing: what he calls a closed text seems to be an open text, and *vice versa:* "'Those texts that obsessively aim at arousing a precise response on the part of more or less precise empirical readers... are in fact open to any possible 'aberrant' decoding. A text so immoderately 'open' to every possible interpretation will be called a *closed* one'" [Hawthorn, 245]. "In contrast, where the author of the text has envisaged the role of the reader at the moment of generation, according to Eco the text is, paradoxically, open to successive interpretations. These interpretations and reinterpretations, according to Eco, echo one another, and operate within certain texually imposed constraints (unlike responses to what he calls closed texts)" [*loc. cit.*]. For Eco, for instance, the 'James Bond' novels of Ian Fleming (1908-64) are closed texts because 'they are open to any sort of reading [or interpretation]. The apparently puzzling paradox in Eco's terminology may be solved with a simple example. Suppose some people are asked to name the thing inside a closed box. Different people will name the thing differently. In this case, according to Eco, the box may be said to be 'open' (i.e., open to various interpretations as to the thing inside). But if the box is held open and the persons are asked to name the thing inside it, all of them will name the thing identically. In this case, the box, according to Eco, will be said to be 'closed'. Examples of closed texts are: 'a whodunit by Agatha Christie, a thriller by Frederick Forsyth or a scientific treatise on lice'. And examples of open texts are: James Joyce's (1882-1941) *Finnegans Wake* and T.S. Eliot's (1888-1965) *The West Land*. Also see *closure.

closure. It is the sense of completion in the mind of the reader at the end of a literary work (or a part of it; e.g., a stanza), including a piece of literary criticism, when he will be satisfied that the work now lacks any force for further continuation of it, and that the work (or a part of it) possesses an aesthetic wholeness. Closure points to a single meaning. Closure is akin to *open text; a *closed text lacks closure. A significant feature of modernist or experimental art and literature is absence of closure in them.

clou [from French *clou* (pronounced: klu), peg, nail, spike]. The central idea, point, situation or episode of a literary work round which the whole work, so to say, spins, or upon which the whole work thrives. It is the chief point of interest in the whole work. The meaning of the term 'clou' is implicit in the phrase 'And thereby hangs a tale'. *Clou* must not be confused with the word 'clue' (or, rarely, 'clew') which means a key, pointer, hint or guide that helps to solve a mystery or conundrum.

cock-and-bull story. A kind of very improbable and quite unbelievable story that is long and rambling, in which the interest is sustained by queer turns and shocking surprises. Cock-and-bull story has strong association with *fable and *bestiary.

code. The term has at least two meanings: (i) code means language (English, Bengali, Hindi, etc.) and dialect; and (ii) code is a set of norms or conventions that govern the thoughts and activities of a group of people; for instance, a particular cultural code controls a certain culture, and a certain literary code provides meaning as well as evaluates a particular work claimed to be literary. The literary code (or the rules, norms and conventions that constitute it) must be shared by the writer and the reader, in order that the writer can communicate his message to the reader through his writing.

code switching. A change by a writer or speaker from one language or *code to another in the course of his writing or speaking. For instance, a writer is said to be doing a code switching when in the course of writing in English he suddenly begins to write in French.

coherence. A form of unity among different parts or elements of a literary work. The idea of structure in a literary work, as spoken of by the structuralists, suggests the presence of a necessary internal coherence in that work. Also see *structuralism.

Collage [from French *collage*, pasting, gluing]. The term has been borrowed from the vocabulary of painting, where it denotes a work which is but a pasting or assemblage of fragments culled from other works. Collage designates both the technique of the pasting or assembling the fragments and the finished product that comes off the pasting or collocation. In literature, a collage signifies a work that incorporates quotations from, and allusions to, other works, foreign phrases, etc. as well as the technique used in creating a collage. The influence of *surrealism on collage is considerable. The works of such writers as Ezra Pound (1885-1972), T.S. Eliot (1888-1965) and James Joyce (1882-

1941) show the presence of collages. Pound's *Cantos*, Eliot's *The West Land* and Joyce's *Ulysses*, Finnegan's *Wake* and even *A Portrait of the Artist as a Young Man* are examples of the use of collage technique. The following paragraph from Joyce's *A Portrait* may illustrate the collage technique: "The word now shone in his brain, clearer and brighter than any ivory sawn from the mottled tusks of elephants. *Ivory*, *ivoire*, *avorio*, *ebur*. One of the first examples that he had learnt in Latin had run: *India mittit ebur*; .... He had learnt what little he knew of the laws of Latin verse from a ragged book written by a Portuguese priest. *Contrahit orator, variant in carmine vates*."

Also see *cut-up, *aleatory writing, *pastiche, **rechauffe*.

collective unconscious. A term introduced by the Swiss analytical psychologist Carl Gustav Jung (1875-1961). It denotes that portion or layer of the unconscious region of the mind of an individual where the forgotten memories of the race to which he belongs are stored, and which is the source of the *archetypes and universal *symbols that surface in legends, dreams, poetry and, rarely in prose narratives. Herman Melville's (1819-91) *Moby Dick*, for instance, contains a good number of archetypes—Queequeg (the image of the noble savage), Pequod (the image of the first Indian tribe exterminated by the white Americans), Elijah (the Apollo-like warner), Moby Dick (the image of the mysterious and cruel darker side of human life), etc. The collective unconscious is not to be confused with individual *unconscious, or, simply, unconscious, which merely contains an individual's painful memories of his own life repressed by himself.

colloquialism. It is the use of colloquial words or language at places of writings where the use is improper. A colloquial word or phrase is one which is below the standard literary language but above the *slang. The colloquial language is not accepted as normal or of good taste, but some colloquial words or phrases may eventually be recognised as formal, or of good taste, or as literary. The word 'flaberghast', for instance, was earlier colloquial, but now it is accepted as formal or literary. A style of language may also be colloquial if it is plain, informal and relaxed, all at the same time. The sentence, 'The man, a dodgy customer with a shifty look in his eye, was clearly up to no good', for instance, is colloquial.

colportage [from French *colporter*, to hawk, to peddle, to spread (news, short stories, etc.)]. The term denotes cheap and popular literature, such as sensational *novels, *thrillers, *romances, broadsides, etc. sold by hawkers or colporteurs.

comedie humaine [from French *comedie*, comedy, pretence, farce, and *humain*, human, humanity]. Literally, the term means 'human comedy' or 'comedy of humanity'. It was invented by the noted French novelist Honore de Balzac (1799-1850) as the title of the 'Furne' collected edition of his *Comedie humaine* (1842-46) which consisted of 91 interlocked novels and stories on the general theme of the mosaic life of the 18th and 19th century French society. Later on, however, the term came to be used "for any literary portrait of the diversity of human affairs, and indeed for those affairs themselves" [Ayto, 68].

comic novel. Originally, the terms 'comedy' and 'comic' (adjectival form of 'comedy') were reserved for the genre of drama (comedy of humours, comedy of manners, etc.); but, later on, the terms invaded the region of narratives, so that, for example, comedy came to denote "a story with a happy ending" [Macdonald, 260]. Now, "As a non-dramatic term, 'comedy' or 'comic' refers broadly to whatever seems calculated to amuse by provoking a smile or a laugh" [Lemon, 16]. So, a *novel, intended for generating, besides other things, a sense of happiness or laughter, may be called a comic novel. In this relatively loose sense of the term, E.M. Forster's (1879-1970) novels may be said to be comedies or comic novels.

committed writer. A committed writer is one who trusts, and is dedicated to, a certain political or social ideology, beliefs and programmes, and writes to advocate and promote those. He does not keep himself neutral but proactively writes to reinforce and fan out his ideological principles, He uses his writing as a propaganda medium. Such dramatists as Jean-Paul Sartre (b. 1905), Bertott Brecht (1898-1956), Gunter Grass (b. 1927), Bernard Shaw (1856-1950) and Arnold Wesker (b. 1932), and such novelists as Jean-Paul Sartre, Gunter Grass, Andre Malraux (b. 1901) and Doris Lessing (b. 1919) are famously committed writers. The committed writers vow or pledge their commitment or *engagement to their ideology and programmes thereof. The committed writer is also known as *_engage_ (French word, meaning engaged or committed) writer.

commonplace book. A note-book or memorandum book in which ideas, themes, points, arguments, questions, etc. and even words and phrases are jotted down by writers for future utilisation of those things. A famous instance of commonplace book is Ben Jonson's (1572-1637) *Timber: Or Discoveries* "which comprises a draft for a treatise on the art of writing and on types of literature, miniature essays, sententiae, pensees (...) and so forth" [Cuddon, 162].

complication. See *Freytag's Triangle.

confessional novel. The term is analogous to the terms 'confessional poetry' and 'confessional literature'. A nebulous term, it is akin to the *autobiographical novel, in which the author actually reveals, or seems to reveal, his self in the first person. The confessional novel may be of three sorts: (i) that in which the novelist himself narrates in the first person; (ii) that in which he enters into the self of the central character who does the narrative, as Albert Camus (1913-60) does in his novel *La chute* (*The Fall*); and (iii) that which follows the *frame story technique and in which the novelist enters into the self of the central character but himself remains the narrator, as Andre Gide (1869-1951) does in his *Les faux-monnayeurs* (*The Coiners*) (in this novel the central character is the novelist Edouard, who is writing an autobiographical *novel—this is the *story within a story, i.e., within the *frame story—but the frame story itself is being narrated by Gide).

confidant, confidante. A *character (confidant is male and confidante is female) of little consequence, generally a close friend of the principal character, to whom the principal character confides his or her private thoughts, feelings, fears, sentiments, longings, etc. which the confidant or confidante is supposed to patiently listen to. The confidant or confidante is a sort of 'side kick' and is to be found both in *novels and plays. For instances, Horatio is the confidant of Hamlet in Shakespeare's (1564-1616) *Hamlet* and Celia is the confidante to Rosalind in his *As You Like It*, and Virgil is the confidant of Bo in William Inge's (1913-73) play *Bus Stop*; and Maria Gostrey is the confidante of Strether in Henry James's (1843-1916) novel *The Ambassadors*.

Whenever a novelist wants to keep himself outside his novel, he, generally, creates a confidant or confidante to whom the central character communicates his innermost thoughts and feelings. Presence of the confidant or confidante is a common feature of the detective story (see *detective novel, detective story).

conflict. It is the opposition or antagonism between *characters or forces in a prose *fiction or play, and is the source of the dynamism that pushes the *plot to its catastrophic end, determines the *action and defines the *theme. The conflict may be thought of as the heart of the *narrative or play. It may be of three kinds: (i) conflict between two persons (or characters) with two contradictory motives (which sometimes arise out of two clashing value systems); for instance, that between the *protagonist's motive (or interest) and the motive of the forces loyal to the deceased king Duncan in *Macbeth*; (ii) conflict between a character and forces external to him; for instance, the struggle or strife in Thomas Hardy's (1840-1928) *Jude the Obscure* between Jude and his contradictory social and supernatural forces; and (iii) conflict between two discordant forces or motives within the same character, or, which is the same thing, between the two contesting halves of the same character; for example, between the two halves (or motives) of Hamlet in *Hamlet*, which is the cause of the Prince's procrastination.

consistency. Consistency in a literary work resides in the compatibility, coherence, harmony, balance and decorum among the parts or elements of it. A comic episode in a comedy, for instance, is consistent in a comedy, but not in a tragedy, unless it is employed as a comic relief. A *character, at a particular moment in a play or *novel, breaks consistency if he behaves as he should not, or does not behave as he should, i.e. if he acts 'out of character'. Consistency also requires keeping the convention. A 'soliloquy in a naturalistic drawing-room comedy', for instance, will violate the *convention of comedy and thus will break the consistency of the play. Breach of *decorum as regards use of words or phrases will amount to violating the consistency of style.

conte [from French *conte*, tale, story]. Broadly, any *story or short prose *fiction, but, specifically, *short story. Examples of the *conte* are Voltaire's (1694-1778) *Zadig* and *Candide*, Jonathan Swift's (1667-1745) *Gulliver's Travels*, (Dr) Samuel Johnson's (1709-84) *Rasselas* and Gustave Flaubert's (1821-80) *Trois Contes*. The *conte* tends to be fantastic, witty, allegorical, comic and moralistic.

controlling image. The image (or metaphor) which is axial or central to a literary work, determining the work's form, meaning or significance, atmosphere, other images, etc. The term particularly pertains to poetry, but is also used in narrative criticism and discourse. The white whale, Moby Dick, in Herman Melville's (1819-91) *Moby Dick*, for instance, is the controlling image of the *novel.

convention. The term particularly refers to the genres of drama and poetry. Convention [from Latin *con*, together, and *venire*, to come] signifies a necessary, or, at least, convenient, set of devices, ideas, beliefs, images, attitudes, *symbols, *codes, etc. that are implicitly agreed upon between the writer and the audience or the reader (they, as if, come together, i.e. closer). For instance, Shakespeare's (1564-1616) *As You Like It* belongs to the pastoral convention and the poetry of the poets before Wordsworth (1770-1850) follows the convention of poetic diction. Convention is a sort of allowance by the audience or reader for the writer "for solving the problems in representing reality that are posed by a particular artistic medium" [Abrams, 47]. Ignorance of the convention frequently stands in the way of fair appreciation and criticism of literary works. Once, even an oblong reference to sex in a piece of literature, for instance, was considered to be egregiously vulgar, but it is now almost "a literary convention to be outspoken on sexual matters" [*loc. cit.*], and so ignorance of the status of sexuality in the convention may tilt one's critical judgement on a literary work. The contrary term of convention is 'invention', but sometimes invention is incorporated into the convention over time. For example, Gerard Manley Hopkins's sprung rhythm was once an invention—something outside convention—but now it has been 'naturalised' and adopted within the poetic convention. The drawbacks of convention are that it may become hardened, mannered, dull and boring, and stylised.

cosmopolitan novel, cosmopolitan writing. The word 'cosmopolitan' [from Greek *kosmos*, world, universe, and *politicos*, citizen] literally means 'citizen of the world or universe'. However, the term cosmopolitan novel denotes a *novel whose theme and attitude are global or universal. A cosmopolitan novel "stresses the global nature of everyday life and tries to depict societies and individuals as globally representative. The use of *myth, *fable and *parable, which tend to have universal parallels and analogies, is a feature of such writing" [Cuddon, 183]. Examples of cosmopolitan novels are : Colin MacInnes's (1914-76) *City of Spades* and Salman Rushdie's (b. 1947) *Midnight's Children* and *Shame*. "Other writers [novelists included] of note who have been described as cosmopolitan are Isabel Allende, Bharati Mukherjee, Derek Walcott, Mario Vargas Llosa and Gabriel Garcia Marquez" [Cuddon, 183]. The cosmopolitan novel is antonymous to the 'national' novel, for while the former goes beyond all national, social, religious and cultural boundaries, the latter's *theme is confined within the confines of a nation or its communities, religions, cultures, etc. Examples of 'national' novels are: Rudyard Kipling's (1865-1936) *Kim*, Joseph Conrad's (1857-1924) *Heart of Darkness*, E. M. Forster's (1879-1970) *A Passage to India*, Graham Greene's (1904-91) *The Heart of the Matter* and Anthony Burgess's (b. 1917) *The Malayan Trilogy*.

counter-turn. Analogous to the antistrophe of the choral song, the term refers to the surprisingly sudden and unexpected turn or twist at the *end* of a play or *narrative.

coup de theatre [from French *coup*, blow, stroke; *de*, of, by; and *theatre*, playhouse]. Literally, the term means 'blow of theatre', but metaphorically it is applicable with a range of significances. For instances, it means a sudden twist or turn in the *plot of a play or *narrative, such as "the unveiling of a disguised character or the reappearance of one assumed by the audience to be dead" [Baldick, 46]; a sudden and dramatic action; and unexpectedly smashing hit in the course of the narrative; etc.

covert plot. Like the major *plot and the minor plot in some play or *narrative, there may also be the covert plot and the *overt plot in a certain play or narrative. As is obvious, the overt plot is easily recognisable, but the covert plot is not—it is a hidden plot. The covert plot is to be found in a *palimpsest text.

cradle book. Any book printed before 1501 is called a cradle book.

creative unconscious. See *Unconscious, the.

crime fiction. A *fiction with a criminal *theme, such as murder, theft, rape, etc. In this sense, the criminal fiction is not a modern invention but prototypes of it may be found in classical epics, for instance in Homer's (c. 8th century B.C.) and in such works as Fyodor Dostoevsky's (1821-81) *Crime and Punishment* (considered by some to be the greatest crime fiction), Shakespeare's (1564-1616) *Hamlet* and Thomas Middleton's (c. 1580-1627) *The Revenger's Tragedy*. Arthur Conan Doyle (1859-1930) and the three queens of crime fiction—Agatha Christie (1890-1976), Dorothy Sayers (1893-1957) and Margery Allingham (1904-66)—have produced many crime fictions.

crisis. It is the point in the course of a drama or *narrative where the generated rising tension reaches the peak, or the growing complication attains its apical stage, and the protagonist needs to make a final and resolving decision on which the shape or nature of the rest of the drama or narrative totally depends. In *Freytag's pyramid, crisis corresponds with the fourth stage of the pyramid called 'climax'. Crisis or climax is followed by 'falling action' and ultimately by *resolution or *denouement or *catastrophe. The term crisis is sometimes used interchangeably with the term *climax.

criticism, literary. The term denotes "the reasoned discussion of literary works" [Baldick, 48]. Criticism is the art or science of defining and determining the qualities of literary works. Criticisms are of various kinds: theoretical, practical, impressionistic, judicial or normative, mimetic, pragmatic, expressive, objective, sociological, Freudian or psychoanalytical, feminine, Marxist, interpretative or analytic, subjective, absolutist, relativistic, comparative, moral, formalistic, Jungian or archetypal, biographical, etc. *Theoretical criticism* aims at determining some general principles of literature and defining some terms, categories, and other tools for analyzing literary works, and also at fixing some norms, standards or criteria for evaluation of literary works. *Practical* or *applied criticism* is concerned with the evaluation of particular literary works and their authors by applying general principles of literary criticism. *Impressionistic criticism* "attempts to represent in words the felt qualities of a particular passage or work, and to express the responses (the 'impression') that the work directly evokes from the critic" [Abrams, 50]. *Judicial* or *normative criticism* "attempts ... to analyze and explain the effects of a work by reference to its subject, organization, techniques, and style, and to base the critic's individual judgements on specified criteria of literary excellence" [*op. cit.*, 51]. *Mimetic criticism* considers literary works as representations or mimeses of human life and the world in miniatures, and so the supreme criterion of criticism, according to it, is the truth in the representation or in the degree of correspondence between the representation and the object represented. *Pragmatic criticism* recognises that the aim of a literary work is to achieve certain desired effect upon its readers or hearers, such as pleasure, arousal of particular emotions, corrections of faults, instructions, etc. Naturally, therefore, such a criticism determines the value of a work basing on the degree of success to which a particular work has achieved its targeted end. *Expressive criticism* is especially concerned with poetry, which, it believes is but the self-expression of the poet, and consequently, it evaluates any poetic creation by the poet's sincerity, vision, imagery, skill of expression. This kind of criticism is principally done by the romantic critics.

Objective criticism is so called because it emphatically considers a piece of literature as an 'object', detached from its author as well as from the world. It wants to be 'scientific', and, in this sense, it is quite divergent from the subjective criticism (*infra*). It "describes the literary product as a self-sufficient and autonomous object, or else as a world-in-itself, which is to be contemplated as its own end, and to be analyzed and judged solely by 'intrinsic' criteria such as its complexity, coherence, equilibrium, integrity, and the interrelations of its component elements" [*op. cit.*, 52]. *Subjective criticism* is just the contrary of the objective criticism in holding that the criteria with which literary works are to be judged proceeds from the person or subject who happens to comprehend it (read or hear it). While in objective (or scientific) criticism the criteria or principles are objective, in subjective criticism these depend on the choice (or whim) of the subject. When a literary work is evaluated from the point of view of its impact on the society, the criticism is called *Sociological criticism*. David Daiches writes that "sociological criticism is that which concerns itself with the whole complex of cultural activities of which the production of literature is only one fragment" [Daiches, 383]. The *Freudian criticism* or *psychoanalytical criticism* views and evaluates literature with the insights of Sigmund Freud's (1856-1939) psychoanalysis: sexuality, unconscious motivation, primary and secondary mechanisms, repression, etc. It is mostly concerned with the latent meanings of literary works, considered as the workings of the unconscious of their authors. The Swiss analytical psychologist C.G. Jung (1875-1961) rejected Freud's theory that literary works and art are ultimately reducible to mere libidinal wish-fulfilments. Jung said that literatures of all climes and all ages abound in the contents of the collective unconscious of all human beings —the contents which he called archetypes. The *archetypal critics* (or the Jungian critics) are interested in identifying the archetypes of literary works.

Marxist criticism, likewise, views and judges literary works from the perspective of Karl Marx's (1818-83) theories of dialectical materialism and historical materialism, according to which art is a part of the 'superstructure' of the society (the 'mode of production' and the 'forces of production' being its base). Marxism believes in social realism as regards art and literature, and "demanded that artists should be committed to the working-class cause of the Party, that literature should reflect a progressive outlook on society, provide a sense of the ideal possibilities of social development, and should be accessible to the masses" [Ousby, 601]. Further, in Marxist criticism, "Modernist tendencies in Western literature were regarded as decadent, subjective and pessimistic in outlook, while the 19th century realist novel was praised as a precursor of the 20th-century socialist-realist novel" [*loc. cit.*]. Marxist criticism has been developed and modified by such critics as Georg Lukacs, Lucien Goldmann, Louis Althusser, those of the *Frunkfurt School, and the two English Marxist critics—Raymond Williams and Terry Eagleton.

Absolutist criticism claims that there are some necessary, self-existent, unchanging and universal ideals, standards or principles under which literary works must be evaluated. This claim is contested by *relativistic criticism* which believes that the principles or standards according to which literary works are judged change, or are modified, from age to age, and differ from one culture to another. *Comparative criticism* evaluates a certain literary work by comparing it with other similar works, either by the same writer or by other writers. *Moral criticism* evaluates a work by judging, among other things, the effect of the work on the morals of readers, which is its chief concern. There is no monolithic *feminist criticism*, but there are varieties of it. Some feminist critics claim that male writers misrepresent female *characters in their works, and so they should refrain from dealing with female characters, some other feminist critics, though, deny their claim. Again, there are feminist critics (like Luce Irigaray and Helene Cixous) who believe that there is such a thing as *ecriture feminine* or 'feminine writing', but other feminine critics would not admit this. *Interpretative criticism* or *analytic criticism* aims at explaining correctly a work by unknotting the complicated web that it is. *Biographical criticism* brings out the hidden relationships between the contents and features of a literary work and the biographical data of its author. Finally, the *formalist criticism* is especially concerned with the formal or structural aspects of a literary work, in almost total disregard of the work's contents in which the realistic and Marxist critics are principally interested. *Formalism, or to be very precise, *Russian Formalism, originated in Moscow in the second decade of the 20th century as a movement that focused on "the formal patterns and technical devices of literature to the exclusion of its subject matter and social values" [Abrams, 102]. Formalist criticism accords with the principles of (Russian) formalism broached and developed by such critics as Boris Eichenbaum, Victor Shklovsky, Roman Jakobson, *et al*.

critifiction. A critical term introduced by Siegfried Mews (and Leo Truchlar) in 1989. It denotes "Novels and short stories, often written by academics, which use academic settings and / or explore, sometimes humorously, issues from current literary-critical theory" [Hawthorn, 59].

critic. One who is a connoisseur or judge of a literary work's quality or value.

critique. An anglicised French word [in French, it, when used a male term, means 'a critic'; but when used as a feminine word, it means 'criticism' or 'review']. Critique signifies a threadbare analysis and evaluation of a literary work, in the shape of an essay or review. The term also denotes a formal treatise, such as the philosopher Immanuel Kant's *Critique of Pure Reason* and *Critique of Judgement*.

crux. Literally, the word means a 'cross', 'something that occasions difficulty or perplexity', that 'on which a decision turns', etc. As a critical term, it denotes a "difficult or ambiguous passage in a literary work upon which interpretation of the rest of the work depends" [Baldick, 49].

culture hero. "A culture hero is a legendary or mythic hero who embodies the idealized values of a particular culture—as Achilles embodied the ideal of Greek warrior" [Lemon, 46].

cultural primitivism. The term refers to the belief that the 'culture' of the primitive society or of the pre-industrial, non-literate, non-urban society is basically better and preferable, as regards values, such as humaneness and happiness, than the culture of the 'so called' cultured society, or of the urban, industrialised and literate society.

cultures, two. The term originated in the novelist Sir C.P. Snow's 1959 Rede Lecture on *The Two Cultures and the Scientific*

Revolution. "In this he contrasted the culture of 'literary intellectuals' and that of 'scientists', and argued that the two had ceased to communicate. He suggested remedy, involving a radical change in the educational attitudes, was savagely attacked by F.R. Leavis for its utilitarian approach to the study of the humanities" [Ousby, 871]. Nevertheless, Snow's idea of two cultures and his remedy for it deserves consideration.

cut-back. Same as *analepsis and *switchback.

cut-up. A peculiar mode of writing *novels in which first a manuscript or written text is made, then that text is cut up into some suitable segments, and then those segments are shuffled and printed in that order to make the book. This *aleatory technique was first adopted by the novelist William S. Burroughs (b. 1914) in some of his novels, particularly in *The Ticket That Exploded*. Also see **collage*.

cyberpunk. [from Greek *kybernetes*, steersman, and punk (a word of unknown origin), a prostitute, balderdash, a fool]. Cyberpunk is "a *postmodern* form of science fiction in which the events take place partially or entirely within the 'virtual reality' formed by computers or computer networks, in which the characters may be either human or artificial intelligences. A well-known instance is William Gibson's (b. 1914) *Neuromancer*" [Abrams, 279]. *Neuromancer*, the ever first cyberpunk novel, was inspired by the famous film (almost cult film) *Blade Runner*.

D

Dada, Dadaism [from French *dada*, gee-gee, hobby, fad]. The term 'Dada' may mean 'hobby horse', and is the curious name of a movement in art and literature that was touched off by the Rumania-born French poet Tristan Tzara (1896-1963) in Zurich in 1916. He could not swallow the Western culture's insouciance about the devastation of the First World War, and this made him a nihilist in the sphere of language and literature. "He sought to destroy conventional language by recording words in the arbitrary order of spontaneous thought, ignoring syntax and logical sequence" [Thorlby, 778]. He believed that from such a disorderly language a new sort of poetry could come out. In course of time, the Dadaists threw to the four winds not only the linguistic conventions but all sorts of traditional ideas, rules and ideals. After the First World War, Dadaism, for a brief period, became considerably popular. It sustained roughly from 1916 to 1920. The word 'nothing' was the basic term of the Dadaists, and the Dadaist literature is characterized by heavy doses of fantasy, symbolic expression, nihilism and satire. Tristan Tzara, the German poet and sculptor Hans Arp (1887-1966) and Hugo Ball (1886-1927), the German poet, dramatist and critic, were the most renowned Dadaists. Around 1919 or 1920 Dadaism made over the world of art and literature to *surrealism as about 1916 it took that over from *futurism.

death of the author. See *author, death of.

decadence [from French *decadence*, decline, decadence, decay]. Decadence originally meant the neglect of established literary canons or standards of excellence in the 19th century French literature. In France, Charles Pierre Baudlaire (1821-67) published his collection of poems *Les Fleurs du mal* (*Flowers of Evil*) in 1857, which may be supposed to be a sort of the manifesto of the decadence movement or cult. The movement or cult was visibly preoccupied with excesses of despair, decay, sadness and sorrow: '—O sorrow, sorrow! Time eats life away, / The Foe obscure which does our hearts consume / Grows stronger from our blood and our decay!' ('The Enemy'). The term at first signified the decline and decay in the regard for the canons of the French literature of the 19th century, but then in course of time it came to mean decline in any literature of any country of any period, so identified. For instance, in America, Edgar Allan Poe's (1809-49) stories and poems are called decadent for the morbidity that is there in them, and in England the works of Oscar Wilde (1854-1900), Dante Gabriel Rossetti (1828-82), Algernon Swinburne (1837-1907) and Aubrey Beardsley (1872-98) are considered decadent. However, besides morbidity and disrespect for convention, decadent literature is also marked by artificiality, egocentricity, sensationalism, bizarreness, self-analysis and conviction of *'art for art's sake'.

deconstruction. The term with its special 'meaning' was coined by the French philosopher Jacques Derrida (b. 1930) and was first introduced by him in his 1966 paper presented at the Johns Hopkins University and then, next year, in his three celebrated critical books: *Writing and Difference*, *Of Grammatology* and *Voice and Phenomenon*. Any attempt at defining the term will be futile because, according to (the theory of) deconstruction, no term, let alone a sentence, can have a fixed meaning. Derrida claims that the meaning of language is limitlessly unstable, but the Western tradition has ever attempted to fix the meaning, to dispel the uncertainty of signification, to create grounds for truth and certainty. Here lies Derrida's objection to the Western tradition. He calls the Western tradition logocentric, the Greek word *logos* here meaning Word, God, Truth, Law or Reason. In the Western tradition, the ultimate meaning of everything, including language, is derived from Logos or God—the ultimate *Centre (hence logocentrism). From Logos or God is derived the authenticity of the self, and from the authenticity of the self is derived the authenticity of speech and the privilege of speech over writing (hence, again, logocentrism), because in speech the self is present (i.e., in speech there is presence) while in writing the self is absent (i.e., in writing there is absence). Deconstruction actually means de-centering. The Western tradition construes, or 'constructs' the meaning of, everything, including language, ultimately relying on the arbitrary concept of Logos or God—the ultimate Centre. Here, Derrida would like to refute the fixity of this ultimate Centre—Logos or God—by saying that the concept of the authenticity of this ultimate Centre is absolutely arbitrary.

Secondly, Derrida says that in the Western tradition meaning or signification depends on the concept of binary opposition and centering or privileging. Human mind, he admits, functions by forming conceptual pairs, such as man/woman, male/female, nature/culture, spirit/matter, white/black, Christian/pagan, etc. The mistake of the Western tradition is that it accepts one of each pair as legitimate or true and excludes the other of each pair. The one of a pair that it accepts is the centre or the privileged. Now, for example, if man is taken to be the centre, the privileged or the ideal, then everything related to human beings will be having a particular meaning than if woman is taken to be the centre. But Derrida argues that neither man nor woman is the centre, that reality—in this case, human being—is both man and woman, and so the system of centering must be stopped for retrieving the legitimate meaning of reality—the centering or the privileging must be deconstructed. The correct meaning, according to Derrida, is a fiction, for the meaning of anything exists in the free play, to and fro, between the two binary opposites of it. The meaning, therefore, is unstable. It is, as if, dancing. The meaning of human being is dancing between the concepts of man and woman. Any centering would be disastrous. This is deconstruction.

decorum. It is the consistency or fitness or appropriateness between the *form and the content of a literary work, or the *consistency among the characters, actions, dialogues and narrations of a play or *narrative. When, for example, a character, who is an extract of the upper class, speaks in a dignified language or behaves in a dignified manner, we may say there is decorum between the character and his language or behaviour. The concept of decorum is believed to have come from Horace's (65-8 B.C.) *Ars Poetica* (*Art of Poetry*), The term *propriety is sometimes used interchangeably with the term 'decorum', but some critics make a difference between the two. They say that propriety has a wider connotation than decorum. Decorum is " consistency with the canons of propriety" and the "canons of propriety are the canons of good taste, good manners and correctness" [Cuddon, 212, 704]. However, decorum or propriety is a set of *a priori* canons, principles or assumptions about the appropriateness of the elements and the relations among them of a literary work.

defamiliarisation. The term is a liberal translation of the Russian word *ostranenie* ('making strange') which was introduced as a literary critical term by the Russian Formalist writer and critic Viktor Shklovsky (b. 1893) in his influential essay 'Poetry as Technique' (1917). Defamiliarisation denotes the act of making the *familiar* perception or thing *unfamiliar*. In our ordinary quotidian life, we become familiar and habituated with hosts of things as well as with hosts of words or expressions. Such ordinary perceptions of things and habituated expressions cannot be the contents or elements of worthwhile literary works, and so both the things and the expressions must be made 'de-familiarised', i.e. unfamiliarised or *singularised*. When things (or perceptions of them) are made unfamiliarised, the act involved is called defamiliarisation, but when expressions are made unfamiliarised, the act involved is known as *foregrounding. In our ordinary conversations, most expressions become so easy of understanding that we understand or cognise the objects of those expressions without paying even moderate attention to them, i.e. we understand the meanings of those expressions, so to say, automatically. In other words, those expressions become automatised. The process in which an expression becomes automatised is called *automatisation. Foregrounding and automatisation are contradictory terms. In automatisation 'the expression itself does not attract any attention' though the object of the expression does; in foregrounding, on the other hand, the expression attracts most of the attention so that the object of the expression becomes marginalised, somewhat shadowed, which process is called *backgrounding. Backgrounding, that is, is a "process whereby certain elements in a literary work are presented in such a way as *not* to stand out or be noticed" [Hawthorn, 69]. By foregrounding "'we mean the use of the devices of the language in such a way that this use itself attracts attention and is perceived as uncommon, as deprived of automization [i.e., automatisation], as deautomized [i.e., deautomatised], such as a live poetic metaphor (as opposed to a lexicalized one, which is automized)'" [*op. cit.*, 68]. However, the two terms 'defamiliarisation' and 'foregrounding' are nowadays often being used interchangeably. Though 'defamiliarisation' is rather a recently inducted critical term, the concept of defamiliarisation is not new. S. T. Coleridge (1772-1834), long ago suggested it in his *Biographia Literaria* when he wrote that a 'film of familiarity' 'blinds us to the wonders of the world' and, being commissioned by William Wordsworth (1770-1850), composed poems for *Lyrical Ballads* where familiar things were metamorphosed into unfamiliar things. In poetry, particularly, the technique of defamiliarization is an ancient concept, as lively today as ever before, and a very important one at that. P. B. Shelley rightly said that poetry "'makes familiar objects be as if they were not familiar' by stripping 'the veil of familiarity from the world'" [Baldick, 54]. But wherever prose will want to be poetical defamiliarisation will be an aid, indeed.

degage [from French *degage*, unconstrained, relaxed, free and easy]. The word is an adjective, and is now used "to mean 'lacking intense personal involvement, not committed to any artistic ideals, political ideology, etc.'" [Ayto, 85]. The term is antonymous with the term **engage*. Most writers are *degage*, i.e. not committed to, or not having a commitment with, any *political*, religious or other ideologies, but some, such as the two left-wingers—G.B. Shaw (1856-1950) and Jean-Paul Sartre (b. 1905)—are.

deixis [from Greek *deixis*, to show]. Deixis means 'showing'. The adjectival form of the term is deictic. Deictic words may be conceived of as "situational 'co-ordinates' of person (*I/you, us/them*), place (*here/there, this/that*), and time (*now/then, yesterday/today*)" and are used "to denote those aspects of an utterance that refer to and depend upon the situation in which the utterance is made" [Baldick, 54].

deja vu [from French *deja*, already, before, and *vu*, seen, observed]. The term, literally, means 'already seen' or 'seen before'. It refers to a psychological condition, characterised by a form of memory disorder, in which the person actually sees a quite new thing or situation but thinks that he saw that thing or situation earlier. In recent times, the meaning of the term has been extended "to connote 'something seen so often before that it has become tedious'" [Ayto, 86].

demotic [from Greek *demos*, people]. The term refers to a kind of writing that is simple both in vocabulary and style, as distinguished from the hieratic, i.e. priestly, scholarly or elegant.

denouement [from French *denouement*, untying, result, solution]. The resolution of the mystery or the untying of the complications at the end of the plot of a play, *novel or *story. Also see *catastrophe.

desert island fiction. A sort of *fiction (*novel, **novella*, *short story, *fable, etc.) in which the *setting of the plot or story is a remote, forlorn, desolate and uncivilised island. Such fictions have special opportunities for presenting ideal places, primitive societies with their innocence, utopian societies, etc. for which reason they have a special appeal or attraction for us. Daniel Defoe's (1660-1731) *Robinson Cruesoe*, Robert Louis Stevenson's (1850-94) *Treasure Island*, Robert Michael Ballantyne's (1825-94) *The Coral Island*, Captain Marryat's (1792-1848) *Masterman Ready*, etc. are desert island fictions.

design. A term introduced by Robert Scholes. Design, he says, is juxtaposition and repetition in the structure (which is close to *plot) of the fictional *narrative. Scholes explains design thus: "When we look at a painting up close, we can see its details clearly and the texture of its brush strokes, but we cannot really see it as a whole. When we back away, we lose our perception of these minute qualities but gain, with this new perspective, a sense of its design" [Scholes, 35]. Juxtaposition is the sequential arrangement of narrative sections, or *events, or *situations. It may or may not be chronological, and this partially determines the design. Repetition is reiteration, duplication, reproduction, rehearsing or echoing of identical or similar images, ideas or situations; for instance the reiteration of the metaphor of drowning in Virginia Woolf's (1882-1941) *Mrs Dalloway*. Repetition also contributes to the design. Also see *pattern, *rhythm.

detached narrator. See *uninvolved narrator.

detective novel, detective story. A detective *novel or *story is one whose *plot is based on a mysterious crime committed and on the clues to the detection of that crime. The mystery is unraveled or solved generally by a professional detective. Adgar Allan Poe's (1809-49) stories, for instance, are examples of the detective story as Sir Arthur Conan Doyle's (1859-1930) four Sherlock Holmes novels are of the detective novel.

de trop [from French *de*, of, from, and *trop*, too much, too many]. In French, the phrase means 'superfluous', 'unwelcome' or 'unwanted'. In English, it generally connotes "the embarrassment caused by superfluity" [Ayto, 91].

dues ex machine [from Latin *dues*, god; *ex*, from; and *machine* pronounced: both *mak-in-a* and *ma-she-na*, machine]. Literally, the expression means 'god from machine'. It refers to the theatrical device in which, in the ancient times, a god (character) would be brought on the stage with the help of a crane to solve a dramatic problem or complication, otherwise, apparently, insoluble. By extension, and figuratively, it now also means "a violent and intrinsic solution of a difficulty in a plot" [Macdonald, 351]. *Dues ex machine* is a device in which an author, generally finding no better way of solving a complex and difficult structural *situation in a *plot, suddenly introduces a 'character', or a trick—such as discovery of a letter, a birthmark (for identity) or an inheritance (to escape penury), etc.—to come out of that difficult situation. From the domain of the drama, the technique of *deux ex machine* was, long afterwards, imported into the domain of the *novel; for instance, the technique is to be found in Charles Dickens's (1812-70) *Oliver Twist* and Thomas Hardy's (1840-1928) *Tess of the d'Urbervilles*.

developing character. A developing *character, which is also called *dynamic character, is one which, unlike a *static character, grows, changes, and develops throughout a play or a *narrative. Static characters never change perceptibly but remain the same all through, i.e. their thoughts and actions follow the same patterns. Static characters are also known as *type characters, and E.M. Forster (1879-1970) calls them *flat characters. The characters of the Morality Plays and Miracle Plays of the medieval period, for instance, are static, type or flat characters. On the other hand, some characters continue to change, grow, develop, in the course of the movement of the story of the *novel or play, due to their new experiences or education in changed *situations. Such characters are developing characters or, what E.M. Forster called, *round characters. For examples, the characters Macbeth, Othello, King Lear, etc. in Shakespeare's tragedies are developing or round characters. Again, Bathsheba in Thomas Hardy's (1840-1928) *Far from the Madding Crowd*, Adam Bede in George Eliot's (1819-80) *Adam Bede* and Lilia Herriton in E.M. Forster's *Where Angels Fear to Tread*, for instance, are developing or round characters.

device. An umbrella term to describe any literary technique or contrivance or ploy used in the *novel or play to achieve some desired effect. For instance, eavesdropping is a device, and Charles Dickens (1812-70) used it in his novels with different ends or effects in view. Also see *function.

dialect. A sort of language inferior to the standard language of a geographical area. Dialect is "a variety of a language, spoken in one part of a country (regional dialect), or by people belonging to a particular social class (social dialect or sociolect), which is different in some words, grammar, and/or pronunciation from other forms of the same language" [Richards, *et al*, 80]. For instance, cockney is a dialect of English, or the Middle English is a dialect. Dialect is used in literary works—in *novels and plays, especially—for creating *verisimilitude in characters. Dialect (*dialecte*) is to be distinguished from *patois* (literally, dialect, lingo). "In French, *patois* means strictly a 'local form of speech used in an area alongside a national variety' (as opposed to a *dialecte*, which is a 'local variety that is the sole form used in a particular area')" [Ayto, 230]. Also see *vernacular.

dialect literature. Literary works written in dialect. Switzerland is rich in dialect literature, because though there standard German is the official language, all the people use a variety of dialect in their ordinary lives.

dialogic novel, dialogical novel. The terms were introduced by Mikhail Bakhtin (1895-1975) in his influential critical book *Problems of Dostoevsky's Poetics* (1929). He also coined the related term 'monologic' in the same book. Bakhtin introduced the terms 'monologic' and 'dialogic' (monologic from Greek *monos*, single, and *logos*, word, speech; and dialogic from Greek *dia*, between, and *logos*, word, speech) with the sole purpose of distinguishing between what he calls 'monologic novel' and 'dialogic novel'. In the monologic *novel, says he, all the characters speak, as if, in the same *voice which is controlled by the author (as though the author himself speaks through the mouths of the different characters). On the other hand, in the dialogic novel, the different *characters speak 'in their own voices' (i.e., each character speaks independently in his or her own voice) and their various voices are not controlled by the author. Bakhtin says that Fyodor Dostoevsky's (1821-1881) characters, for instance, speak in their different idiosyncratic and independent (uncontrolled by the author) voices, and so his novels are both* polyphonic and dialogic. Leo Tolstoy's (1828-1910) characters, contrarily, speak as though in one single voice (as if Tolstoy himself is speaking through their various mouths, controlling their idiosyncracies), and, therefore, Bakhtin calls his novels monophonic and monologic. However, Bakhtin is cautious to point out that even the monologic novel is not absolutely monologic as even the dialogic novel is not totally dialogic. "In Bakhtin's view, however, a novel can never be totally monologic, since the narrator's reports of the utterances of another character are inescapably 'double-voiced' (in that we can distinguish therein the author's own accent and inflexion), and also dialogic (in that the author's discourse continually reinforces, alters, or contests with the types of speech that it reports)" [Abrams, 63].

didacticism. The term denotes the presence of a definite moral direction—'moral' in its widest range of meanings—in literary works, including the *novel, consciously hinted at by the author. John Bunyan's (1628-88) *The Pilgrim's Progress*, for instance, is a didactic work, for it preaches the need to be pure at heart and aspire after Christian ideals. Literary works that are not didactic are called *autotelic.

diegesis. The term 'diegesis' and the term *mimesis are used in modern *narratology to designate the narrative account and the mimetic (from mime) representation in a fictional narrative, respectively. "Both the terms are to be found in the third book of Plato's (c. 429-347 B.C.) *Republic*, in which

Socrates uses them to distinguish between two ways of presenting speech. For Socrates, diegesis stands for those cases where the poet himself is the speaker and does not wish to suggest otherwise, and mimesis stands for those cases in which the poet attempts to create the illusion that it is not he who is speaking. Thus a speech spoken by a character in the play would represent mimesis, whereas if the writer spoke 'as him or herself' about *characters, we would have a case of diegesis" [Hawthorn, 78]. In short, diegesis simply refers to "the narrated events or story (...) as a 'level' distinct from that of the narration. The diegetic level of a *narrative is that of the main *story, whereas the 'higher' level at which the story is told is extradiegetic (i.e., standing outside the sphere of the main story). An *embedded tale-within-the-tale constitutes a lower level known as hypodiegetic" [Baldick, 57]. Diegesis may have a far wider spectrum of meanings. J.A. Cuddon writes: "In drama and film diegesis can take the form of voice-over, choric intervention, and on-stage description of mimetic action. Similarly, music or sound-effects not emanating from the mimetic action but superimposed on it: sonnets and songs performed by characters in Shakespeare are mimetic; atmospheric background music is diegetic" [Cuddon, 225]. Novelists may incline more either towards diegesis or towards mimesis. Jane Austen's (1775-1817) *novels, for instance, show her tendency towards diegesis while the novels of Dame Ivy Compton-Burnett's (1892-1969) show her's towards mimesis, for they "are built on dialogue—they contain the very minimum of descriptive writing" [Kettle, 1999, 167].

digression. It is that part of a literary composition which is not strictly related to the main point or the main course of the *narrative. To digress is to move away temporarily from the principal subject, or the *theme or *plot. In *novels and *short stories, resorting to digression is a valuable technique, and this technique is rather frequently adopted especially in novels, as Laurence Sterne (1713-68) did in *Tristram Shandy*.

dime novel. The term was coined by combining 'dime', meaning 'a tenth part of the American dollar' or 'a little money', and 'novel'. Dime novel was so called for its cheapness—it would cost a dime. It is sensational, melodramatic, and romantic, and is full of adventures and violence. It was much in vogue in the latter half of the 19th century. E.J.C. Judson, Prentiss Ingraham, Edward L. Wheeler and J.R. Coryell are some of the successful authors of dime novels [Cuddon, 226]. Also see *shilling shocker, *penny dreadful.

Dionysian, dionysian. The term derives from the name of Dionysus, the Greek god who presides over drunken revelry, vegetation, fertility and licentiousness. Dionysian literature is instinctive, stormy, turbulent, frenzied, uninhibited, orgiastic and romantic as opposed to *Apollonian literature which is creative, imaginative, rational, measured, serene, sunny and classical. Frederich Nietzche (1844-1900), the philosopher, thought that tragic drama was born in a certain combination of the Apollonian and Dionysian. D.H. Lawrence's (1885-1930) *novels are said to be Dionysian as the novels of Stendhal (1783-1842) and Andre Gide (1869-1951) are thought to be Apollonian.

discours [from French *discours*, discourse, speech, talk, language, treatise]. A critical term introduced by Emile Benveniste. *Discours* denotes 'subjective' mode of speech or writing as **historie* denotes 'objective' mode of speech or writing. "In *discours*, the present situation of speech or writing is indicated by signs of deixis (e.g., the pronouns/and *You*, the adverbs *here*, *now*, *there*, etc.) and by the use of tense (*she has gone* rather than *she went*). While *discours* thus displays its nature as an enunciation involving a relationship between a speaker/writer and a listener/reader, *historie* conceals this by its concentration on the enonced (...). Confusingly, another distinction is made between these two terms in narratology, where *historie* is story, and *discours* is language or narration" [Baldick, 59]. Also see **enonce*, *enonciation*.

discourse. The term is very loosely used. It generally signifies a learned discussion on any topic of any subject: literature, philosophy, politics, religion, etc. In linguistics, the term signifies a unit or stretch of language larger than a sentence, such as a paragraph, conversation and interview.

dissident writers. After the revolution of 1917 and the consequent creation of the Soviet Union, the writers of the Soviet Union and other communist countries were obliged to write in such a manner that the Marxist ideology and Marxist principles of philosophy and political economy are not in any way infringed. But some refractory writers did not heed to the warning and in their literary works violated this *diktat* of the communist rulers. Such writers of the Soviet Union and other communist states were called dissident writers. Boris Pasternak (1890-1960) and Aleksander Solzhenitsin (b. 1918), the two novelists of the Soviet Union, and Milan Kundera (b. 1929), the Czech dramatist, for instance, were dubbed dissident writers. The Russian poetess Anna Akhmatova (1889-1967) and the Russian humorous writer Mikhail Zoshchenko (1895-1958) were also dissident writers.

distance. A critical term to refer to the emotional involvement of the reader with the *characters of novels: the more the involvement, the less the distance or the interspace between the reader and the characters, and the other way round. For instance, "whereas readers of Dickens's novels typically became (and become) very involved in the fate of characters in the course of reading (...), much of Joseph Conrad's fiction encourages the reader to observe character and events more dispassionately, at more of an emotional distance" [Hawthorn, 93].

documentary novel. The term signifies a kind of *novel "which, like documentary drama, is based on documentary evidence in the shape of newspaper articles, legal reports, archives, and recent official papers" [Cuddon, 233]. The documentary novel is also known as *instant fiction. In the 1860s, this form of novel was first produced by the two French writer brothers styled The Goncourt Brothers: Edmond Goncourt (1822-96) and Jules Goncourt (1830-70). These two brothers always wrote in collaboration. They invented the **roman documentaire* or *documentary novel, in which they depicted the 'history that might have happened', taking historical facts, real details, real conversations, etc. as their materials. For instance, for their novel "*Saeur Philomene* (1861) they studied hospital life from inside, and for *Germinie Lacerteux* (...) they made a study of one of their own servants who had served them faithfully for years while leading unknown to them a life of debauchery revealed only after her death from consumption" [Thorlby, 322]. Some other documentary novels are: Theodore Dreiser's (1871-1945) *An American Tragedy* ('based upon an actual murder case of 1906'); Truman Capote's (b. 1924) *In Cold Blood* ('about the slaughter of a respectable Kansas farming family by two wandering psychopaths'); Graham Greene's (b. 1904) *The Quiet American* (whose setting is Vietnam during the country's war of liberation against the French), and V.S. Naipaul's (b. 1932) *In a Free State* (based on modern notion of freedom, which, the author says, is illusory).

domestic novel. The domestic novel is that sort of *novel which deals with domestic themes —love, marriage, inter-sibling relationship and other matters related to the family circle. Jane Austen's (1775-1817) *Pride and Prejudice*, *Sense and Sensibility* and *Emma* and Louisa May Alcott's (1832-88) *Little Women* are instances of domestic novel.

donnee [from French *donnee*, datum, fundamental idea, theme]. Donnee literally means 'that which is given', but as a technical term of literature it signifies 'the fundamental idea or motif of a story'. The donnee of a *novel may be a particular *vecu* or lived or authentic, experience; a simple idea or notion of a *character or incident; a stray conversation; or simply the face of a person. Such an 'atomic' thing may be so powerful as to be able to ignite the imagination of an author so as to compel him to write out a complete novel. What Henry James (1843-1916) called 'the speck' is not different from the donnee.

Doric, Doricism. The term 'Doric' is the adjectival form of the name Doris which belonged to a district or region in the southern part of the ancient Greece. Doris was all pastoral, its people being rustic, innocent and unsophisticated as opposed to the refined, urbane, sophisticated and complex people of the region of the ancient Greece called Attica or Athens. The Doric architecture shows conspicuous simplicity and heaviness, while doricism in literature is marked by rustic simplicity of language and execution, pastorality and pristine purity of ideas. Also see *Atticism.

double-decker novel. The term roughly signifies the greater length of a *novel. In the 19th century, on the demand of the readers, the novel tended to be considerably long, so that the publisher had to accommodate it in two volumes: Such a novel is called double-decker novel. Likewise, a novel printed in three volumes is called three-decker novel. Louis May Alcott's (1832-88) *Aunt Jo's Scrap-Bag*, for instance, is a multi-volume novel.

double plot. Double plot is an uncommon narrative phenomenon. When two *plots, instead of one, are present in a *narrative, almost independent of one another, it is called a double plot. Lee T. Lemon writes: "A double plot occurs when two independent or semi-independent stories of almost equal magnitude and interest exist side-by-side in the same narrative (as in Bennett's *The Old Wives' Tale*, which follows the separate lives of two sisters, one of whom stays home and one of whom lives an adventurous but comparatively empty life)" [Lemon, 42].

drama-novel, dramatic novel. A form of *novel that took its birth at the hands of the dramatist and novelist Sir J.M. Barrie (1860-1937), the author of the famous play *Peter Pan*. In 1929, Barrie drastically revised his sixteen long plays and twenty-two one-act plays, "adding supplementary scenes or characters and sprinkling the texts with descriptive notes on the action" [Long, 585] and published them as the Complete Edition. "Thus appeared a new type, called 'the drama-novel', which in Barrie's hands became the most readable of its kind in modern literature" [*loc. cit.*]. The drama-novel is not designed to be staged for it is hard to perform; it is intended only for reading, like the closet drama, such as John Milton's (1608-74) *Samson Agonistes*, Lord Byron's (1788-1824) *Manfred*, P.B. Shelley's (1792-1822) *Cenci*, Thomas Hardy's (1840-1928) *The Dynasts* and G.B. Shaw's (1856-1950) *Man and Superman*. Yet there is a difference between the closet drama and the drama-novel: the closet drama contains nothing non-dramatic but in the drama-novel there are opinions, explanations, oneiric or hallucinatory scenes, etc. Barrie's own drama-novel *Dear Brutus*, for instance, contains a scene 'through which characters move like shadows from another world'. Edwin Muir, in his *The Structure of the Novel*, says that Jane Austen's (1775-1817) novels may be said to be 'dramatic novels' because in them there are more intensifications of actions than emphases on characterizations.

Muir differentiates the dramatic novel from the novel of action and the novel of character saying that in the dramatic novel the "characters are not part of the machinery of the plot [as in the novel of action]; nor is the plot merely a rough framework round the character [as in the novel character]. On the contrary, both are inseparably knit together. The given qualities of characters determine the action, and the action in turn progressively changes the characters, and thus everything is borne forward to an end. At its greatest the affinity of the dramatic novel is with poetic tragedy, just as that of the novel of character is with comedy" [Muir, 41]. According to Muir, there is a 'hiatus' between the *plot and the *characters in both the novel of action and the novel of character, but there should be no such hiatus in the dramatic novel. Muir says that Jane Austen's *Pride and Prejudice* closely approaches the concept of the dramatic novel.

dramatisation of novel. Sometimes (generally popular) *novels are transformed into plays or dramas, i.e. the matters of novels are utilised to write dramas or plays. This transmogrification is called dramatisation of novels. It is not something quite new, for in the medieval English literature we find biblical stories transformed into Mystery Plays or Morality Plays. Shakespeare (1564-1616) dramatised the chronicles in Plutarch's (c.46-c.127 A.D.) *Parallel Lives* and Raphael Holinshed's (d.c.1580) *Chronicles*. Since the 18th century, dramatists began to transform novels into dramas. Richardson's *Pamela* was perhaps the first novel to be dramatised. After this, "There followed dramatization of novels by Mrs Radcliffe, Walpole, Godwin, 'Monk' Lewis and Clara Reeve. In the 19th century Dickens and Scott were the authors most used; so were Lord Lytton, Charlotte Bronte, Charles Reade, Wilkie Collins, and many more" [Cuddon, 241]. Besides all these, some other novels which were dramatised are: James M. Barrie's (1860-1937) *The Little Minister* (dramatized by himself), Thomas Hardy's (1840-1928) *The Return of the Native*, E.M. Forster's (1879-1970) *A Passage to India* (dramatised by Santha Rama Rau) and Carson McCullers's (1917-67) *The Members of the Wedding* (dramatised by herself). Further, the playwrite Edward Albee (b. 1928) dramatised Carson McCuller's novel *The Ballad of the Sad Café*, James Purdy's (b. 1923) novel *Malcolm* and Vladimir Nabokov's (1899-1977) novel *Lolita*. Like Albee, the actor-dramatist William Gillette (1855-1937) dramatised Arthur Conan Doyle's (1859-1930) two short stories, 'A Scandal in Bohemia' and 'The Final Problem', and also Doyle's novel *A Study in Scarlet*. The detective fiction writer Agatha Christie (1890-1976) herself dramatised some of her own short stories, such as 'The Mousetrap' and 'Witness for the Prosecution'.

dramatised narrator. Wayne C. Booth, in his *The Rhetoric of Fiction*, tells of two categories of *narrators: dramatised narrators and *undramatised narrators. The dramatised narrator is presented as a *character, unlike the undramatised narrator, i.e. he is personalised. As soon as a narrator refers to himself as 'I', he becomes a dramatised narrator. The level of the personalisation or dramatisation of the narrator of course vary from one *novel or *short story to another. However, the difference between the dramatised narrator and the undramatised narrator is, in fact, only one of degree of personalisation: the more the personalisation, the more a narrator moves towards the pole of the absolutely dramatised narrator, and the less the personalisation, the more a narrator moves towards the opposite pole. But Booth cautions us that "Stories are usually not so rigorously impersonal as 'The Killers'; most tales are presented as passing through the consciousness of a teller, whether an 'I' or a 'he'" [Booth, 151]. Booth elaborates on the point: "In a sense even the most reticent narrator has been dramatized as soon as he refers himself as 'I', or like Flaubert, tells us that 'we' were in the classroom when Charles Bovary entered. But many novels dramatize their narrators with great fullness, making them into characters who are as vivid as those they tell us about (*Tristram Shandy*, *Remembrance of Things Past*, *Heart of Darkness*, *Dr. Faustus*)" [*op. cit.*, 152].

duende [from Spanish *duende*, 'imp, goblin, ghost']. In English, the term generally means 'frenzied artistic inspiration' [Ayto, 96].

duration. In *narratology, duration signifies either *storytime or *texttime. The storytime is the duration covered by the story or the event of it (i.e., a part of the story). The story may cover a long duration; for instance, from the young age of the principal *character to his death, though the text of this story may require only two or three pages. In this case, the storytime is long but the texttime is short. Another case may be just the opposite of this: the storytime may be short, but the texttime may be long, i.e. the text may require unexpectedly more pages. "On a rough basis it is possible to note that three years of story-time may be covered by three pages of text, while further on in the same text one hour of story-time may occupy fifty pages" [Hawthorn, 96].

dynamic character. See *developing character.

dysphemism. A term contradictory to *euphemism. Dysphemism denotes a statement or expression that overtly or emphatically points out a defect or failing. For example, the expressions 'a filthy dirty face' and 'a dirty slushy, sloppy day' are dysphemistic. It should be noted that while euphemism tries to cover up a failing and to convert a unpleasant expression into a pleasant one, dysphemism does not strive to transform a pleasant expression into an unpleasant one—it simply underlines the defect or failing.

dystopia. See *utopia.

E

economic novel. Same as *money novel. *Novels are sometimes loosely classified into different categories, depending on their subject-matters, such as political novel, *money novel or economic novel, *sociological novel, *historical novel, *international novel, religious novel, *existentialist novel, etc. However, economic novels deal with economic matters or matters somehow related to economics, money-making process, finance, etc. Daniel Defoe's (1660-1731) *Robinson Crusoe* and Upton Sinclair's (1878-1968) *The Money-changers* are examples of the economic novel or money novel.

ecphrasis, ekphrasis [from Greek *ek*, out of, and *phrases*, speech]. The Greek word *ekphrasis* means 'description' and hence the terms ekphrasis and ecphrasis, in literary discourses, mean 'intense pictorial description of an object'. "A more generous account would define *ekphrasis* as virtuosic description of physical reality (objects, scenes, persons) in order to evoke an image in the mind's eye as intense as if the described object were actually before the reader" [Cuddon, 252].

ecriture [from French *ecriture*, writing, documents, records]. The word literally means simply handwriting. But Roland Barthes (1915-80) uses it as a critical term to denote that form of writing which is absolutely free of all sorts of historical, social, institutional, political, linguistic and personal associations and influences—a form of writing that he calls 'writing zero degree' or 'colourless writing'. Barthes sets *ecriture* in opposition to *litterature* (literature) which, he thinks, is contaminated with those associations and influences. Barthes holds that *litterature*, that is (bourgeois) literature, is replete with bourgeois myths, historicity and political implications. In his Inaugural Lecture at the College de France, in 1965, Barthes admitted that he himself could not ordinarily steer clear of those influences: "There is't a day when reading a newspaper, watching a TV programme, listening to a taxi driver, I don't to transform what I read or hear into what I call mythological material, that is precisely into a discourse which is between criticism and the novel" [Simons, 70]. Barthes calls the writing, which is adulterated with those historical, linguistic and other influences, literature; and the writing, which is clean of these, *ecriture*.

ecriture feminine [from French *ecriture*, writing, and *feminine*, feminine]. The term can be translated into English as 'feminine writing'. It was introduced as a critical term by the French fiction writer, playwright, feminist and critic Helene Cixous (b. 1937). Through the concept of *ecriture feminine* or *feminine ecriture* she protests against the binary oppositions (he/she, activity/passivity, culture/nature, head/heart, father/mother, etc.) in the space of writing or discourse; against *phallocentrism in the Western philosophy and literature; and against the patriarchal culture, which treats women as the marginalised and oppressed 'other'. To bring justice to the feminine, she thinks that the site of writing is of central importance, and proposes, in her most influential book *The Newly Born Woman* and elsewhere, adoption of *ecriture feminine* which "denotes writing which is typically, characteristically feminine in style, language, tone and feeling, and completely different from (and opposed to) male language and discourse" [Cuddon, 248]. Cixous means to say that *ecriture feminine* is natural for human expression and so it should be the model. She says that the child first identifies itself with the mother (the feminine) *freely* and only latterly comes under the impact of the father, (the phallic norm) who imposes various codes and laws and norms upon it, as a result of which it becomes deprived of its former *freedom*. The adult's language is therefore codified, symbolical and normative. It is unnatural, extraneous. The mother's language, on the other hand, is natural, uncodified, free. This is Cixous's principal argument for *ecriture feminine*. It should be noted that, according to her, it is not true that only women can do *ecriture feminine*, for some great male writers have shown their excellent *métier* in *ecriture feminine*—writers such as Shakespeare (1564-1616), Heinrich Kleist (1777-1811) and Jean Genet (b. 1910). The writings of such writers are not trammelled and controlled by the laws, codes, logic, order and rationality of the patriarchal culture—they are free and uninhibited as the *ecriture feminine* should be.

ecrivain [from French *ecrivain*, 'intransitive' writer]. The critical term was introduced by Roland Barthes (1915-80) to refer to the 'intransitive' writer who wants the reader keep himself fixed to the writing itself, i.e. keep his attention glued to the writing. The three novelists, Marcel Proust (1871-1922), James Joyce (1882-1941) and Samuel Beckett (1906-89), are instances of the *ecrivain*. Also see **ecrivant*.

ecrivant [from French *ecrivant*, 'transitive' writer]. A critical term, it was introduced by Roland Barthes (1915-80) to denote the 'transitive' writer who wants to lead the reader beyond the contour of his writing—to lead the reader towards an ulterior purpose of his not obvious in the writing itself. Gustave Flaubert (1821-80), Emile Zola (1840-1902) and Ernest Hemingway (1898-1961) are only three among the novelists who may be called *ecrivants*. Also see **ecrivain*.

education novel. The term designates the kind of *novel in which the principal character(s) confronts altered, novel, alien, unfamiliar *situations and is forced to believe that his earlier knowledge, or angle of view, of the worldly affairs was faulty, and so resorts to a totally new perspective and acquires new knowledge of life and the world. Daniel Defoe's (1660-1731) *Robinson Crusoe*, Thomas Hardy's (1840-1928) *Far from the Madding Crowd* and E.M. Forster's (1879-1970) *Where Angels Fear to Tread* and *The Longest Journey* are instances of the education novel. Also see **Bildungroman*, **Erziehungsroman*.

Edwardian period. The period between the death of Queen Victoria (1901) and the end of the reign of King Edward VII (1910). Some of the important novelists and *novels of this period are: Joseph Conrad (1857-1924: *Nostromo*), Henry James (1843-1916: *The Golden Bowl*), Arnold Bennett (1867-1931: *The Old Wives' Tales*), H.G. Wells (1866-1946: *Tono-Bungay*) and E.M. Forster (1879-1970: *Howards End*).

effect. It is the special impression intended by the writer to create in the mind of the reader through his writing [effects (plural), however, means sound and lighting devices that contribute to the illusion in the theatre or cinema].

Einfuhlung [from German *Einfuhlung*, feeling with some one else]. See *empathy.

eiron [from Greek *eiron*, a dissembler]. A *stock character in ancient Greek comedies, who, somewhat like Socrates, feigned to be a dullard, tongue in cheek, before a stock braggart or **alazon* for some secret purpose. The term 'irony' derived from the term *eiron*. Northrop Frye defines the term as "A self-deprecating or unobtrusively treated character in fiction, usually an agent of happy ending and of the catastrophe in tragedy" [Frye, 365].

Elizabethan period. The period during which Queen Elizabeth I reigned, i.e. from 1558 to 1603. The period saw the thriving of drama and poetry. No notable *novel or *fiction is to be found in this period except John Lyly's (?1554-1606) romance *Euphues, or The Anatomy of Wit* (1579).

ellipsis, ellipse [from Greek *ellipsis*, leaving out]. In rhetorics the term means a figure in which one or more words are omitted. The term is extended to the narrative where it denotes an omission of a passage of time or of information. "We never learn anything concrete, for example, of Heathcliff 's history prior to his discovery in Liverpool by Mr Earnshaw, nor of what he does to become rich between the time of his disappearance and reappearance in *Wuthering Heights*. In this case the ellipsis is relatively *unmarked* (or implicit) as it covers information not known to the personified narrators. But when in Charles Dickens's *Bleak House* Esther Summerson seeks to explain why she finds Mrs Woodcourt irksome, and breaks off with the words, 'I don't know what it was. Or at least if I do, now, I thought I did not then. Or at least—but it don't matter', then we have a clearly *marked (or explicit) ellipsis*: the reader's attention is drawn to the fact that something that is known to the narrator is withheld from him or her" [Hawthorn, 101].

embedded narrative. A *narrative enclosed or framed within another narrative, like a tale-within-a-tale. The stories in Geoffrey Chaucer's (c.1343/4-1400) *Canterbury Tales* are embedded narratives because they are introduced by the beginning story, in the General Prologue, told by Chaucer himself—the story or account of the journey of the pilgrims to Canterbury. The embedded narrative is also called *Chinese Box narrative.

emmendation. Correction of an author's printed work, generally by an editor, usually for the purpose of clarifying or elucidating meanings of words, sentences or passages.

emotive language. The sort of language that especially expresses or arouses emotion. It is to be differentiated from the cognitive or referential language which is intended only for expressing emotion-neutral statements.

empathy. *The Encyclopedia of Psychology*, by H.J. Eysenck, *et al.* writes about the word: "A term used for the endeavour to add to extraneous behaviour with the object of understanding the other person. The way to experience is primarily through linguistic communication, but it can also come through a spontaneous expression of feeling" (Eysenck, 324]. In empathy, one identifies, to a certain degree, with another person or even with an inanimate object, so that the other person's sensation, feeling and emotion are realised or experienced by him, or, in the case of the inanimate object (for instance an art object), the sensation, feeling and emotion suggested by the object are shared or experienced by him (by the viewer). Empathy must be differentiated from *sympathy. Sympathy is compassion; in sympathy one feels *like* another, but *not identically:* when one becomes sympathetic to a widow, he feels like her but does not identify himself with her. But if he also identifies himself with her, he may be said to be empathetic. In German, empathy is **Einfiihlung*. Empathy is an important aid to writers for creating lively characters.

emplotment. Jeremy Hawthorn has explained the term thus: "A term much used within historicist writing which refers to the textualizing of historical 'facts' or 'events' to create a plot or narrative. Just as a novelist may create any amount of novels from a given set of characters and events, so too (certain radical historians have argued) a given set of historical data can be emplotted in innumerable manners, all of which will present that material in different ways" [Hawthorn, 102].

encyclopaedic form. The term has been coined by Northrop Frye and he has explained it in the Glossary of his *Anatomy of Criticism* saying that it is a "genre presenting an anagogic [i.e., pertaining to mystical interpretation or to the strivings in the unconscious towards morally high ideals] form of symbolism, such as a sacred scripture, or its analogues in other modes. The term includes the Bible, Dante's *Commedia*, the great epics, and the works of Joyce and Proust" [Frye, 365].

***engage* writer** [from French *engage*, engaged]. The term literally means 'engaged writer', but in literary and critical discourses it denotes a writer who is committed to certain artistic, philosophical, social, political or religious ideology. Also see *committed writer.

engagement [from French *engagement*, engagement, commitment]. The status of a writer of being committed to a particular ideology—artistic, philosophical, social, political, etc. Also see **engage*, **degage*.

Enlightenment. The term refers to the particular philosophical, artistic and literary movement in the Western Europe and England from around 1660 to about 1770. In Germany, the movement was known as *Aufklarung* (clearing, supposedly of some misunderstanding or false knowledge) and in England the period covered by the movement was called 'the Age of Reason'. The characteristic features of the movement were: rejection of dogma and superstition, rational attitude, scientific enquiry, empirical and critical philosophizing, faith in humanity and human progress. Great figures, such as Kant, Newton, Locke, Hume, Diderot, Gibbon, Voltaire and such others adorned the period. Some of the noted novelists and *novels of the Enlightenment period are: Daniel Defoe (1660-1731: *Robinson Crusoe*, *Moll Flanders*), Jonathan Swift (1667-1745: *Gulliver's Travels*), Samuel Richardson (1689-1761: *Pamela*, Part I and *Clarissa*), Henry Fielding(1707-54: *Joseph Andrews* and *Tom Jones*), Laurence Sterne (1713-68: *Tristram Shandy*) and Oliver Goldsmith (1730-74: *The Vicar of Wakefield*).

enonce, enonciation [from French *enonce*, statement]. The two terms belong to *structuralism or the structuralist theory. *Enonce* is what is said or a statement, and *enonciation* is the act or process of saying what is said or stated. Enonciation is "a process by which a speaker (or writer) adopts a position within a language as an 'I' addressing a 'you' and perhaps referring to a 'they'. Whenever I say 'I', however, the I who speaks can be distinguished (as the 'subject of *enonciation*') from the 'I' that is thus spoken of (the 'subject of the *enonce*')" [Baldick, 69]. The concepts of *enonce* and *enonciation* are helpful in identifying the narratorial *voice and the voice of the subject of the *narrative. The narratorial voice or the narrator's voice, it should be kept in view, is the *enonciation*, which voice is more marked in the *first-person narrative than in the *third person narrative, where it is generally subdued and sometimes hardy recognisable.

entelechy [from Greek *en*, in, and *telos*, end, perfection]. Literally, the word means the final actuality or realised existence. Aristotle used the word in this sense in his philosophy. In literary discourse, it was later on "used by writers to signify what helped to develop perfection" [Cuddon, 263].

epic novel. In the strict traditional sense, the epic is a considerably long narrative poem, on a great and serious subject, written in an elevated style and having at its centre a supermanly warrior-hero. The *narrative is 'polygonal', in the sense that it incorporates *folk tales, history, *myths, *legends, and in the sense that it has wide ramifications in the form of organically related sub-narratives. *Ramayana*, *Mahabharata*, *Illiad*, *Odyssey*, *Gilgamesh*, *Beowulf*, *Aeneid*, *Pharsalia*, *Divina Commedia*, *Os Lusiadas* and *Paradise Lost* are examples of the epic. The epic ultimately "aspires to grandeur of no common sort; to a state where men transcend their human limitations and, for a time at least, become more obviously in the image of God-like creatures. In epic the men are ten feet tall. In epic, to apply Wordsworth's lines from Book I of *The Prelude*,

> no familiar shapes remain,
> no pleasant images of trees,
> Of sea or sky, no colours of green fields;
> But huge and mighty forms, that do not live
> Like living men". [Cuddon, 273]

Later on, the principal features of the epic were introduced in the drama. Thus the epic drama came into being in Germany in the 1920s, chiefly at the hands of Bertolt Brecht (1898-1956). But those features were revealed in the genre of the *novel much earlier than that. Novels such as Herman Melville's (1819-91) *Moby-Dick*, Leo Tolstoy's (1828-1910) *War and Peace*, James Joyce's (1882-1941) *Ulysses*, John Steinbeck's (1902-68) *The Grapes of Wrath*, Patrick White's (b. 1912) *Voss*, Boris Pasternak's (1890-1960) *Doctor Zhivago* and Ivo Andric's (b. 1892) *The Bridge on the Drina* may be called epic novels.

epigon, epigone [from Greek *epi*, after, and *gone*, birth]. The words mean one of a later generation. But in literary criticism or discourse it denotes a writer or poet, generally of inferior quality, who is considerably influenced by the style, thoughts and other things of his preceding writer or poet, generally of superior quality. A later generation of writers and poets who follow the styles, thoughts and other things of their distinguished preceding generation of writers and poets are collectively also called Epigon (generally with capital E).

epilogue. The term denotes a short speech at the end of a play (as the *prologue denotes one at the beginning), or the end of a *fable where the moral of it is stated, or a concluding section of a literary work in the form of an after-thought. The epilogue was not an uncommon feature of the Elizabethan plays. *Novels also sometimes contain epilogues. For example, Herman Melville's (1819-91) *Moby Dick* and H. G. Well's (1866-1946) *The Time Machine* have each an one-page epilogue.

epimythium [from Greek *epi*, and *mythos*, story]. A succinct moral instruction at the end of a *fable. If it occurs at the beginning of the fable, it is called *promythium. Also see *epilogue.

epiphany [from Greek *epi*, to, and *phainein*, to show]. According to Christian belief, epiphany is the *manifestation* of Christ (after his demise) to the wise men of the East. This Christian notion was secularised by James Joyce (1882-1941) and employed in literary discourse and criticism. In his *novel *Stephen Hero*, which was actually a part of his later novel *A Portrait of the Artist as a Young Man* Joyce meant by epiphany "'a sudden spiritual manifestation' in which the 'whatness' of a common object or gesture appears radiant to the observer" [Baldick, 72]. For instance, one eavesdrops an almost inaudible short conversations between a young lady and a young man at an umbrageous corner and it suddenly occurs to him that the two are a representation of Adam and Eve in paradise. By epiphany, as Joyce has taught us, may be meant the (gradual) revelation of the central drift, import, significance, idea or force of a *narrative—of a novel or *short story. Joyce's notion of epiphany is illustrated in the short narratives (22 epiphanies) of his *Epiphanies*. It is not true that only Joyce experienced epiphany, for such poets as George Herbert (1593-1633), Henry Vaughan (1621/22-95), G.M. Hopkins (1844-89), W. Wordsworth (1770-1850) and P. B. Shelley (1792-1822) as well as the essayist De Quincey (1785-1859) admitted to have realized epiphanies. Wordsworth called the phenomena of epiphanies 'spots of time', Shelley 'moments' and De Quincey 'involutes'.

episode. In classical Greek dramas, the term referred to "the sections of action and dialogue that alternate with the choral odes. Today the term can mean anything from an incident to a whole scene" [Mobley, 50]. There is no difference of meaning between the two terms, episode and incident. The two terms are also used about *novel. In Henry Fielding's (1707-54) *Joseph Andrew*, for instance, Mrs Slipslop's failed attempt to seduce Joseph is an episode or incident. The episode may be as short as a paragraph, or short bits of dialogue, and as long as dozens of pages, or a long sequence of actions.

episodic novel. The term denotes the kind of *novel in which the *plot is either absent or very thin or imperceptible, and where the incidents or episodes are lineally or chronologically so arranged that they do not reveal any causal relationship between them, nor are they integral to any single continuing story. The episodic novel is said to have episodic structure. Picaresque novels are mostly episodic. R.K. Narayan's (b. 1907) *The Bachelor Arts* and *Swami and Friends*, for instance, are episodic novels. The *short story also may be episodic, in which case the *story is called episode short story or episodic short story. D.H. Lawrence's (1885-1930) *A Sick Collier*, for instance, is an episodic short story. Also see *episode.

epistolary novel. A form of *novel built on exchanges of series of epistles (or letters, communications, missives, notes, etc.) among the *characters. Epistolary novels were much in demand both in England and in France in the 18th century. Notable examples of the epistolary novel are: (in England) Samuel Richardson's (1689-1761) *Pamela* and *Clarissa*, Tobias Smollett's (1721-71) *The Expedition of Humphry Clinker*, Algernon Swinburne's (1837-1909) *Love's Cross-Currents: A Year's Letters* and John Barth's (b. 1930) *Letters*; and (in France) Jean-Jacques Rousseau's (1712-78) *La Nouvelle Heloise* and Choderlos de Laclos's (1741-1803) *Les Liaisons dangereuses*.

eponym, eponymous [from Greek *epi*, upon, and *onoma* or *onyma*, a name].The name of a *character, or an epithet of a character, after which a *novel or play is entitled, is called eponym, and the character is called eponymous. 'Anna Karenina' (after the character Anna Karenina), for instance, is the eponym of Leo Tolstoy's (1828-1910) novel *Anna Karenina* and so the character Anna Karenina is eponymous. Likewise, the title of Thomas Hardy's (1840-1928) novel *The Mayor of Casterbridge*, an epithet of the hero or protagonist Michael Henchard, is an eponym and the character is eponymous.

erased character. In *novel, if a *character is drawn realistically, i.e. the character exhibits verisimilitude with the reality, and then the achieved verisimilitude is subsequently denied in the same novel, then that character will be called erased character. "Thus an erased character would be a character accepted by the reader as 'real' according to realist conventions, but who was shown later to be not-real in some sense, either within the achieved world of fiction or by a transference of the character from this world to the extra-fictional world of the text" [Hawthorn, 107-08]. Erased character is a post-modernist concept. Also see *erasure.

erasure [from French *sous*, under, and *rature*, erasure]. Literally, the term means 'under erasure' (i.e., under suspicion or erasement). It was introduced by the French philosopher Jacques Derrida (b. 1930) in his theory of *deconstruction. Erasure is technique of writing as well as crossing out—both at the same time—a word that is being used for expressing a concept which is both essential or indispensable and doubtful or suspected. Erasure reveals a paradox or vacillation in the mind of the writer (or speaker) about a concept. It is to be noted that in erasure a word is crossed out but not removed. Erasure is shown with a X-mark over the whole length of the word. "The erasure marks thus act in a manner similar to what are known colloquially as scare quotes; that is, quotation marks placed round a word with the similar intention of drawing attention to its inadequacy or questionable validity" [Hawthorn, 107].

erotic literature. The sort of literature which involves frank, uninhibited and elaborate descriptions or overt suggestions of carnal love.

Erzahlung [from German *erzahlen*, to tell a story, etc.]. The German word means 'narration' or 'story-telling'. In literary discouse, it denotes the actual process, method or operation of telling a story. However, the word is sometimes used to mean a *short story or a **nouvelle*.

Erziehungsroman [from German *erziehen*, to bring up, to educate (a child), and *Roman*, novel]. Same as **Bildungsroman*, *education novel.

escape literature. See *literature of escape.

ethos [from Greek *ethos*, custom, character]. Literally, the word means 'habitual character and disposition of individual, group, race, etc.' or 'moral significance'. E.B. Tylor, in his *Dictionary of Anthropology*, writes that 'ethos' is "The totality of the distinctive ways of living that separate one group from another, especially its values. Ethos also denotes the emotional quality possessed by socially patterned behaviour. Ruth Benedict, adopting Oswald Spengler's terminology, has suggested that an ethos may be characterized as either Apollonian or Dionysian" [Tylor, 193]. However, Northrop Frye, in his *Anatomy of Criticism*, writes that, in literary criticism, the term refers to the "internal social context of a work of literature, comprising the characterization and setting of fictional literature and the relation of the author to his reader or audience in thematic literature" [Frye, 365]. Also see *Apollonian, *Dionysian, dionysian.

euphemism. See *dysphemism.

euphuism [from Greek *euphues*, well-grown, fertile]. The term was taken from the name of the hero of John Lyly's (?1554-1606) two prose *romances, *Euphues, or the Anatomy of Wit* and *Euphues and His England*. Euphuism refers to the prose style of those two romances, which is richly ornate, heavily decorated with rhetorical figures, laden with frequent uses of clauses, prone to circuitous and artificial expressions, and filled with biblical and classical allusions. The following sentences taken from a soliloquy of Euphues may partially illustrate the euphuistic style: 'Ah Euphues, into what misfortune art thou brought! In what sudden misery art thou wrapped! It is like to fare with thee as with the eagle, which dieth neither for age nor with sickness but with famine, for although they stomach hunger, thy heart will not suffer thee to eat.' Also see *mannerism.

event. In *narratology, two kinds of things of *novel are distinguished: the physical elements or the 'existents' which are, or which exist, in the novel; and the happenings or occurrences in the *plot or *story, or the 'events'. "It is conventional in narratology to distinguish between 'existents' (those things that are, such as characters, settings, etc.), and 'events' (the things that are done or which occur)" [Hawthorn, 110]. Event is to be distinguished from *action which is the main series of events. Robert Scholes writes about event and action in *fiction: "If a single *action* is presented in a simple, chronological arrangement, the order of *events* is not likely to assume any special significance. But if the *action* is not arranged in time so that we encounter *events* out of their chronological sequence—through flashbacks or some other device—then the order should be given some attention" (italics mine) [Scholes, 35-36].

exciting force. The energy, efficacy, incident or power that initiates the *action of the protagonist in a play or *novel. The exciting force or the *inciting force is responsible for the progress of the *story, for it brings in the *events. The appearance of the ghost in *Hamlet*, for instance, excites or incites Hamlet for action, and so it is the exciting force or the inciting force.

excursus [from Latin *ex*, out, and *cursum*, to run]. Literally, the word means 'running out', but as a term in literary discourse it denotes an incidental digression or divergent discussion in which the writer or speaker goes off at a tangent to the main topic that provides detailed analysis or examination of a point taken over from the main body of the text. An excursus is usually placed at the end of a work, as an appendix.

exegesis [from Greek *ex*, out, and *hegeesthai*, to guide]. The term signifies interpretation or interpretative guidance, especially of biblical passages, but also of literary passages or works, such as *allegories. One who practises exegesis is called exegete or exegetist.

exemplum [from Latin *exemplum*, example]. A didactic *story of short length to illustrate a moral point. Geoffrey Chaucer's (c. 1343/4-1400) two tales, *The Pardoner's Tale* and *The Nun's Priest's Tale*, for instance, are exemplums. Also see *allegory, *fable, *parable.

existentialism. A modern revolutionary philosophical doctrine which holds up the primacy of existence over essence. Man, for instance, first exists, and only then can we contemplate his essence. The traditional philosophy is, therefore, topsyturvied by existentialism, which, further, believes that man has, in fact, no essence—man is only *becoming*. He is always becoming something, according to his project of making himself something. Man is a free being with a free will with which he has to shape his project of the future, shape what he will be. "The central doctrine [of existentialism] is that man is what he makes of himself: he is not predestined by a God, or by society, or by biology. He has a free will, and the responsibility which goes with it. If he refuses to choose or lets outside forces determine him, he is contemptible. Hence the literary works of existentialism insist on action—including acts of will—as the determining things" [Brown, 157-58]. But man has no models, yardsticks, principles or ideals before him for choosing his future, and by choosing his own future indirectly choosing the futures of others as well, and, nevertheless, he has the responsibility of choosing, as a free being, his own future and that of others. Hence arises man's anguish or sort of agony or mental distress. Again, man is ever conscious of his finitude. Man is, as if, thrown in this world at his birth without his consent, and at his death he is relegated to the limbo, again without his nodding. This is the human condition—the absurdity of human existence. The French philosopher, novelist and playwright Jean-Paul Sartre (1905-80) is the hierophant of existentialism which he has expounded in his philosophical masterpiece *L'Etre et la neant* (*Being and Nothingness*). Also see *existentialist novel.

existentialist novel. A *novel which is written from the point of view of existentialism or which has a slant for the existentialist mode of thinking. The novels (as well as the plays) of Jean-Paul Sartre (1905-80), *La nausea* (*Nausea*) and the trilogy *L'age da raison* (*The Age of Reason*), *Le sursis* (*The Reprieve*) and *La mort dans l'ame* and Albert Camus's (1913-60) *L'etranger* (*The Outsider*) and *Le mythe de Sisyphe* (*The Myth of Sisyphus*) are instances of the existentialist novel. The novels of Jean Cayrol (b. 1911) Simone de Beauvoir (b. 1908) and Samuel Beckett (b. 1906) are also considered as existentialist novels. Also see *existentialism.

experimentalism. The *oeuvre* of going beyond the conventional literary ideas, forms, genres, modes, techniques, etc. and seeking after all these which are quite novel, modern. *Dadaism, *expressionism, *impressionism, *anti-novel, **nouveau roman* and such other modern and post-modern concepts and *oeuvres* fall within the category of experimentalism. Also see *experimental novel.

experimental novel. A *novel which deliberately skips over or disregards traditional novelistic codes of theme, form, language, technique, etc. and assays new ones in their stead. James Joyce's (1882-1941) *Finnegans Wake* (a congeries of plotlessness, *stream of consciousness technique, oneiric imagery, extremely whimsical linguistic experiments, etc.) and Gertrude Stein's (1874-1946) *Three Lives: Stories of the Good Anna, Melanctha, and the Gentle Lena* (with its highly unconventional prose style—repetition of phrases, sentences and even paragraphs; disregard of normal punctuation marks; idiosyncratic use of words, even those that bear no significance; etc.) are only two exemplars of the experimental novel. The novels of Dorothy Richardson, (1873-1957), Virginia Woolf (1882-1941) and William Faulkner (1897-1962) are also considered as experimental novels. Also see *experimentalism.

exposition. The introductory or opening part of a *novel, *story or play in which the writer provides the reader or audience with necessary informations about background, setting, characters, initial relations among characters, etc. with a view to preparing him for following the main part of the work. Exposition follows *complication. In *Freytag's pyramid, exposition refers to the *introduction or the introductory part of a play. The term also denotes a systematic account or description of a topic or subject-matter.

expressionism. The term is borrowed from the art of painting. Between about 1910 and 1924, expressionism in painting, poetry, drama and *novel [at the hands of Franz Kafka (1883-1924)] was a violent protest against realism as well as idealism. Realistic art demands verisimilitude with the real and idealistic art aspires after some transcendental image. On the contrary, expressionistic art or expressionism "is that type of art which strives to depict, not the objective facts of nature, nor any abstract notion based on those facts, but the subjective feelings of the artist" [Read, 1936, 118]. Expressionism is, by definition, individualistic, and Van Gogh is thought to be the founder of expressionist art. "Expressionism lives up to its name; that is to say, it expresses the emotions of the artist at any cost—the cost being usually an exaggeration or distortion of natural appearances which borders on the grotesque" [*op. cit.*, 119]. The expressionist writer is engaged in giving vent to his personal feelings, moods, emotions and ideas; he is not interested in representing the reality all faithfully. The expressionist technique or expressionism may be found in the plays of Ernst Toller (1893-1939), Georg Kaiser (1878-1945) and Bertolt Brecht (1898-1956); in the poetry of Georg Trakl (1887-1914), Gottfried Benn (1886-1956) and T.S. Eliot (1888-1965) (*The Waste Land*); and in the novels of Franz Kafka and in the 'Circe' episode of James Joyce's (1882-1941) novel *Ulysses*. Also see *impressionism, *realism, *surrealism.

expurgated edition. An edition of a book from which objectionable words, sentences or passages have been removed. For instance, an expurgated edition of D. H. Lawrence's (1885-1930) *Lady Chatterley's Lover* was published in 1932 (the unexpurgated edition of the book, i.e. the full version of it, was published in 1960).

extrinsic criticism. See *intrinsic criticism.

eye dialect. A term for how writers sometimes spell or write some words to represent a semblance of the pronunciation of those words by the rustics or the uneducated. For instance, 'enough' is written (and printed) as *enuff*, 'women' as *wimmin* and 'animals' as *animulz*.

F

fable. A fairly short *tale in verse or prose, mostly with talking birds and animal as*characters, illustrating a moral principle that is succinctly, clearly and proverbially stated usually by one of the characters or by the author himself. Fables with beast characters are also called beast fables. Aesop's (6th c. B.C.) fables are perhaps the oldest. In India the fables in *Panchatantra*, in England Geoffrey Chaucer's (c. 1343/4-1400) 'Chanticleer and the Fox', and the fables (in *Fables*) of John Gay (1685-1732), and in Russia the fables of Ivan Krylov (1769-1844) are famous. Some of the modern fabulists are: Rudyard Kipling (1865-1936), (*Just So Stories*); George Orwell (1903-53), (*Animal Farm*); and Gotthold Lessing (1729-81), (Nathan's fable in they play *Nathan the Wise*). But La Fontaine (1621-95) is considered by some to be the greatest fabulist of the world. The term 'fable' is used, rarely though, to denote the *story of a *novel or play.

fabliau [from French *fable*, fable, story, tale, myth]. A raw humour-containing satirical *story in verse, prevalent in France in the 12th and 13th century, that was generally directed against cuckoldry, the clergy and sexual promiscuity. In England, the genre was practised by Geoffrey Chaucer (c. 1343/4-1400) in his *Miller's Tale* (in which an Oxford carpenter is tricked by miller Nicholas to let his wife Alisoun sleep with him) and its sequel *The Reeve's Tale* (in which two carpenters trick the miller into letting his daughter and wife sleep with them). The plural form of the term is fabliaux.

fabula [from Latin *fibula*, story, tale]. The term was introduced in *Russian Formalism to distinguish clearly between the *plot and the *story. The Russian formalists conceived of the *fibula* as the raw materials of *narrative, i.e. the *events which *actually occur* chronologically or sequentially, while they conceived of the *plot (which they called **syuzhet* or **sjuzet*) as the order in which events are *actually presented* in *narrative.

fabulation. A term used by some critics, notably by Robert Scholes in his *The Fabulators* (1967), to refer to the *anti-novel or the kind of *novel which is essentially comical, allegorical, romantic or picaresque, and in which the writer indulges in verbal jugglery and surrealistic devices. "Fabulative novels violate, in various ways, standard novelistic expectations by drastic—and sometimes highly effective—experiments with subject matter, form, style, temporal sequence, and fusions of the everyday, the fantastic, the mythical and the nightmarish, in renderings that blur traditional distinctions between what is serious or trivial, horrible or ludicrous, tragic or comic" [Abrams, 196]. Some of the fabulative novelists are: John Barth (b. 1930) (*The Floating Opera*, *The End of the Road*, *Chimera*); Thomas Pynchon (b. 1937) (*Gravity's Rainbow*); William Grass (b. 1924) (*Omensetter's Luck*, *Willie Master's Lonesome Wife*);

Ishmael Reed (b. 1938) (*Flight to Canada*, *The Terrible Twos*) and Robert Coover (b. 1932) (*The Origin of the Brunists*). Also see *surfiction.

facetiae [from Latin *facetiae*, jest]. An euphemistic term of booksellers and librarians for obscene or pornographic books—a "code-word used in catalogues to disguise pornography" [Ayto, 119].

faction. A fictional novel which is built on verifiable historical or factual contents. The term is derived from the fusion of the two words: fact and fiction. Notable instances of the faction are: Truman Capote's (1924-84) *In Cold Blood* (in which there is 'an investigation of the apparently motiveless murder of a Kansas family by two youths') and Norman Mailer's (b. 1923) *Armies of the Night* (which describes 'the 1967 protest march on the Pentagon').

fairy tale. A *folk tale which involves such characters as fairies, elves, witches and such other supernatural beings (but usually not deities) and which is set in an eerie, magically strange space—in a never-never land. W.M. Thackeray (1811-63), Oscar Wilde (1854-1900) Charles Kingsley (1819-75) and some other novelists have produced a good number of fairy tales. In German, the fairy tale is called *Marchen. Also see *folk tale.

falling action. A term of dramatic criticism that refers to the action that succeeds the *climax and precedes the *denouement or *resolution, and contributes to lessening of dramatic tension. In *Freytag's pyramid, it is the 5th stage in the course of a play.

fantastic, the. The term denotes "a mode of fiction in which the possible and the impossible are confounded so as to leave the reader (and often the narrator and/or central character) with no consistent explanation for the story's strange events" [Baldick, 81]. The fantastic is a commixture of the natural and the supernatural that confounds understanding. In this sense, it is different from *allegory, *ghost story, *science fiction as well as from *utopia and *dystopia: "it is different from *allegory*, which is more controlled and more directly corresponds with the familiar, from *ghost stories*, which show the supernatural impinging on the natural without creating a different world or world-view, from *science fiction* (as distinct from science fantasy), which is usually set in possible worlds, accessible through great but measurable distances of space or time, and from *utopias* and *dystopias*, which are often futuristic or based on a recognizably human community" [McArthur, 399]. Henry James's (1843-1916) *The Turn of the Screw* and Alexey Tolstoy's (1882-1945) *The Vampire* are, for instance, two fantastics. Novels, such as Franz Kafka's (1883-1924) *Metamorphosis*, are fantastic. In *Metamorphosis*, we are baffled as to how to understand the novel: "Are we to read Kafka's *Metamorphosis* (1916) as a description of mental illness from the inside, a metaphor for some kind of alienation, or a literally true story (the protagonist turns into an insect, but the objective third-person narrative is remarkably matter-of-fact)?" [Fowler, Roger, 88]. Tzvetan Todorov, in his *The Fantastic*, "argues that fantastic narratives involve an unresolved hesitation between the supernatural explanation available in marvelous tales and the natural or psychological explanation offered by tales of the uncanny" [Baldick, 81]. Also see *marvelous , the; *uncanny, the; *fantasy.

fantasy, phantasy [from Greek *phantasia*, how things seem, what is sensed, appearance, apparition, imagination]. In psychology, the "term refers to subjective imagining, including waking and sleeping imagery, and hallucination. This may be visual, auditory, tactile, or a composite of these and other sense modes" [Eysenck, 367]. Briefly, an inclusive definition of 'fantasy' would be a 'mental image without objective reality'. In literature, on the other hand, the term denotes "any kind of fictional work that is not primarily devoted to realistic representation of the known world" [Baldick, 81]. So, the term may signify *fairy tales, *Gothic novels and *tales, *science fictions, *fables, etc. The fantasy is distinguished for its highly imaginative nature and the presence of elves, fairies and such other supernatural beings. The 'fantasy' should be distinguished from the *fantastic, for while the construction or structure of the latter is of necessity *illogical*, that of the former is *logical*: "Fantasy must be logically developed, so that acceptance of an initial premises allows the reader to enter fully into what follows. The narrative style should convey a credible story, even while normal expectations of narrative are being defeated" [McArthur, 399]. E.M. Forster (1879-1970), in his *Aspects of the Novel*, however, does not understand by 'fantasy' any genre or sub-genre of literature but an element or aspect of some *novels. According to him, the novel has all together six aspects: *story, people, *plot, fantasy, *prophecy, and *pattern and *rhythm. Fantasy, to him, is something unnatural, like ghosts, angels, etc., which sometimes exist in a novel as a 'side-show', as something 'extra' for the reader to appreciate.

farceur [from French *farceur*, wag, joker, humorist]. A 'performer in or writer of farces' [Ayto, 121].

fashionable fiction. A form of fictional *narrative that deals especially with *characters who represent the people who are economically affluent and are powerfully drawn to the prevailing customs, manners, dresses, etc. of the upper class of the society. Fashionable *fictions were popular in England from 1825 to 1850. Examples of the fashionable fictions are: Theodore Hook's (1788-1841) *Sayings and Doings*, *Maxwell*, *Gilbert Gurney* and *Jack Brag*; Susan Ferrier's (1782-1854) *Marriage* and *The Inheritance*; Bulwer Lytton's (1803-73) *Pelham*; etc. Benjamin Disraeli (1804-81) and Ouida or Marie Louise (1839-1908) also wrote several fashionable fictions.

feigning. Literally, the word means pretending, counterfeiting, dissembling or simulating. As a literary term also the word retains this connotation. Feigning is falsehood, and, in a sense—in the superficial sense, rather—most genres of literature—poetry, drama and novel —are feignings, in so far as they do not carry photocopies of the realities but only their verisimilitudes, though they, of course, contain a kind of *truth through imitating the realities.

fellow travelers. A term coined by the Russian radical leftist political writer and activist Trotsky (1879-1940) to designate those Soviet authors who accepted the 1917 Revolution but did not blindly subscribe to the Bolshevik political ideology. "In fact they maintained that literature should not be subject to political tenets or coercion." [Cuddon, 314] "The term was later extended to describe sympathizers with communism (specifically with the social system of the USSR as they take it to be), whether they confess their sympathy or do not confess it or even openly deny it. It is now used yet more widely, to cover those who sympathize with, and advance, a political cause, while not overtly belonging to it" [Scruton, 170-71]. Also see **engage* writer, *committed writer.

feminism. A radical belief in the absolute equality between men and women in all spheres of life and a striving to achieve that equality. Feminism is the "advocacy of the rights of women and of their social, political and economic equality with men" [Scruton, 171]. Feminism believe that the presently existing notion of inferiority of women is due to the capitalist mode of production relations which considers women only for such activities as child-bearing, raising the child, domestic works, providing sexual release to men, etc. It vehemently denies that the inferiority of the woman to the man is justified due to her muscular inferiority only. Originally, the term referred to the movement of *women* for establishing equal rights for men and women, but, in course of time, it admitted *men* also as equal partners in their struggle for achieving those equal rights, so that a man can be as good a feminist as a woman. The idea of feminism originated in the latter half of the 18th century and particularly in such revolutionary works as: Mary Wollstonecraft's (1759-97) *A Vindication of the Rights of Women* and *The Wrongs of Women* (novel); John Stuart Mill's (1806-73) *The Subjection of Women*; and Margaret Fuller's (1810-50) *Woman in the Nineteenth Century*. The suffragette movement at the beginning of the 20th century pushed the notion of feminism to the forefront of public consciousness. Also see *feminist criticism.

feminist criticism. It is an offshoot of the feminist 'movement' that surfaced somewhat clamorously in the 1960s, for a short period, though, but the spirit of the 'movement' has never died down. The feminist criticism "is an attempt to describe and interpret (and reinterpret) women's experience as depicted in various kinds of literature—especially the novel (...); and, to a lesser extent, poetry and drama. "It questions the long-standing, dominant, male, phallocentric ideologies (which add up to a kind of male conspiracy), patriarchal attitudes and male interpretations in literature (and critical evaluation of literature). It attacks male notions of value in literature—by offering critiques of male authors and representations of men in literature and also by privileging women writers. In addition it challenges traditional and accepted male ideas about the nature of women and about how women feel, act and think, or are *supposed* to feel, act and think, and how in general they respond to life and living. It thus questions numerous prejudices and assumptions about women made by male writers, not least any tendency to cast women in stock character (...) roles" [Cuddon, 315]. Though feminist criticism revolts against *phallocentrism and *phallogocentrism, it is not identical with *gynocriticism.

Some of the works supporting, or contributing to, the feminist criticism are: Virginia Woolf 's (1882-1941) *A Room of One's Own* (an essay in which she suggests that 'If one is a man, still the woman part of the brain must have effect, and a woman also must have intercourse with the man in her'), Simon de Beauvoir's (b. 1908) *The Second Sex* (an impressive survey of the history of psychological oppression of woman), Mary Ellmann's *Thinking About Women* (1968), Julia Kristeva's *Revolution in the Poetic Language* (1986), Helen Cixous's *Stigmata. Escaping* (1998) and Luce Irigaray's *An Ethics of Sexual Difference* and *To Speak is Never Neutral*.

festschrift [from German *Fest*, festivity, celebration, and *Schrift*, script]. Literally, the term means 'festival writing'. Festschrift is generally a collection of learned essays, articles or papers published in honour of some distinguished person on some memorable occasion. The custom of *festschrift* originated in Germany in the 19th century.

feuilleton [(pronunciation: *fae-to*) from French *feuille*, leaf, sheet (of paper), and *ton*, style, manner]. Literally, the term denotes a 'serial story', but, in fact, it refers to a section of a daily newspaper (originally at the bottom of the front page, but now at more pages) kept apart for literary (mainly drama) criticisms. When a *novel is serially published in the *feuilleton*, it is called *roman-feuilleton*. Some novels of Honorie Balzac (1799-1850), Alexander Dumas (*pere*: 1802-70) and George Sand (1804-76) were first published serially in the *feuilletons*. The custom of the *feuilleton* was in high vogue in France in the 1840s.

ficelle [from French *ficelle*, string, pack-thread, twine, trick, dodge]. *Ficelle* generally means the string(s) with which puppets are manipulated, and it is in this sense that the term is used in literary discourse—the sense of string, trick or manipulation—(of several *characters through the help of one single character—the *confidant or *confidante, who may be conceived of or imagined as a string or a bunch of strings). The term was coined by Henry James (1843—1916) to denote the confidant or confidante through whom the novelist provides the reader with informations directly, bypassing the narrator. Characters disclose informations secretly to the confidant or confidante, and thus those informations are conveyed to the reader (while the narrator is, as if, ignorant about those informations). Here the confidant or confidante is like the string of a puppet. "The *ficelle* was described by Henry James as the author's friend; the ficelle draws out other characters, manages stage business, is present to liven up action or dialogue, and so on" [Lemon, 47]. An example of the *ficelle* is the character Maisie Farange in Henry James's *What Maisie Knew*—Maisie "the naïve but preternaturally wise child in whom all the warring parents, step-parents and lovers casually confide, and through whose eyes the story is told" [Cuddon, 320].

fiction [from Latin *fictio* or *fictionis*, a shaping, forming, fashioning,which are from *fingere* or *fictum*, to shape, form or fashion]. Literally, the word means anything created, shaped or fashioned (by man). But, as a literary term, 'fiction' signifies something which is not a fact or reality but is invented; or something which is not a fact and yet is partially real; or which is a 'special kind of fact' (for instance, the 'fact' of a *novel or *crime fiction). "In an inclusive sense,fiction is any literary *narrative*, whether in prose or verse,which is invented instead of being an account of events that in fact happened. In a narrower sense, however, fiction denotes only narratives that are written in prose (the *novel* and *short story*), and sometimes is used simply as a synonym for the novel" [Abrams, 94]. (There are three adjectival forms of the term with three distinctive meanings: (1) fictional, which means 'relating to fiction', (2) fictitious, which means 'full of falsehood' and (3) fictive, which means 'imaginative' or 'inventive'.

fiction and truth. The term 'truth' is a complex and debatable one in both philosophy and *fiction. In philosophy, there are at least three main theories of truth: the *correspondence theory*, according to which an idea or knowledge or statement is true if it corresponds (fits, matches, agrees or correlates) with fact; the *coherence theory*, which maintains that an idea or knowledge or statement is only partially true in so far as it coheres (unites, adheres, joins or coalesces) with the 'absolute truth' or the 'ultimate truth' that relates to everything that be; and the *pragmatic theory* (of William James), which holds that an idea or knowledge or statement is true if it "proves the best for us in the long run" [Flew, 355]. It is obvious that the correspondence and pragmatic theories are not applicable in the case of a fiction to find out if it is true or false, for the notions of 'absolute truth' falls within the perview of philosophy and that of pragmatism within the concern about our practical life, from both of which the fiction is apart. The correspondence theory is also not applicable in the case of the fiction, for by definition it is not a fact, and neither is it a true representation of a fact, in so far as it is built on imagination. "Some thinkers have asserted that 'fictional sentences' should be regarded as referring to a *special world*, 'created' by the author, which is analogous to the real world, but possesses its own setting, beings, and mode of coherence.... Others, most notably J.A. Richards, have held that fiction is a form of *emotive language* composed of pseudostatements; and that whereas a statement in 'referential language' is 'justified by its truth, i.e. its correspondence...with the fact to which it points,' a pseudostatement 'is justified entirely by its effect in releasing or organizing our attitudes.... Most current theorists, however, present an elaborated logical version of what Sir Philip Sidney long ago proposed in his *Apology for Poetry* (published 1595) that a poet *'nothing affirmes, therefore never lyeth*. For, as I take it, to lye is to affirm that to be true which is false.' Current versions of this view hold that fictive sentences are *meaningful* according to the rules of ordinary, nonfictional discourse, but that, in accordance with conventions implicitly shared by the author and reader of a work of fiction, they are not put forward as assertions of fact, and therefore are *not subject to the criterion of truth or falsity* that applies to sentences in nonfictional discourse" (emphases added) [Abrams, 95]. One workable solution of this unending debate is perhaps to agree that if there are assertions or generalisations in a fictional work, they are but suggestions, opinions or inferences about the reality, and whether the reader should accept them as true depends all upon his readiness to believe in them —upon his belief system, that is.

fin de siecle [from French *fin*, finish, end; *de*, of; and *siecle*, century, age, period]. The French phrase literally means 'end of the century or age or period'. But in literary discourse it specifically refers to the end of the 19th century or, to be more specific, to the 1890s which "were viewed at that time, and later, as a decade of world-weary decadence and overblown sophistication whose epitome amongst writers and artists was perhaps Oscar Wilde" [Ayto, 126-27]. This means that the period of the 1890s was distinguished from its preceding and succeeding periods by its (inordinate) decadence, and that it ended there. The decadent writers, such as Pierre Baudlaire (1821-67), Algernon Swinburne (1837-1907), Oscar Wilde (1854-1900) and the illustrator Aubrey Beardsley (1872-98), along with the French *symbolists raised the slogan, 'Art's for art's sake' and "adopted a 'decadent' rejection of moral and social function for art. Reacting against realism and naturalism, they sought a pure beauty entirely removed from the imperfections of nature and from the drabness of contemporary society" [Baldick, 84]. According to some critics the *fin de siecle* includes the 1880s as well. Also see *decadence.

fioritura [from Latin *flos* or *floris*, flow, flowing]. A French term, it signifies florid embellishment or flourish in writing. The plural form of the word is *fioriture*.

first-person narrative. A *narrative whose author is a *character who identifies himself as 'I'; or a narrative that is filtered through the consciousness of one of its characters who is directly or indirectly involved in the action of the narrative. The first-person narrative is so called because its narrator speaks or narrates in the first person. Charlotte Bronte's (1816-55) *Jane Eyre*, Daniel Defoe's (1660-1731) *Robinson Crusoe* and Charles Dickens's (1812-70) *David Copperfield*, for instance, are first-person narratives. The narrator of a first-person narrative is called *first-person narrator. The first-person narrator of course relates the narrative in the first person but when he refers to the other characters he of necessity has to use the grammatical third person (he either names the characters or uses third-person pronouns: he or they). Also see *third-person narrative, *point of view.

first-person narrator. See *first-person narrative.

first-person perspective. See *point of view.

first-person point of view. See *point of view.

flaneur [from French *flaneur*, idler, loafer]. "A (normally male) idler who wanders along crowded city streets and observes without involvement" [Hawthorn, 124]. The term bears a "sense of semi-lonely detachment in the midst of the crowded urbane scene" and thereby expresses "something essential about modern life" [*ibid*]. The term was brought into vogue by Charles Baudlaire (1821-67).

flashback. In a non-linear *narrative or *plot, it is the technique of interrupting the forward continuity of the narrative in order to relate an *episode or incident that occurred earlier but was not narrated so far. It is particularly used in narratives that are began *in media res*. The technique is a good aid for the narrator to give background informations about *characters and events at appropriate times. The term was borrowed from the motion picture, and it is synonymous with *analepsis, *switchback. Also see *flashforward, *foreshadowing.

flashforward. It is antonymous with *flashback. In flashforward, *characters are imaginatively shown in some future background or as involved in some future incident or event, i.e., in flashforward something is narrated that has not yet actually taken place. Synonymous terms are *prolepsis, *foreshadowing.

flat character. See *developing character, *round character.

flicker. "The effect achieved by a sort of ambiguity, in which rather than having two clear alternatives between which to choose, the reader is disturbed by flashes of alternative meanings. The term is Brian McHale's, and he relates it to Roman Ingarden's concept of iridescence or opalescence, found where two alternative worlds are struggling for supremacy in a text but neither is capable of achieving it" [Hawthorn, 124]. Also see *four levels of meaning.

focalisation. The term is related to *point of view and *perspective and signifies a focal point from which, or an aperture through which, the *characters and their *actions are to be viewed.The term is now widely used. A narrative may have focalisation or may have no focalization, i.e. may have *zero focalisation*. The *first person narrative is *focalised*, for in it we experience what is being narrated through the consciousness of the narrating character or the *focaliser*. Daniel Defoe's (1660-1731) *Robinson Crusoe*, for instance, is a *focalized *narrative*, as in it we experience what is being narrated through Crusoe. But "a narrative which has zero focalization is one in which it is impossible to fix the perspective in terms of which the narrated characters, events and situations are being observed and presented. Many works of fiction which were traditionally described as characterized by an *omniscient* point of view are described by modern narratologists as having zero focalization" [Hawthorn, 258]. George Eliot's (1819-80) *Middlemarch*, for instance, is a *non-focalised narrative* or a narrative having *zero focalisation*. The character through whose consciousness a narrative is focalised is called *focaliser*. "Thus a *focaliser* is a character or consciousness *in* a work who or which offers the reader 'positions' from which that which is narrated can be experienced" [*ibid*.].

foil. A *character with contrasting questions designed to contradict the course of action of some more important character—usually that of the protagonist—and thus emphasizes the qualities and actions of that character. In *Hamlet*, for instance, Laertes is the foil to the Prince of Denmark and in Charlotte Bronte's (1816-55) novel *Jane Eyre* Helen Burns (very docile and obedient to Jane) is the foil to Jane (very rebellious) herself.

folk literature. A vague and umbrella term that denotes such diverse things as *fairy tales, *legends, ballads, folk songs, riddles, dramas, etc.—all created by primitive or illiterate people, and handed down generation to generation through oral tradition and then written down (till they are not written down they are not considered as folk literature).

folk tale. The term refers to a broad category that comprises *fairy tales, *fables, *tall stories, *legends, etc.—all of which are orally handed down from generation to generation. Magic and *myths generally enrich the folk tale. Despite the name of this sub-genre, it is not a fact "that 'folktales' are invented by the 'folk' in any mystic sense. Every single element of a given folktale was invented by some specific artisan somewhere in the tale's past history" [Hockett, 562]. The folk tales are rarely though used by writers as their materials or *themes. The Faust legend, for instance, has been utilised by such great writers as Christopher Marlow (1564-93), Wolfgang von Goethe (1749-1832) and Thomas Mann (1875-1955). The German word **Marchen* is often used for folk tale.

foregrounding. The term is an English rendering of the Czech word *aktualisace*. Foregrounding is the act of pushing the language or expression, rather than the content, of a literary work (poetry as well as *narratives) into prominence, i.e. making it dominant in perception or making it 'palpable'. When the language is thus foregrounded, the content is automatically and concomitently 'backgrounded'. Foregrounding is an important term in *Russian formalism, according to which the degree of literariness of a work depends on the degree of its foregrounding (the content of the work may be altogether ignored). Foregrounding is very much related to estrangement or *defamiliarisation. "The primary aim of literature in (thus) foregrounding its linguistic medium, as Victor Shklovsky put it in an influential formulation, is to estrange or defamiliarize; that is, by disrupting the modes of ordinary linguistic discourse, literature 'makes strange' the world of everyday perception and renews the reader's lost capacity for fresh sensation" [Abrams, 103]. This is of course nothing more than what S.T. Coleridge (1772-1834) wrote long before Shklovsky in *Biographia Literaria*. If poetry is the primary field of foregrounding, *novel is certainly the secondary. The importance of foregrounding in novel may be seen in such novels as Laurence Sterne's (1713-68) *Tristram Shandy*, Samuel Beckett's (1906-89) *Molloy* and *Malone Meurt*, Jame Joyce's (1882-1941) *Ulysses* and *Finnegans Wake* and William Faulkner's (1897-1962) *Absalom, Absalom!* and *The Sound and the Fury*. The supreme importance of foregrounding may be obvious in the following retort of Samuel Beckett. "Beckett, in answering [James] Joyce's detractors, once wrote: 'You complain that this stuff is not English. It is not only to be read. It is to be looked at and listened to. His writing is not about something; it is that something itself [...]'" [Cuddon, 326].

foreshadowing. See *flashforward, *prolepsis.

form. A complex and confusing term, having a variety of meanings. A literary work has two essential aspects: content or subject matter and form. The content refers to what an author says, and form refers to the manner in which he says what he says. The content is paraphrasable, i.e. the content can be revealed to the reader in a manner or mode (style) other than the author's. But the form cannot be changed, since any change in the form of a literary piece will render it metamorphosed into a quite new literary piece. But what then is this form? "Perhaps the most useful description of the form unique to particular works considers it to be the total of all patterns present in the work—including such diverse kinds of pattenrs as rhyme scheme, metrical and intonational patterns, grammatical peculiarities, motifs, image clusters, semantic relationships, and so on" [Lemon, 94]. This description of form may seem rather clear, only once we understand what *pattern is. But there are other notions about form. The "neoclassic critics, for example, thought of the form of a work as a combination of component parts, matched to each other according to the principle of *decorum*, or mutual fittingness" [Abrams, 101]. Here, we can understand form only if we understand **decorum*. Thus we see that the notion of form is complex.

Form is of two kinds: *organic form* and *imposed form*. If the form seems to have grown out of the content or the subject matter then it is called organic form, but if certain premeditated form is imposed on some content then the form is an imposed form. The form that is there in a sonnet is an imposed form. Again, form must be either *structural* or *textural*. "Structural form is a matter of memory, textural form of sensibility. Structure at its most obvious (plot, story, argument) may be said to be the skeleton of the work, texture (diction, rhythms, imagery, syntax) the skin" [Rodway, 175].

formalism. See *Russian formalism.

formulaic literature. Literature that contains formulaic or prescribed elements, such as stock phrases, epithets, etc. and follows the common mode of introduction, speech, conclusion, etc. Epics, for instance, are generally formulaic, for, all epics begin with an invocation. Simply, formulaic literature is stereotypical.

Forsterian. The term refers to the characteristics of the style and attitude of E.M. Forster's (1879-1970) prose *narratives or *novels and *short stories, such as (all novels) *Where Angels Fear to Tread*, *A Room with a View*, *Longest*

Journey, *Howards End* and *A Passage to India*. His style is visibly relaxed and his attitude humanistic and liberal.

four levels of meaning. Traditionally, there may be four types or levels of meaning of *narratives or poems: literal or historical meaning, moral meaning, allegorical meaning, and analogical meaning. These meanings must be distinguished from I. A. Richard's brand of *four meanings* "(a) the sense—what is actually said; (b) feeling—the writer's emotional attitude towards it; (c) tone—the writer's attitude towards his reader; (d) intention—the writer's purpose, the effect of his aiming at" [Cuddon, 329]. The four levels of meaning may be found in George Orwell's (1903-50) *Animal Farm*.

frame narrative, frame story. A frame *narrative or *story is one that comprises within its fold one or more other narratives or stories. The 'inner' story or narrative that is nested or contained in the 'outer' story or narrative (i.e., framed by the 'outer' story) is called *framed*, **embedded* or *nested* story or narrative. Boccaccio's (c. 1313-75) *Decameron*, *The Arabian Nights* (authorship unknown) and Chaucer's (c. 1343/4-1400) *Canterbury Tales* each has a frame narrative or frame story and multiple framed narratives or stories. Some novels are as well structured like the frame story. For example, Mary Shelley's (1797-1851) *Frankenstein* and Emily Bronte's (1818-48) *Wuthering Heights* "employ a narrative structure in which the main action is relayed at second hand through an enclosing frame story" [Baldick, 87].

frame narrator. The narrator of the frame narrative or story, who is also called *outer narrator*. Also see *frame narrative, frame story.

Frankfurt School. A pro-modernist, anti-Stalinist and critical Marxist ideological and cultural movement associated with the Institute for Social Research founded within the University of Frankfurt in 1923. It rejected the view that revolution was possible by the global working class, for it believed that the working class cadres of the industrially advanced countries were no longer a revolutionary force. The prominent members of the School in its initial stage were Max Horkheimer, Theodor Adorno, Herbert Marcuse, etc. The uniting idea of the School was "the need for a critical Marxism, construed as involving rejection of positivism, value-freedom, and (crude) materialism, while stressing the actual Hegelian and alleged idealist side of Marx himself" [Flew, 125]. Late sympathizers of the School include such thinkers as Jean-Francois Lyotard, Gilles Deleuze, Felix Guattari, Michel Foucault, Jean Baudrillard, Jurgen Habermas, Frederic Jameson, Jacques Lacan, Luce Irigaray, Helen Cixous, Julia Kristeva, etc.

free association. A psychological term that refers to the "non-purposefully linked course, trend or flow of thoughts, ideas and memories that arises, in dreams (...), daydreaming, and free fantasy, in psychotherapy (...) and psychoanalysis" [Eysenck, vol. I, 88]. For instance, if the thought of a dirndl or even of a pen occurs in the consciouness of a person, the image or thought of his beloved may arise in his consciousness as well and immediately. Here, the image or thought of the beloved is said to be freely associated with the thought of the dirndl or pen. In free association, no logical connection exists between the first and the second thoughts.

The term has been introduced into literary criticism to refer to the technique of writing that appears to be the result of free association. The following quotation from James Joyce's (1882-1941) *Ulysses* may illustrate how logically unconnected thoughts, words, images, etc. may follow one after another as if in a cascade, i.e. how they are 'freely' associated with one another. "'Ineluctable modality of the visible: at least that if no more, thought through my eyes. Signatures of all things I am here to read, seaspawn and seawrack, the nearing tide, that rusty boot. Snotgreen, bluesilver, rust: coloured signs. Limits of the diaphane. But he adds: coloured. How? By knocking his sconce against them, sure. Go easy. Bald he was and a millionaire, *maestro di color che sanno*. Limit of the diaphane in. Why in? Diaphane, adiaphane. If you can put your five fingers through it, it is a gate, if not a door. Shut your eyes and see'" [Cuddon, 330]. The term is cognate with, or related to, the term *stream of consciousness.

free indirect style, free indirect discourse. The terms are translations of French *le style indirect libre*, the name of the style or technique that Gustave Flaubert (1821-80) first adopted in his novel *Madame Bovary* and since then has become a common style. Discourse normally can be of two sorts: direct discourse or speech and indirect discourse or speech *Rama thought, 'I will stay here tomorrow'* is a direct discourse or sentence and *Rama thought that he would stay there the next day* is an indirect discourse or sentence. In free indirect style or discourse or sentence, the two modes of expressions (discourses or sentences) are combined in such a way that the *person* and *tense* of the indirect discourse ('Rama would stay') have the *time* and *place* appropriate to the direct discourse ('here tomorrow'). The result of this arrangement, in this case, would be the new sort of sentence, which will be called a free indirect discourse or a sentence in free indirect style, and that sentence would be the following: *Rama would stay here tomorrow*. This form of statement allows a *third-person narrative to exploit a *first-person point of view.

Freudian criticism. See *psychological criticism, psychoanalytical criticism.

Freytag's Triangle. A graphic illustration on a triangle's five parts or points the five acts of a five-act drama by the German dramatist and novelist Gustav Freytag (1816-95). The five parts are named introduction, inciting moment or rising action or *complication, *climax, *falling action or *denouement and *catastrophe. In most cases, the concept of the Triangle is applicable to the plots of novels as well.

frisson. [from French *frisson*, shiver (in cold, for example), thrill]. A special sort of pleasure in moments of great excitement, suspense or danger. Also see **duende*.

function. In *narratology, the term denotes an *action of a *character that significantly contributes towards the unfolding of the *plot or *story.

futurism. A short-lived *avant-garde* literary movement launched by the Italian poet and novelist Filippo Tommaso Marinetti (1876-1944) at the beginning of the 20th century. In 1908, Wilbur Wright *flew across* the English Channel and about the same time Bugatti was designing *recing automobiles*, while the *motion picture* industry was flourishing feverishly. Marinetti was impressed and influenced by the craze for dynamism of the 20th century man—the craze that looked desperately forward into the future. In 1909, he published the first manifesto of futurism in *Le Figaro*, in Paris, after which several others followed. The futurist manifestoes "advocated a complete break with tradition and aimed at new forms, new subjects and new styles in keeping with the advent of a mechanistic age. They extolled dynamism, the machine (and machinery in general), speed (there was a speed cult) and the splendour of war and patriotism" [Cuddon, 336]. The futurist cult was aggressively masculine and anti-tradition. It was soon to be exploited by the warmonger Mussolini and by the Russian Revolutionists. In Russia, Vladimir Mayakovsky (1893-1930), the poet and playwright, was the foremost futurist as Guillaime Apollinaire (1880-1918), the poet, was in France. The futurist movement died down around 1920, but before it ceased to exist, it provoked the emergence of *Dadaism and *Vorticism. The adjectival form of the term futuristic "usually has no reference to this movement, but is applied to fictional works (usually of science fiction or utopian fantasy) that describe some imagined future society" [Baldick, 89].

G

galanter Roman [from German *galant*, gallant, brave, amorous adventure; and *Roman*, novel]. "A minor genre in German fiction which is fundamentally erotic in content and tone and is concerned with amorous intrigues and exploits often treated in fairly light-hearted fashion" [Cuddon, 338].

Gallicism. The use of French words expressions as if they are English words or expressions, sometimes making slight changes in them and sometimes doing nothing. For instance, the following English words are Gallicisms (the original French words appear in parentheses): actuality (*actualite),* banality (*banalite*), redaction (*redaction*), living pictures (*tableaux vivants*), marriage of convenience (*mariage de convenance*), etc. The term also denotes the use of French customs, manners, turns of thought in English *narratives and ambiences.

***gaucho* literature** [*gaucho* from Spanish *gaucho*, cowboy]. The term refers to the literature in Spanish—poetic and fictional—that deals with the life of the nomadic cowboys or herdsmen (*gauchos*) on the plains of the River Plate in Argentine. *Gaucho* literature stresses the courage, endurance, skill, and love of horses and cattle of the nomadic *gauchos* and portrays their colourful life.

gaze. An important modern critical term with somewhat loose meaning. Jacques Lacan (b. 1901), the most influential psychoanalyst, since Freud, writes in his *The Four Fundamental Concepts of Psychoanalysis*: "In our relation to things, in so far as this relation is constituted by the way of vision, and ordered in the figures of representation, something slips, passes, is transmitted, from stage to stage, and is always to some degree eluded in it—that is what we call the gaze" [Hawthorn, 137]. Admittedly, from this we do not clearly understand what gaze is beyond the fact that gaze belongs to subjectivity, or, better, to the *desire* of the subject, the viewer. The subject or the viewer wants *something* to see in the object of his vision, and in his fantasy he confers that *something* on to the object, whereby the object is changed, metamorphosed—stylised—in his imagination, as a result of which he views not the object as it is but the stylised object. Here the desire-ladden view of the subject is called gaze. For instance, generally, the determining (active) male gaze projects its fantasy onto the (passive and exhibited) female figure, whereby the female figure is stylised. And, contrarily, "In their traditional exhibitionist role women are simultaneously to be looked at and displayed, with their appearance coded for strong visual and erotic impact so that they can be said to connote *to-be-looked-at-ness*" [*op. cit.*, 138]. Gaze has to be distinguished from *look*. Look is desire-free, neutral, unlike gaze. Look may be a two-way process (I see you and you see me) but gaze is a 'one-way subjective vision' (I see you with my desire-ladden vision actively while you stand before me passively, stylised by my fantasy). The subject of gaze has centrality which is absent in look. The matter may be clearer from the following quotation from E. Ann Kaplan's 1997 book *Looking for the Other: Feminism, Film, and the Imperial Gaze*: "The imperial gaze reflects the assumption that the white western subject is central much as the male gaze assumes the centrality of the male subject.... The gaze of the colonialist (thus) refuses to acknowledge its own power and privilege: it unconsciously represses knowledge of power hierarchies and its need to dominate, to control. Like the male gaze, it's an objectifying [or metamorphosing] gaze, one that refuses mutual gazing, mutual subject-to-subject recognition [because it assumes a 'centrality']" [*op. cit.*, 139].

Geistesgeschichte [from German *Geist*, mind, spirit, and *Geschicht*, story, history, anecdote]. Literally, the term denotes 'spirit-history' or 'mind-history'. In 1808, Friedrich Schlegel (1772-1829), the German poet and thinker, used this term to denote 'the sciences of the spirit'. Now the term means understanding and interpretation of the prevalent 'spirit' and 'mind' of an epoch or age as expressed in its literature, art, culture, etc. The term is cognate with **Zeitgeist*.

genius loci [from Latin *genitum*, to beget, and *locus*, place]. The Latin phrase (*loci*, plural of *locus*) literally means 'spirit of places' or the peculiar character of places or the distinctive impressions places make on the mind. Sometimes the *genius loci* may provide a creative writer with inspiration. For instance, the very place, Tintern Abbey, was the *genius locus*—the source of inspiration—for William Wordsworth (1770-1850) for composing the poem 'Tintern Abbey' and the *genius loci* of the Figsbury Rings inspired E.M. Forster (1879-1970) to write his novel *The Longest Journey*. Also see **duende*.

genre. A type, species, class or category of literary works showing distinctive *form, technique or purpose. The term is used for the basic modes of literary art (lyric, dramatic or *narrative) or for the broadest categories of composition (poetry, prose, *fiction). There is no agreed rules of grouping literary works into some fixed genres. There are also *sub-genres or sub-categories of literary works which are grouped following other different criteria. For instance, according to formal structure (sonnet, *picaresque novel) or according to length (*novel, **novella*) or according to origin (*folktale) or according to effect (*comedy, *tragedy) or according to subject-matter (*pastoral, *science fiction).

Gesellschaftsroman [from German *Gesellschafts*, social (class, order, novel, etc), and *Roman*, novel]. The term literally means 'society novel'. Gesellschaftsroman is a kind of *novel that depicts either a particular society or illustrates what 'society' (in the abstract) means, and in which society is as important (if not more) as its *characters. Thomas Mann's (1875-1955) *Der Zauberberg* (*The Magic Mountain*), for instance, is a *Gesellschaftsroman*.

Gestalt [from German *Gestalt*, figure, form, shape]. The German term is occasionally used in literary criticism to refer to the organic unity or unified whole of a literary work.

ghost novel, ghost story. A fictional *narrative in which ghosts or spirits, embodied or disembodied, are *characters. Ghost stories were very popular in the 19th century. Some of the famous ghost stories are: Edgar Allen Poe's (1809-49) *Tales of the Grotesque and Arabesque*, Charles Dickens's (1812-70) *A Christmas Carol* and

The Trial for Murder, R.L. Stevenson's (1850-94) *Thrawn Janet*, Margaret Oliphant's (1828-97) *The Open Door*, Wilkie Collins's *After Dark* and *The Queen of Hearts*, Rudyard Kipling's (1865-1936) *The Return of Imray* and *The Phantom Rickshaw*, etc. Ghost stories of *novel length or ghost novels are rare but not non-existent. Kingsley Amis's (b. 1922) *The Green Man* and Susan Hill's (b. 1942) *The Woman in Black*, for example, are ghost novels.

ghost writer. A writer who does not publish his works in his own name but in the name of some famous or popular artist, politician, athlete, etc. in order to attract the attention of readers and earn more money. Sometimes also such persons employ ghost writers to write and publish in their names with a view to enhance their worth in the eyes of the public.

god trick. The term "refers to the way in which God (or any divinity) can be used as a centre to fix the meaning of all the experience of the believer. Normally the divinity referred to is a metaphoric rather than a literal one: the term tends to be used in a sarcastic or dismissive manner" [Hawthorn, 39]. Also see *centre.

Gothic novel, Gothic romance. The Goths were one of the ancient (roughly from the 12th century to the 16th) barbarous people of the southern part of Germany. The adjective 'Gothic' primarily refers to those people's style of architecture and their romantic attitude. The term 'Gothic architecture' "now denotes the medieval type of architecture, characterised by the use of the high pointed arch and vault, flying buttresses, and intricate recesses" [Abrams, 110]. The Gothic *novel, *romance and *fiction flourished in the late 18th and 19th centuries to the popular taste, bearing a reaction against the sedate neoclassicism of the 17th and early 18th centuries. Gothic novels, for convenience, may be divided into two groups: early and recent or late. "The early Gothic novels were characterized by settings remote in time (usually the Middle Ages) or place (Turkey was common) where mysterious and magical events could be given an air of plausibility. The details of setting (dungeons, monstrous statues, dark corridors and trap doors, omens and ancestral curses) emphasize morbid gloom; the central conflict is usually between a genteel but courageous young man and the forces of evil—often aided by magic" [Lemon, 11]. Some of the early Gothic novels are: Horace Walpole's (1717-97) *The Castle of Otranto*, Mrs Ann Radcliffe's (1764-1823) *The Mysteries of Udolpho*, M.G. 'Monk' Lewis's (1775-1818) *The Monk*, Mary Shelley's (1797-1851) *Frankenstein* and Charlotte Bronte's (1816-55) *Jane Eyre*. Recent novels that have the features and elements of the early Gothic novels—wildness, mystery, barbarousness, crudity, gloom, supernatural beings and events, magic, horror, ghastliness, adventure, etc.—are also called Gothic (or neo-Gothic) novels or romances. Edgar Allan Poe's (1809-49) horror tales, Ernst Theodor Hoffmann's (1776-1822) grotesque and bizarre novels and tales, William Faulkner's (1897-1962) *Sanctuary* and *Absalom, Absalom* and Isak Dinesen's [pseudo. of Mrs Karen Blixen (1885-1962)] *Seven Gothic Tales* may be taken to be examples of recent or late Gothic novels, romances, tales or fictions.

grace. An easy elegance in *form or manner, which is a mysterious quality in literary works and which contributes to their beauty. Beauty is the outward sign of inward grace. Grace was highly prized by the classical writers.

Grand Guignol [from French *grand*, great, tall, majestic, and *guignol*, puppet show, Punch and Judy show]. The term denotes a kind of extremely sensational melodrama, featuring bloody murders, rapes, tantrums, etc. that was once popular in France. The audience derived a sort of sadistic pleasure from the ghastly scenes of the *Grand Guignol*. "'Guignol' originally was a puppet in a sort of French Punch-and-Judy show. The genre of play to which he lent his name flourished particularly in Montmartre in the 1890s and 1900s; London saw a famous season of *grand guignol* plays staring Sybil Thorndike in 1920-2" [Taylor, 114]. "The term is now often applied to horror movies: while in contemporary fiction, several of Angela Carter's [b. 1940] stories are studies in *Grand Guignol*" [Baldick, 93].

grotesque. As an adjective, the term means bizarre, highly fantastic or extravagantly formed, and as a noun it signifies that which is so. The grotesque is far from realistic and it evokes our laughter, for it produces a comic, sardonic, exaggerated effect on us. The literature of the grotesque freakishly caricatures human figures and behaviour, brings to the fore the gross similarities between men and animals, distorts emotions by exaggeration, etc. A classic example of the grotesque is to be found in Gregor Samsa's metamorphosis into an insect during sleep in Franz Kafka's (1883-1924) *novel, *Metamorphosis*. The grotesque elements are also present, for example, in the works of the following novelists: Jonathan Swift (1667-1745), Tobias Smollett (1721-71), Charles Dickens (1812-70), Evelyn Waugh (1903-66), Victor Hugo (180-85), Emile Zola (1840-1902), Samuel Beckett (b. 1906), Jean Genet (b. 1910), etc.

Grub Street, grub street. The term was taken from the name of a street near Moorfields in London where many hack writers once lived. It now signifies any literary hackwork or trash. The term 'Grub Street' or its variant 'Grubean' has been used since the 18th century. The present name of the street is Milton Street. Also see *hack.

Gruppe 47 [from German *Gruppe*, group, team]. The name of a "group of predominantly left-wing German writers founded by Hans Richter in 1947. They gathered annually between 1947 and 1967 when they read each other's work and offered criticism" [Cuddon, 369]. The German novelist and poet Gunter Grass (b. 1927) was one of those writers. Also see **Gruppe 61*.

Gruppe 61 [from German *Gruppe*, group, team]. "A group of left-wing revolutionary German writers centred on Dortmund (c. 1961). Their principal objective was to promote writing—particularly fiction—about work by working men" [Cuddon, 369]. Also see **Gruppe 47*.

gynocentrism [from Greek *gune*, woman, and *kentron*, a sharp point]. A term opposed to *androcentrism. The term was introduced by feminist theorists to denote the feminine perspective. Gynocentrism insists on respecting female attitudes and experiences alongside male attitudes and experiences in literary works.

gynocriticism [from Greek *gyne*, woman, and *kriticos*, judgement]. Gynocriticism points to a "criticism exclusively pre-occupied with the production, motivation and analysis of writing by women on women" [Seturaman, 570]. Gynocriticism must be distinguished from *feminist criticism, for while the latter criticizes and evaluates male authors as to their dealing with female characters and female psychology, the former focuses on women as writers. Feminist criticism is also called feminist critique. Gynocriticism, however, is a distinct "branch of modern feminist literary studies that focuses on women as writers" [Baldick, 93].

H

hack. In literary discourse, the term denotes a low-grade or hackneyed literary work or a low-grade writer who produces such works often for a pittance (called hack writer). Also see *Grub Street, *potboiler.

hamartia [from Greek *hamartia*, error of judgment]. According to Aristotle's *Poetics*, hamartia is the single fatal flaw in the judgment, in a critical situation, of the hero (or heroine) of a tragedy that brings in his irreversible downfall. This fatal flaw is to be imputed to the **hubris* or **hybris*, i.e. the overbearing pride or self-confidence of the hero that goads him to violate the inviolable universal moral law or order even disregarding divine warnings. Also see **hubris*, **hybris*, **peripeteia*.

happening. A sort of improvised theatrical production that consists of discrete events, elements of everyday life, etc. put together in a non-realistic way. In happening, there is no finished script and no full-scale rehearsal, and audience participation is a frequent feature. An example is John Cage's (b. 1912) *Sonata Six*. The term is also used in art where such junks as rags, broken mirror, electric bulbs, painted paper, plastic film, cords, etc. are fabricated to make the art object. The happening bears a message; the message generally is that of chaos. The happening, both in art and the theatre, came to prominence in the 1950, particularly in America. "In a few short years the happening has become a part of American folk culture, perhaps because it reflects the sense of chaos we observe in our society" [Russell, 381].

Harlem Renaissance. The term refers to the buoyant and vibrant movement of the African-Americans in the fields of literature, music, painting, sculpture, etc. from the end of the First World War in 1917 till the Great Depression of 1929. The centre of the movement was Harlem, an area of New York City with predominantly black population or African-Americans. The movement is also known as 'New Negro' and 'Black Renaissance', and it emphasised the African heritage of the American blacks. The movement was fostered by poets (such as Sterting Brown, Countee Cullen, Claude McKay, etc.) dramatists, essayists, etc. as well as novelists, such as Langston Hughes (1902-67) (who was also a poet and dramatist), Jean Toomer (1894-1967) (whose remarkably inventive *Cane* is a peculiar creation in the sense that though it is a *fiction yet it includes not only verse but also drama) and Jessie Fauset (1882-1961). The Black American editor, critic, philosopher and art historian Alain Locke's 1925 literary anthology *The New Negro* reflects the spirit and partial achievement of the movement. Though during the Great Depression the movement lost its steam it continued into the 1930s when two other black novelists flourished: Arna Bontemps (1902-73) and Zora Neale Hurston (1903-60).

Hebraism. The term denotes a strictly moralistic attitude of life that subordinates all other things to ethical ideology, like the orthodox Jews or Hebrews. Hebraism is antonymous with *Hellenism which prizes beauty and intellect the most over everything else. The antinomy between the two attitudes or ideologies "was celebrated by Matthew Arnold in Chapter IV of [his] *Culture and Anarchy* (1869). Arnold sees the essence of Hebraism as 'spontaneity of consciousness'. He regards a combination of these two as a necessary pre-requisite to a mature life. They are not contradictory, as he puts it, 'the desire, native in man, for reason and the will of God, the feeling after the universal order' is their common aim" [Cuddon, 347-75].

Hellenism. See *Hebraism.

hermeneutics [from Greek *hermeneus*, an interpreter]. The term has an association with the Greek mythological figure Hermes, son of Zeus and Maia, and patron of art and thieves. He is noted for his *inventiveness* and hence hermeneutics signifies, or is related to, interpretation of texts. Originally the term meant interpretation or exegesis of especially the Bible but since the 19th century it has come to assume a wider meaning so that philosophical and literary texts also come under its perview.

hero, heroine. The most important *character, or structurally the central character, of a dramatic or narrative work—if male, the hero; if female, the heroine. It is wrong to assume that the central character must be morally or otherwise superior to the other characters or that it possesses 'heroism'. To fight shy of this possible misinterpretation, the more neutral term, *protagonist, is commonly employed.

heterodigesis. A term of *narratology that refers to a narrative sequence or part that relates a *theme that is different from the principal theme of the main *narrative. But if a sequential narrative part dovetails with the main narrative as regards its principal theme, then that narrative part is called *homodigesis.

heteroglossia [from Greek *hetero*, different, other, and *glossa*, tongue]. The Russian critic Mikhail Bakhtin (1895-1975) introduced this term "to describe the variety and diversity of languages used in epic and in the *novel. He distinguished between the language used to represent the attitudes and opinions of the author and that used by individual *characters in *fiction and epic" [Cuddon, 381]. In the novel, heteroglossia presents only two basic sorts of language: that of the author or narrator and that of the characters. But if there are more than two languages within the same *narrative, it is called *polyglossia* (where, for instance, the characters speak in different languages).

high mimetic. The term, according to Northrop Frye, denotes the "mode of literature in which, as in most epics and tragedies, the central characters are above our own level of power and authority, though within the order of nature and subject to social criticism" [Frye, 366]. If the central characters are *not* above, but equal or below, our level of power and authority, the mode of literature is called *low mimetic.

historical fiction, historical novel. A sort of *fiction or *novel that deals with some historical event or action that actually took place at least one—in some cases several—century before the time of the writer, which event or action exists in the living memory of the reader. The objective of the historical novel is to reconstruct and re-enact the past event as accurately as possible, along with a verisimilar depiction of the social *setting, customs, mode of life, personal relations, etc. of the specified historical period. The *characters may be both real and imagined. Sometimes the writer of historical novel or fiction does extensive research works for gathering the materials of that period as well as capturing its spirit or **Zeitgeist*. Some of the outstanding historical novels or fictions are: Sir Walter Scott's (1771-1832) *Waverly*; William Makepeace Thackeray's (1811-63) *Vanity Fair*; Charles Kingsley's (1819-75) *Hypatia*, *Westward Ho!* and *Hereward the Wake*, Victo Hugo's (1802-85) *Notre-Dame de Paris*, Gustave Flaubert's (1821-80) *Salammb* and Leo Tolstoy's (1828-1910) *War and Peace*. There is another kind of narrative that also exploits historical periods, like the historical novel or fiction, but its exploitation is limited, in the sense that it "tends to employ the period setting only as a decorative background to the leading characters" [Baldick, 100]. Such a *narrative is called *historical romance or 'costume' romance.

historical romance, 'costume' romance. See *historical fiction.

***historie*.** See **Discours*.

holograph [from Greek *hilos*, whole and *graphe*, a writing]. The word literally means 'whole or entire writing'. Holograph is a "manuscript or letter written entirely by the person in whose name it appears" [Cuddon, 385].

homodigesis. See *heterodigesis.

horizon of expectations. The term was coined by the German critic Hans Robert Jauss "to denote the criteria which readers use to judge literary texts in any given period. It is a crucial aspect of Jauss's aesthetics of reception, and the term designates the *shared set of assumptions* which can be attributed to any given generation of readers. The criteria help constitute readers' judgments of, say, a poem (e.g., pastoral or elegy) in a trans-subjective way. Horizons of expectation change. The poetry of one age is judged, valued and interpreted by its contemporaries, but the views of that age do not necessarily establish the meaning and value of the poetry definitively. Neither meaning nor value is permanently fixed, because the *horizon of expectations of each generation will change*. As Jauss puts it: 'A literary work is not an object which stands by itself and which offers the same face to each reader in each period. It is not a monument which reveals its timeless essence in a monologue.' Each age reinterprets poetry (and literature in general) in the light of its own knowledge and experience, its own cultural environment. Literary value is measured according to 'aesthetic distance', the degree to which a work departs from the 'horizon of expectations' of its first readers" (emphases added) [Cuddon, 387]. The reader has always a more or less definite set of expectations from a particular text, and that set of expectations is conditioned by his time and place, his ideology and socio-political environ, etc. Briefly, the reader has a particular personal set of cultural norms, assumptions, and criteria with which he will understand and judge a literary work.

horror story. Simply stated, it is a story that arouses in us alarm, dread, fright, panic or terror due to the presence in it of such hair-raising things as murder, madness, torture, suicide, ghosts, witchcraft, succubi, incubi, voodoo, poltergeists, lycanthropy, talekinesis and such other horrifying supernatural or preternatural objects or events. Horror stories have always been popular, may be due to man's some innate peculiar drive for the horrific. Some horror stories, for instance, are the following: Geoffrey Chaucer's (1340?-1400) *Perdoner's Tale*, Christopher Marlowe's (1564-93) *Dr*

Faustus, Edgar Allan Poe's (1809-49) *Tales of the Grotesque and Arabesque*, R.L. Stevenson's (1850-94) *The Strange Case of Dr Jekyll and Mr Hyde*, Henry James's (1843-1916) *The Turn of the Screw*, Saki's (H.H. Munro's) (1870-1916) *The Music on the Hill* and *The Open Window* and H.G. Wells's (1866-1946) *The Abyss* and *The Sea-Riders*, *The Valley of the Spiders* and *The Empire of the Ants*.

hubris, hybris [from Greek *hybris*, insolence, arrogance]. A sort of overconfidence in oneself that grows pride and pushes towards violation of all authority, including that of God, and also of universal moral laws, and thereby brings in his doom. In ancient Greek tragedies hubris was the reason of the downfall of the heroes. Hubris generally generates out of **hamartia* or error in judgment or cognition. Macbeth in *Macbeth*, for instance, wrongfully judged or cognised that 'none of woman born can harm Macbeth' and this grew hubris in him.

humanism. A new philosophical, artistic, cultural and literary phenomenon of Europe in the 16th and 17th centuries that showed a topsyturvification of the earlier predominance of religion in which humans were treaded, or conceived of, as critters, and that showed the blooming of human beings in the eyes of the philosophers, artists and creative writers. Humanism in Europe was almost coeval all the way through with European Renaissance which was the delayed consequence of the Italian Renaissance. The European Renaissance continued from the beginning of the 16th century to the dawning of the modern era, or, if earlier than that, to the end of the 17th century. Humanism restored the lost dignity, freedom, hope, spirit and ideality of man. The essence of humanism is well expressed in the following exhortation of Alighieri Dante (1265-1321) to man in his *Divine Comedy*: "Thy will is free and whole and upright and now it would be wrong to rein it in. Be thy own Emperor and thine own Pope" [Russell, 200]. Or, in the famous soliloquy of Hamlet: '... What a piece of work is a man! How noble in reason! How infinite in faculties! In form and moving, how express and admirable! In action, how like an angel! In apprehension, how like a god! The beauty of the world! The paragon of animals!' Earlier, the finite man was thought to be a tiny and insignificant thing in the infinite universe of God, but humanism taught him that finite though he really is he can prove himself infinite at least in his imagination and that rather than cowering before God he can stand chin up in his own imaginatively created universe, if he only wills. Earlier, God was the centre of the universe, but humanism brought in man centre stage in the universal drama, sending God to the green house. And some of the great thinkers and writers who brought in this sort of Copernican revolution are: Desiderius Erasmus (1466-1536), Sir Thomas More (1478-1535), Michel Montaigne (1533-92), Sir Philip Sidney (1554-86), Edmund Spenser (?1552-99) and John Milton (1608-74).

In the 1920s a new wave of humanism emerged in America, known as *new humanism. In the vanguard of this new humanistic movement were the critic Irving Babbitt (1865-1933), the critic Norman Foerster (b. 1887), the critic and philosopher Paul Elmer More (1864-1937), etc. Babbitt, Foerster and More were hugely influenced by the critic W.C. Brownell's (1851-1928) stern emphasis on the need of rationality, discipline and morality in life and literature, the former two also by the ancient classical literature. The new humanism upheld four cardinal principles. First, the new humanists "believe man's true nature is that of a controlled and rational being, so that the individual's proper business is the discriminating cultivation of all his faculties. 'The humanist, then as opposed to the humanitarian, is interested in the perfecting of the individual rather than in schemes for the elevation of mankind as a whole, and although he allows largely for sympathy, he insists that it be disciplined and tempered by judgement' (Babbitt). Second, they wish to encourage and inhabit a society based on reason and control.... Third, they believe that a literature which truly reflects and explores man's nature will be primarily ethical and concern itself with moral values, and not with the ideal of self-expression introduced by romanticism.... Fourth, they reassert the supreme value of literature and the study of moral experience in education, and oppose the fashionable rise of the natural sciences. 'The humanities need to be defended today against the encroachments of physical science, as they once needed to be against the encroachments of theology' (Babbitt)" [Mottram, 193].

humours [from Latin *umor*, to be moist]. The term was first used by the Father of Medicine, Hippocrates (460-357 B.C.) of Thessaly in Central Greece. Hippocrates divided human beings into four categories, each category having the predominance of one of the four basic humours or bodily fluids—blood, phlegm, choler (yellow bile) and black bile. He believed that though all men have all the four fluids, a predominance of a particular fluid over the other three in a man gives rise to a particular temperament in him. Thus the predominance of blood would make a man sanguine; of phlegm, phlegmatic; of choler, choleric; and of black bile, melancholic. Ben Jonson (1572-1637) first brought the concept of humours in literature by contrieving the kind of play called the comedy of humours, the ever first instance of which is his play *Everyman in his Humours*. The concept of the humour is now obsolete.

hybris. See **hubris, hybris*.

hyperreality. An important postmodern critical term and a central concept in Jean Badrillard's (b. 1928) explanation of the life in postmodern era. The concept of the hyperreal or hyperreality has come into literary discourse only after the advent of the electronic media—TV, computer, internet, etc.—which have radically changed our concept of reality. The real is that which truly exists, which is not counterfeit or assumed, which is ontologically genuine, or which is authentic. The electronic media have changed this earlier concept of reality by providing simulacra (plural of simulacrum) or images or semblances for each and every component of the actual reality. For instance, you have your real car in your garage, and you can have a simulacrum or image of that car in your computer. And, which is more subterfusing is that your frequenter engagement with the car in the computer may render it more 'real' than the real car in the garage. In this case, the car in the computer is hyperreal or a component of the hyperreality (i.e., the sum total of all the hyperreals or simulacra). The electronic media have been so much successful in simulating or counterfeiting the real reality that, for instance, the computer has become life and life has become a computer. This is so because not only do *you see* images in the computer but the *images also do see you* (say, you can talk with your friend in the computer). Now, your frequenter intercourse with the images in the computer or T.V. has pushed off the real reality into the limbo and brought a live all the simulacra into your focus. Consequently, the real reality has become less real or non-reality and the simulated 'reality' of the simulacra has become more 'real' than the real reality, or has become hyperreality. A classic instance of this is the postmodern movie *Bladerunner*, in which a gang of artificially created 'humans' or 'replicants' are the cast, and which movie successfully presents a hyperreality, such that for a moment, at least, we become oblivious of our real, work-a-day, reality. The devious and devilish trick of the hyperreality is explicated in Badrillard's definition of the simulacrum: it is that which is so close to the original that the original is no longer required. And he very rightly thinks that "reality is increasingly removed as we move through history, a process that culminates in simulation replacing reality with 'hyperreality', the more real than real" [Simons, 204].

hypertext. Conventionally, a creative text (of *novel, play, *short story, etc.) is unidirectional: it has a 'beginning' and an 'end', and, moreover, it is fixed—it does not change (revisions must be ignored). A hypertext, on the other hand, is something fluid, changing. The changes take place due to continuous interaction between the reader and the author. Further, the hypertext contains not only the text but also subsidiary informations about the text and the author. "Fundamental to the idea of the hypertext is the replacement of linear and unidirectional progression [of a text, for instance, of a novel] between two fixed points ('beginning' and 'end') with a very large number of potential journeys through text-mass which is continually being added to, amended, and re-signposted and re-mapped.... "A conventional literary text such as a play by Shakespeare or a novel by Dickens can be made part of a hypertext by being linked electronically with such things as linguistic information about words and grammatical formations in the work, biographical information about the author, contextual information about the author's time, generic information about the literary tradition within which the author was working, and so on" [Hawthorn, 161]. The cardinal criterion of a text being a hypertext is its moving away from the linear progression, even if it is not electronically manipulated or stuffed with informations extraneous to the text. B.S. Johnson's (1933-73) novel *The Unfortunates*, for instance, may be called a hypertext, for it was "published in a box of 27 stapled gatherings [a gathering is a number of signatures or printed sheets folded into pages], which could be read in any order" [*ibid*.]. Some other experimental novelists, besides Johnson, have produced hypertexts. Also see *subtext, *IF (interactive fiction).

hypocorism [from Greek *hypo*, inadequate, and *koros*, boy]. A diminutive or abbreviated pet name or term of endearment, such as Will Shakespeare (William Shakespeare), Willie Yeats (William Butler Yeats), Tom Eliot (T.S. Eliot), 'honey', 'chuck', 'cherry blosson' 'sweetie pie', 'Susie', (all terms of endearment), etc.

hypostatisation. The term literally means to treat as hypostasis or basis, foundation or substance. Hypostatisation, in literary discourse, means a form of personification in which an abstraction or an abstract quality is treated as something human. For instance, in 'Truth insists I tell the story' and 'Decency compels me to admit the truth', 'Truth' and 'Decency' are hypostatized.

hypotyposis [from Greek *hypo*, under, and *typos*, blow, stamp, mark, model]. In rhetoric, the term connotes a 'vivid description of a scene'. It is a "figurative device by which something is represented as if it were present. For example: John of Gaunt's dying speech in *Richard II* (II, I, 31) in which he 'sees' England as a sceptred isle and creates a general word image of the country" [Cuddon, 407].

I

ideal reader. The term is equivalent in meaning to the *ideal spectator of the play, who is a neutral *character observing the events within the play without being affected by them like Horatio in *Hamlet* and Kent in *King Lear*. The ideal reader is an imaginary person who, a writer expects, will fully understand his purport in his particular literary work. The term 'ideal reader' originated in the concept of *reader-response (theory) and is synonymous with the term *optimal reader. Jeremy Hawthorn writes: "The optimal/ideal reader is a term used to refer to that collection of abilities, attitudes, experience, and knowledge which will allow a reader to extract the maximum value from a reading of a particular text" [Hawthorn, 291]. Also see *actual reader, *implied reader.

ideal spectator. See *ideal reader

idée fixe [from French *idée*, idea, fancy, whim, and *fixe*, fixed, fast, firm]. Literally, the term means a 'fixed idea'. *Idée fixe* denotes an idea that has become fixed or ingrained in the consciousness of a person, such that it dominates one's behaviour and cannot normally be shaken off. In literary discourse, however, a symbol, image, theme or word complex that frequently recurs in a literary work is deemed to have been associated with an *idée fixe*.

idée recue [from French *idée*, idea, fancy, notion, conception, and *recu*, received, admitted]. Literally, the term means 'received or admitted idea'. *Idée recue* denotes an idea or opinion that has been accepted uncritically as valid, though on deeper inquiry it may prove to be invalid.

idiolect. The term signifies all the speech habits of a person taken together. Charles F. Hockett defines idiolect thus: "Generally speaking, the totality of speech habits of a single person at a given time constitutes an idiolect" [Hockett, 321]. Though linguisticians normally restrict the term to speech only, it applies by extension to written language as well. Idiolect must be distinguished from *dialect which is just 'a collection of more or less similar idiolects', and also from *language* which is not very different from dialect. Hockett distinguishes between dialect and language thus: "A *language*...is a collection of more or less similar idiolects. A *dialect* is just the same thing, with this difference: when both terms are used in a single discussion, the degree of similarity of the idiolects in a single dialect is presumed to be greater than that of all the idiolects in the language" [*op. cit.*, 322]. A dialect generally marks out the distinctive language characteristics of a community (geographical, social educational, weaving, fishing, etc.).

idyllic. The quality of being ideally pastoral or having the ideal pastoral characteristics.

IF. A standard abbreviation for *interactive fiction.

illusion (dramatic). A deception or false-impression of something actually present in a drama or narrative. "The dramatic illusion is the feeling that the action, characters, scene, and so on of a drama or narrative are, for the moment at least, real. Its result is what Coleridge called the 'Willing suspension of disbelief' [Lemon, 50].

imagery [from Latin *imago*, image, and *imitari*, to imitate]. Image is "a mental copy of a sensory quality or experience in the absence of any sensory stimulus" [Eysenck, I, 499]. This is how the term is understood in psychology. But in literary discourse the term has a wider range of meanings: "Imagery as a general term covers the use of language to represent objects, actions, feelings, thoughts, ideas, states of mind and any sensory or extra-sensory experience. An 'image' does not necessarily mean a mental picture" [Cuddon, 413]. Imagery is images in general or collectively, and an image, as has been said, is not necessarily a mental picture, for it may as well appeal to senses other than that of sight. *The Concise Oxford Dictionary of Literary Terms* writes about 'imagery' that it is "a rather vague critical term covering those uses of language in a literary work that evoke sense-impressions by literal or figurative reference to perceptible or 'concrete' objects, scenes, actions, or states, as distinct from the language of abstract argument or expression" [Baldick, 106]. Lee T. Lemon, in his *A Glossary for the Study of English*, very clearly distinguishes between *image* and *imagery*. Lemon writes: "In literary study, an image is a verbal imitation of a sensory reality—visual, auditory, gustatory, etc. Imagery is language calculated to re-create in the minds of the readers the sight, touch, taste, smell, or whatever, of physical things. It tries less to make the reader understand than to make him imagine the appropriate aspects of physical reality. To say, 'My love is 5' 2" and weighs 98 pounds' does not present an image; to say, 'My love is as small and light as a hummingbird' does" [Lemon, 73]. Imagery must be distinguished from imagism, which is a short poetic movement, or doctrine, of the early 20th century. Imagism rejected cloudy and verbose poetry and demanded clarity and exactitude in poetry through clearly contoured images. Also see *imagination, *symbol.

imagination. The term denotes the mental act or function by which one creates 'pictures' in the mind of, objects, situations, relations among objects, etc. all that are not present before him at the moment. Or, in other words, the term refers to "mind's capacity to generate images of objects, states, or actions that have not been felt or experienced by the senses" [*op. cit.*, 107]. The term should not be confused with its related term 'fancy', though before S.T. Coleridge's (1772-1834) *Biographia Literaria* the two terms were used interchangeably. According to Coleridge, fancy is "merely 'a mode of memory emancipated from the order of time and space' and was thus able to combine and reassemble ready-made images in new spatial and temporal arrangements, but not able to dissolve or unite them in new creations as the imagination could" [Baldick, 81]. Of course both fancy and imagination are devoid of reason or judgment, but while imagination is creative, fancy is mechanical. In fancy, different parts or components do not dissolve into one another, but in imagination the parts or components unrecogniseably dissolve into one another and make a new whole. Centaur—half man (an undissolved part) and half horse (another undissolved part)—is, for example, the creation of fancy. On the contrary, Shakespeare wrote *Hamlet* taking materials from *ur-Hamlet*, Holinshed's *Chronicles*, courtesy books, etc. but those materials dissolved into one another in the play so imperceptibly that they lost their identities and made a new whole, i.e. the play itself. *Hamlet*, therefore, is a creation of imagination.

imitation. The term is generally used as a synonym of *mimesis, but it is also employed as the name of a literary *genre. *The Wordsworth Companion to Literature in English* writes about the term: "As a literary genre, the term signifies the attempt by one writer to rework the structure and theme of an earlier writer's work, recast in a contemporary mood" [Ousby, 465]. The term must not be confused with *translation*.

impassibilite [from French *impassibilite*, impassibility, impassiveness, unfeeling, unimpressionable, unperturbed]. The term was introduced by Gustave Flaubert (1821-80) to mean "an unmoved or unimpassioned feeling toward the characters and events of one's [a writer's] story" [Booth, 81]. The term is distinct from both *neutrality* and *impartiality*. It is not neutrality of judgment about values, for "an author could be committed to one or another value and still not feel with or against any of his characters. At the same time, it is clearly distinct from impartiality, since the artist could feel a lively hate or love or pity for all of his characters impartially" [*op. cit.*, 81-82]. *Impassibilite*, simply, is absolute objectivity on the part of an author—the objectivity that is quite untouched by any passion.

implied author. Same as *voice. But Wayne C. Booth prefers to use the term 'implied author' rather than the term 'voice' "in order better to indicate that the reader of a work of fiction has the sense not only of the timbre and tone of a speaking voice, but of a total human presence. Booth's view is that this implied author is 'an ideal, literary, created version of the real man'—that is the implied author, although related to the actual author, is nonetheless part of the total fiction, whom the author gradually brings into being in the course of his composition, and who plays an important role in the overall effect of a work on the reader" [Amrams, 219]. The reader, in the course of reading a text gradually creates a picture of a writer, other than the actual writer of the text, on the basis of the timbre, tone, attitude, etc. of the narrating or speaking voice, and this pictured writer is the implied author. Also see *implied narrator.

implied narrator. An implied narrator is one who always remains such and who does not emerge as a *character at any point in the whole course of the *narrative. For instance, the narrator of Fyodor Dostoevsky's (1821-1881) *Brothers Karamazov* is an implied narrator, for he always remains in the background and never emerges as a character, or intrudes or participates in the *actions or dialogues of the *novel.

implied reader. See *actual reader.

impressionism. The term, as it is used in literary discourse, was borrowed from the impressionistic movement in painting, in the vanguard of which movement were Edgar Degas and Claude Monet. Degas's painting *The Rehearsal on the Stage* (1878-79) [Russell, 251] and Monet's *impression: Sunrise* (1872) [*op. cit.*, Plate 26] are supreme examples of the impressionist painting. It was from the title of Monet's *Impression: Sunrise* that the impressionist movements both in painting and literature got their names. The impressionist painters were trying to capture *momentary subjective impression* of an object from a particular point of view rather than showing the real object or in giving a sharp and idealized representation of the form and colours of the object. The impressionist painters were not interested in precise representation of objects—static objects—rather they were eager to capture fleeting impressions of objects from subjective point of view in momentary, transitory plays of light, in order to betray the inward (not outward) essence of those objects. In literature, impressionism signifies a mode of writing that is highly personal and that describes *characters and *scenes as they *appear to the writer and not as they really happen to be*. In this sense impressionism is a term quite contradictory to realism.The term impressionism is used in *narratology to describe the novelist's *oeuve* of concentrating on, and portraying, the inner life of characters rather than of their externalities. The impressionistic mode of writing is to be found in the works of Dorothy Richardson (1873-1957), James Joyce (1882-1941), Virginia Woolf (1882-1941), Marcel Proust (1871-1922), and such other novelists. Virginia Woolf's most experimental novel *The Waves*, which traces the inner lives of six characters from their childhood to old age, through series of interior monologues, is an excellent instance of the impressionistic novel, or of impressionism. Also see *expressionism, *surrealism, *realism.

inciting force. Same as *exciting force.

incunabulum. A book printed before 1500, i.e. in the early days of printing; or the birthplace, cradle, or origin of a thing. The plural form of the term is incunabula.

indeterminacy. The term may remind one of the uncertainty principle or indeterminacy principle of the great physicist Werner Heisenberg (1901-76) that 'There is a fundamental limit to the precision with which a position coordinate of a particle and its momentum in that direction can be simultaneously known.' In literary criticism, particularly in reader-response criticism, the term refers to those elements in a text (a *novel, *short story, play, etc.) which offer no fixed meaning or interpretation so that readers may interpret them in various ways. The degree of the indeterminacy of a text depends on the length and complexity of it. But in no case does the indeterminacy of a text suggest that it has got no meaning at all; the meaning simply depends on the individual reader. The term is also employed in *deconstruction, where it denotes "a principle of uncertainty invoked to deny the existence of any final or determinate meaning that could bring to an end the play of meanings between the elements of a text" [Baldick, 109]. Also see *reception theory, *reader-response theory, *flicker.

ingénue [from French *ingénue*, unsophisticated, artless or guileless girl]. An artless, simple or unsophisticated, guileless or innocent young, attractive and somewhat romantically tilted girl or female lead in a play or *narrative. Examples of the ingénue in plays are: "Muriel in Eugene O'Neill's *Ah, Wilderness*!, Kim in Michael Stewart's *Bye Bye Birdie*, and Dominica in Barbara Shotenfeld's *Catch Me If I Fall*" [Mobley, 74]. Also see **soubrette*.

initiation story. An initiation story is one in which a significant change occurs in the character of its *young* *protagonist as a result of his some critical experience that informs his future *adulthood*. Mordecai Marcus, in his essay 'What Is an Initiation Story', writes: "An initiation story may be said to show its young protagonist a significant change of knowledge about the world or himself, or a change of character, or of both, and this change must point or lead him towards an adult world" [Kumar, 186]. Ernest Hemingway's (1898-1961) 'The Killers', Katherine Mansfield's (pseudo. of Kathleen Mansfield Beauchamp: 1888-1923) 'The Garden Party' and William

Faulkner's (1897-1962) 'The Bear' are three examples of the initiation story. Also see *education novel.

inkhornism, inkhorn term. The noun form of the word inkhorn, meaning an ink-holder (formerly made of horn), is now obsolete. The adjectival use of the word inkhorn means pedantic or bookish, so that the phrase 'inkhorn term' signifies a pedantic or bookish term, and inkhornism signifies the derogatory use of bookish, pedantic or bombastic words and expressions.

in medias res [from Latin *in*, in; *medias*, midst; *res*, things]. The Latin phrase literally means 'into the midst of things'. The phrase signifies the technique of beginning a literary work not from the initial stage or starting point but at a crucial point of the whole *narrative or *story or *action, i.e. in the midst of it or in the middle of things. In such a case, the earlier part of the narrative, story or action may be related later on through the method of *flashback. John Milton's (1608-74) *Paradise Lost* is a classic example of the use of this technique. Ancient Greek dramas frequently used this technique. The term *in medias res* originated in an injunction of the Latin lyric poet Quintus Horace (65-08 B.C.) to other poets (in the sense of those who create any genre of literary works). Horace urged them to hasten to the issue and hurry to drive their hearers (or readers) into the midst of the story as if they knew it already: '*Semper ad eventum festinat et in medias res / Non secus ac notas auditorem rapit*.'

inspiration. Any powerful full or fragmentary fleeting or stable idea, image, sensation, etc. that acts as the seed of a full-scale literary work; for instance, a *novel. Originally, inspiration was a theological term, meaning divine breath or stimulation (inspiration from Latin *in*, into, and *spirare*, breath) that informs a person and goads him in the way of god. Later on, the term signified supernatural beings or forces that animated, elevated, imbued or inflamed a person to write creatively, as if under duress. For instance, Sir Walter Scott (1771-1832) said that he used to write under the aegis of a demon: "I think there is a demon who seats himself on the feather of my pen when I begin to write, and leads it astray from my purpose" [Allott, 145]. C.G. Jung, the depth-psychoanalyst also confessed that he wrote under the direction of some supernatural being, but he did not call it a demon, like Scott did, but a daemon. In Henry Fielding's (1707-50) *Tom Jones* (BK XIII, ch. i), the novelist suggests the influence of the genius (in the sense of a spirit that is supposed to preside over every person) in creative writing: "... Genius; thou gift of Heaven;.... Come, thou that hast inspired thy Aristophanes, thy Lucian,... thy Swift, thy Marivaux, fill my pages with humour; till mankind learn the good-nature to laugh only at the follies of others, and the humility to grieve at their own" [*op. cit.*, 154]. William Faulkner (1897-1962) writes about the inspiration behind his *The Sound and the Fury*: "[The book] began with a mental picture. I didn't realize at the time it was symbolical. The picture was the muddy seat of a girl's drawers in a pear tree, where she could see through a window where her grand mother's funeral was taking place and report what was happening to her brothers on the ground below. By the time I explained who they were and what they were doing and how her pants got muddy, I realized it would be impossible to get all of it into a short story and it would have to be a book" [Koch, 9]. And a book it really became, and due to the inspiration of that mental picture. E.M. Forster (1879-1970) also believed in inspiration, and, moreover, had his own theory of inspiration, which he delineated in his short essay *Anonymity*. In his *Aspects of the Novel* also Forster touched on the phenomenon of inspiration. He writes that some writers "may decide to write a novel upon the French or the Russian Revolution, but memories, associations, passions, rise up and cloud their objectivity, so that at the close, when they reread, some one else seems to have been holding their pen and to have relegated their theme to the background. That 'some one else' is their self no doubt, but not the self that is so active in time and lives under George IV or V. All through history writers while writing have felt more or less the same. They have entered a common state which it is convenient to call inspiration" [Forster, 28]. Also see **duende*, *moment.

instant fiction. Same as *documentary novel.

intentional fallacy. The fallacy that is committed when it is supposed that "a literary work can be judged successful in the degree to which it corresponds to the intention of the author" [Rodway, 175-76]. There are various reasons why the author's actual intention is not reflected in his work. For one thing, the writer may deliberately write something which he does not at all want to say or believe. And secondly, and more importantly, how can we know the actual intention of the writer? The term 'intentional fallacy' is "the name given by the American New Critics W.K. Wimsatt Jr and Monroe C. Beardsley to the widespread assumption that an author's declared or supposed intention in writing a work is the proper basis for deciding on the meaning and the value of that work" [Baldick, 110].

interactive fiction. A sort of *fiction that is in a sense incomplete and that gets continually changed or modified, or that continually develops, with feedbacks of its readers. "Interactive fiction allows for the possibility of revising and expanding a text by means of the incorporation of reader feedback. The electronic media offer the most fully developed possibilities for such interaction, both with regard to speed and to the number of participants, but the genre or sub-genre apparently predates the computer. In common with the hypertext, IF [interactive fiction] challenges certain traditional and conventional qualities of the text, such as autonomy, linearity, and a sharp distinction between author and reader" [Hawthorn, 169]. Also see *hypertext, *IF.

intercalary chapter. A chapter in a *narrative that is not actually related to the sequence of chapters which are essentially comprised in the narrative but is inserted, intercalated or interpolated between two essential chapters, one succeeding the other. The intercalary chapter is usually short, and is supposed to provide the reader with the physical, historical, social and political background of the *story of the narrative, in order to facilitate his comprehension. John Steinbeck's (1902-68) *The Grapes of Wrath*, for instance, has numerous intercalary chapters, as chapter 35 of E.M. Forster's (1879-1970) *A Passage to India* is one. Intercalary chapter is also called *interchapter. Also see *interpolation.

interchapter. Same as *intercalary chapter.

interior dialogue. A dialogue between two well-defined voices within the single consciousness of a literary character (or, in a wider usage, of a real human being), and the narrative representation of this process. "Interior dialogue involves more than the representation of a character's verbalised thought processes in which questions are asked and answered. To count as genuine interior dialogue the questions and answers must stem from two voices which represent different and as it were personified attitudes, beliefs, or characteristics. A good example occurs towards the beginning of the tenth chapter of Charlotte Bronte's *Jane Eyre*, in which we have represented a long dialogue between different and personified aspects of Jane Eyre's personality or identity" [Hawthorn, 176]. Also see *interior monologue.

interior monologue. The term is believed to have been taken from the French novelist and essayist Valery-Nicolas Larbaud's (1881-1957) essay on James Joyce (1882-1941). The term signifies a verbalised unbroken chain of thoughts, impulses, impressions and associations of all these, of a certain *character in a *narrative, immaculately or realistically reproduced. In Joyce's *Ulysses*, for instance, Molly Bloom makes an interior monologue at the end of it. The chain of thoughts, impulses, impressions, etc. may be activated by some conscious experience, as in the case of Marcel Proust's (1871-1922) *novel *A la recherché du temps perdu* (*Remembrance of Things Past*), which is a sort of interior monologue and which was activated by Proust's dipping a meringue in wine, or the chain may be coming out of subconscious automatically. It is generally agreed that the term 'interior monologue' is synonymous with the term *stream of consciousness', but some critics believe that interior monologue is of wider significance, for it includes not only stream of consciousness but also 'dramatic monologue', i.e. a poetic soliloquy in which a speaking character reveals his thoughts before another who is present either actually or in the imagination of the speaking character.

internal dialogue. The term is M.M. Bakhtin's. Same as *interior dialogue.

internal evidence. A term of textual criticism especially concerned with the problem of deciding on the date of composition or writing of a literary work from available proofs from within the work itself.

international novel. A *novel that deals with no regional or national theme but with an international one, like most of Henry James's (1843-1916) novels: *The American*, *The Europeans*, *The Ambassadors*, etc. Henry James is generally acknowledged as the international novelist. Also see *regional novel.

interpolation. Interpolation literally means inserting or wedging something in between two things. In literary discourse interpolation signifies inserting a passage between two moments of a narrative. The passage thus interpolated is called *interpolated narration* or *intercalated narration*. *Epistolary novels, for instance, Samuel Richardson's (1689-1761) *Pamela*, rather frequently comprises interpolations. Also see *intercalary chapter, *interchapter.

intertext. See *intertextuality.

intertextuality. The term signifies the status of a literary work's being an *intertext, i.e. a text within which there is the presence or echo of other texts. Jeremy Hawthorn writes about intertextuality that it is "A relation between two or more texts which has an effect upon the way in which the *intertext* (that is, the text within which other texts reside or echo their presence) is read. In some usages the term *transtextuality* is reserved for more overt relations between specific texts, or between two particular texts, while *intertextuality* is reserved to indicate a more diffuse penetration of the individual text by memories, echoes, transformations, of other texts" [Hawthorn, 182]. The term was coined by Julia Kristeva.

intrinsic criticism. The term denotes that sort of criticism which limits its jurisdiction within the bound of a text. It evaluates a text so to say from within itself. Intrinsic criticism is contradictory to *extrinsic criticism which goes beyond the bound of the text in order to evaluate it. Jeremy Hawthorn distinguishes between intrinsic and extrinsic criticisms saying that intrinsic criticism is a "general description of those critical theories which countenance, and those critical methods which attempt to practise, a criticism which attends primarily or exclusively to the evidence of the individual literary work itself. The term is normally set in opposition to *extrinsic criticism*: criticism which does not limit itself to what is to be found 'inside' the work but which goes outside it and brings for example historical, biographical, or sociological evidence to bear upon the reading and interpretation of the work" [Hawthorn, 184].

intrusive narrator. A narrator who goes beyond his legitimate limit of narration and intrudes into the narration itself in order "to comment upon a character, event or situation—or even to introduce opinions not directly related to what has been narrated" [Hawthorn, 184]. The term is generally held to be pejorative, because such intrusions mostly impede the natural development of the *story, *plot, *actions or *characters. Also see *uninvolved narrator, *involved narrator, *detached narrator.

invention. The meaning of the term as it is technically used in modern literary criticism is not very different from the literal meaning of it: devise, contrivance, originality, etc. However, in literary criticism it signifies the quality of originality in thought and expression.

involuted novel. See *self-reflexive novel.

involved narrator. The narrator who is not all through a narrator but sometimes involves himself or herself, i.e. participates, in the *action of the *story of a *narrative. When the *protagonist, or his *confidant (or *confidante) or any other *character, who participates in the action, is the narrator, then that character is called involved narrator. Also see *implied narrator, *detached narrator, *uninvolved narrator, *intrusive narrator.

ipse dixit [from Latin *ipse dixit*, he himself said it]. The Latin expression literally means 'he himself has said' or 'he himself said it'. The expression is used in critical parlance to signify a brief dogmatic statement or a brief statement emphatically uttered.

irony. A term rather not clearly defined. Irony is thought to be of various kinds, such as Socratic irony, dramatic irony, romantic irony, rhetorical irony, cosmic irony or irony of fate, etc. The essential meaning of the term may be supposed to reside in the factor or element common among these and other kinds of irony, and the common factor is suggested by the Greek source word of the term, *eiron*, which means 'a dissembler'—one who says something but means something else. Socrates used to dissemblingly profess his ignorance and to ask a passerby to define a certain concept. The passerby found the definition quite easy and pronounced it, when Socrates pointed out the inadequacy of the definition and requested the passerby to redefine the concept, which he did. Socrates again pointed out the inadequacy of his revised definition and again requested further modified definition. And this process went on and on until the passerby confessed his ignorance about the definition of the concept, his comfortableness about the definition being gone. This is Socratic definition. Dramatic irony is achieved when the audience (or the reader) knows more about, and more accurately, the situation of a *character than the character himself—the character who is confident about his knowledge of the situation. In romantic irony, one is wafted by his imagination, so much so that he fails to notice the discrepancy between his vision of the reality coloured by imagination and the (actual) reality itself. Professor Sedgewick defines romantic irony as "'the attitude of mind held by a philosophic observer when he abstracts himself from the contradictions of life and views them all impartially, himself perhaps included in the ironic vision'" [Kumar, 365]. Simply perhaps may we say that the romantic's *Weltansicht* or world view is illusory, but, nonetheless, he clutches at it with 'some ardor and affection'. In rhetorical irony antiphrastic words and expressions, i.e. words and expressions that bear implications opposite to their usual meanings, are employed, giving rise to humorous or sarcastic effect. And cosmic irony or irony of fate "is attributed to literary works in which a deity, or else fate, is represented as though deliberately manipulating events so as to lead the protagonist [of a drama or novel] to false hopes, only to frustrate and mock them" [Abrams, 137]. Irony in short, works over the paradoxes and absurdities of the human situation, leading man to the trap of deception, as, for instance, the clever Emma in Jane Austen's (1775-1817) novel *Emma*, who plays tricks on others, is ultimately reduced to a victim of her own trickery or beguile. Some of the great ironists are: Socrates, Plato, Jonathan Swift (1667-1745), Jane Austen, Daniel Defoe (1660-1731), Henry James (1843-1916) and Thomas Hardy (1840-1928).

isochrony [from Greek *isos*, equal, and *chronos*, time]. The term has recently been introduced by *narrative theorists to denote "an *unvarying* or an *equal* relationship between narrating-time and story-time. The two are not the same: if a story covers three hours and each hour is narrated by means of five thousand words, then the relationship between narrating-time and story-time is unvarying. But if a story covers three hours and each hour of the story takes approximately an hour to read, then the relationship between narrating-time and story-time can be said to be equal. It should be clear that whereas the former relationship can be measured with some degree of precision, the latter cannot [because different readers read at different speeds]" [Hawthorn, 185].

J

Jacobean period. The period from 1603 to 1625, during which period James VI of Scotland reigned as King James I of England. It was a period of plays and poetry, not of *novel.

jargon. The term usually signifies the special language of a group or profession; for instance, the jargon of thieves, the jargon of law, medical jargon, etc. The term 'jargon' is typically used by those who are unfamiliar with the particular type of language that belongs to a particular group or profession, generally in a pejorative sense.

jeremiad [from Jeremiah, the name of the author of the *Book of Lamentations*]. A tale of grief or a *story of sadness, heartbreak, sorrow, such as to be found in Shakespeare's (1564-1616) *Timon of Athens*.

jest book ['jest' from Latin *gesta*, things done, doings]. A jest book is a collection of funny *stories, witty and satirical anecdotes, or jokes, sometimes with moral tags. It was very popular in the 16th century England. Examples of jest books are: *Alphabet of tales*, *A Hundred Merry Tales*, *The Geystes of Skogan*, etc.

jeu d'esprit [from French *jeu*, play, and *d'esprit*, of spirit or mind]. The French term literally means 'play of the spirit or mind', but in literary discourse it signifies a brief witty play of words, marked by flight of fancy and producing humour. Oscar Wilde (1854-1900), for instance, was an adept in the use of *jeu d'esprit*.

Johnsonese, Johnsonian [from the name of Samuel Johnson (1709-84), the English lexicographer, poet, critic, and man of letters]. The term refers to the style or manner of Samuel Johnson's writing that is characterised by ponderousness, balanced phrases, abundance of antitheses, words of classical origin, martial splendour, verbosity, pompousness, melodious resonance, didactic tone, etc.

jouissance [from French *jouissance*, enjoyment, bliss delight]. A French word and a critical *jargon introduced by Roland Barthes (1915-80) it literally means a sort of bliss having the qualities of ecstasy and sexual delight. It is closely associated with another French term **plaisir*—meaning 'pleasure'—, also a critical jargon and introduced by Roland Barthes. Barthes says that a text may give us one of two sorts of enjoyment: *plaisir* and *jouissance*. He differentiates between the two suggesting that "*plaisir* taken in a text comes through the more or less straightforward processes of reading, while *jouissance*, a heightened form of pleasure, derives from a sense of interruption, a 'breakdown' or gap, where, perhaps, something unorthodox or unexpected occurs. The comforts of *plaisir* are compatible with texts which are *lisible* while the comforts and surprises of *jouissance* arise from the *scriptible*. He elaborates with a kind of erotic analogy, suggesting that the focus of erotic pleasure is the place where the naked flesh meets a garment, where 'the garment gapes'. This is analogous to *jouissance*. However, he also suggests that the 'text of bliss' may impose a 'state of loss'; it is a text that discomforts and 'unsettles the reader's historical, cultural, psychological assumptions, the consistency of his taste, values, memories, brings to a crisis his relation with language" [Cuddon, 672]. Barthes's distinction between *plaisir* and *jouissance* may be briefly summarized as follows:

plaisir

i. pleasure
ii. no 'sexuality' or 'body'
iii. no ecstasy
iv. derived from **lisible* text
v. received through straightforward process of reading
vi. nothing 'unorthodox' or unexpected occurs in the text

Jouissance

i. bliss
ii. 'sexuality' or 'body'
iii. ecstasy
iv. derived from **scriptable* text
v. not received through straight forward process of reading
vi. something 'unorthodox' or unexpected occurs in the text.

Barthes says that unlike textual *plaisir*, "textual jouissance is an orgasmic experience in which the reader is so enrapt (or enwrapped) that objectivity and distance necessary for judgement is impossible" [Hawthorn, 186]. The famous psychoanalyst Jacques Lacan (b. 1901) also used the term *jouissance*, however, in the sense of pleasure which 'is sexual, spiritual, physical, conceptual at one and the same time'. Also see **ravissement*.

journal. The term is used in two senses. One, it signifies a magazine or periodical. And two, it denotes a daily record of events or personal impressions; sometimes even fictionalised daily record of events or personal impressions, as Daniel Defoe's (1660-1731) *A Journal of the Plague Year*, but not Henry Fielding's (1707-54) *The Journal of a Voyage to Lisbon* which is just a record of facts. Also see *journalese, *journalism.

journalese. See *journalism.

journalism. The profession or occupation of writing for newspapers in contradistinction to the occupation of writing a literary work, and hence the occasional pejorative use of the term. Nevertheless, many writers—even some distinguished ones, including distinguished novelists—had had the experience of doing journalism before and even after concentrating on literary works, such as (only novelists) Charles Dickens (1812-70), Rudyard Kipling (1865—1936), Mark Twain (1835-1910), Aldous Huxley (1894-1963), Ernest Hemingway (1898-1961), Jean-Paul Sartre (b. 1905), Albert Camus (1913-1960) and Francois Mauriac (b. 1885). The style and manner in which the journalists write is called *journalese. Journalese or journalistic writing is marked by the presence in it of clichés, occasional neologism, archness, sensationalizing adjectives, unusual or faulty syntax, etc.

Joycean. The term refers to the characteristic features of the writing of James Joyce (1882-1941), marked by high degree of stylistic and technical inventiveness, noticeable use of puns and portmantu words, original and striking symbols, habitual joining up of multiple words without hyphenations, writing of sentences on pages on end without any punctuation marks, etc. and the use of virtually a 'private language', plus, and most importantly, the use of the *stream-of-consciousness technique—all of these being obvious particularly in his *Ulysses* and *Finnegans Wake*. Also see *Kafkaesque.

Jugenstil [from German *Jugend*, youth, adolescence, and *Stil*, style]. The German word literally means 'adolescence style' or 'youth style'. In literary discourse, it "denotes a style of the late 19th century decorative art characterized by long curling sinuous lines and stylized natural forms" [Ayto, 168]. *Jugenstil* was popular in the literary art of Germany between 1890 and 1910, perhaps because it was felt to be a means "to escape from academic tradition" [Cuddon, 439]. The French counterpart of *Jugenstil* is **art nouveau*.

juvenalia [from Latin *juvenilia*, 'works done in one's youth']. The term refers to the collection of works of a writer done in his youth or adolescence, i.e. done before his mature creative period. Examples of juvenalia are (all from poets): John Dryden's (1631-1700) 'Upon the Death of Lord Hastings' (he was then 18), Alexander Pope's (1688-1744) 'Pastorals' (he was then 16) and Lord Byron's (1788-1824) 'Hours of Idleness' (he was then 18).

K

kaffeeklatsch [from German *Kaffee*, coffee, and *Klatsch*, smack, gossip]. The term literally means 'coffee-gossip'. Originally it meant a gossip among friends "sitting round a café table putting the world to rights over a cup of coffee.... These days the coffee element is optional, the essential point of the kaffeeklatsch being the gossip" [Ayto, 170].

Kafkaesque. The term refers to the characteristic features of the consciousness of, as well as the style, manner, attitude and tone of the creative writings of, the Austrian novelist Franz Kafka (1883-1924), especially marked by a feeling of loss of identity, a sense of guilt and fear and sinistrality, and a sense of absurdness of the human situation, as is obvious in his novels, such as *The Trial*, *Metamorphosis* and *The Castle*. Also see *Joycean.

Kailyard school [from Scottish *kailyard*, 'a cabbage patch or kitchen garden attached to a cottage']. The term denotes a group of Scottish writers of the late 19th century who wrote about the ordinary people of Scottish villages in dialect. "The term derives from a Scottish Jacobite song 'There grows a bonnie brier bush in our kailyard', which Ian Maclaren chose as a motto for his book Beside the Bonnie Brier Bush (1894)" [Cuddon, 441-42]. Some of the other notable writers, besides Maclaren, pseudo. of John Watson (1850-1907), who belonged to the Kailyard school were: Sir J.M. Barrie (1860-1937), S.R. Crockett (1860-1914) and John Joy Bell (1871-1934)—all Scottish novelists. "Their books about, humble, homespun topics, often written in the vernacular, promoted a sentimental image of small-town life in Scotland and were, briefly, extremely popular" [Ousby, 498].

***katharsis*.** See *catharsis.

key novel. See **livre a clef*.

King's English. The term denotes "correct, standard [English] speech" [Macdonald, 725] or "English as it should be spoken" [Cuddon, 444] or the form of the English language that is the best and purest. Sometimes, if the occasion demands, the term 'Queen's English' is also used as a substitute for the term 'King's English'. The principles and guidelines of King's English may be found, for instance, in H.W. & F.G. Fowler's *The King's English* [Fowler, 1993].

***kitsch*.** [from German *kitsch* (singular and plural), kitsch, trash]. In literary discourse, the term denotes a literary work that is pretentious, inferior and of no or little merit—something that is purported to gratify the low popular taste. The term is also used to refer to a *potboiler.

Knickerbocker Group, knickerbockers group. The term does not derive from the word 'knickerbockers' (in plural), meaning loose breeches or woman's undergarment; nor from the word 'knickerbocker' (singular), meaning a 'descendant of one of the original Dutch settlers of New York; nor from the word 'Knickerbocker' (capital K), meaning simply a New Yorker; but from the American writer Washington Irving's

(1783-1859) pseudonym Diedrich Knickerbocker. The Knickerbocker Group was an early-19th century school of American writers whose writings are marked by 'sophistication in style and conservatism in politics'. Some of the Knickerbocker writers, besides Washington Irving, were: the poet William Cullen Bryant (1794-1878), the man of letters James Kirke Paulding (1778-1860) and the poets Fitz-Greene Halleck (1790-1867) and Joseph Rodman Drake (1795-1820). The common location of the Group was New York City.

Kraftgenie [from German *Kraft*, force, power, and *Genie*, genius]. The term literally means 'power genius'. During the **Sturm und Drang* or *'storm and stress' movement, the term 'denoted creative and imaginative originality and dynamic energy'. Writers as well as *characters of literary works were called *Kraftgenies*. For instance, Goethe (1749-1832) thought himself a *Kraftgenie* and the character of Gotz in Goethe's *Gotz von Berlichingen* is a *Kraftgenie*.

Kunstlerroman [from German *Kunstler*, artist, and *Roman*, novel]. Literally, the term means 'artist novel', but in literary discourse it signifies a novel in which the central *character is an artist who develops in the course of the narrative, such as Somerset Maugham's (1874-1965) *The Moon and Sixpence* and James Joyce's (1882-1941) *A Portrait of the Artist as a Young Man*. Also see **Bildungsroman*.

Kunstmarchen [from German *Kunst*, art, and *Marchen*, fairy tale, tall story]. A *fairy tale or *folk tale that, after being carried over through oral transmission, has been written down. Also see *Marchen.

kurzgeschichte [from German *kurz*, short, and *Geschichte*, little story]. A *short story which is brief and terse.

L

lacrimae rerum [from Latin *lacrimae*, tears, and *rerum*, things]. The term literally means 'tears of things', but allusively its import is that "there are tears in the very nature of things and man's affairs touch the heart" or that "'sorrow is part of the scheme of things'" [Ayto, 178]. Also see **Weltschmerz*.

langue* and *parole [from French *langue*, language, and *parole*, utterance, speech, speaking]. The terms were introduced in literary criticism following their use in linguistics by Ferdinand de Saussure (d. 1913). Saussure used the term *langue* "to mean the system of a language, that is the arrangement of sounds and words which speakers of a language have shared knowledge of or, 'agree to use'" [Richards, *et al*, 161]. Briefly, *langue* is the *ideal* form of a language as opposed to the *actual* form that people use in speech or writing. Saussure called the actual use of language by people in speech *parole*. *Parole* is speaking, speech, language-behaviour or the sum of all actual as well as possible utterances.

Latinism. The term refers to the use in English of the Latinate style, or the use of Latin diction, grammar and form of expressions, such as periodic sentence, syntactic inversion, etc. Examples of Latinism may be found in the following line of *Paradise Lost*: 'His far more pleasant garden God ordained'. Or in the following sentence from Edward Gibbon's (1737-94) *Memoirs*: "'It was in Rome, on the 15th of October, 1764, as I sat musing amidst the ruins of the Capitol, while the barefooted friars were singing vespers in the Temple of Jupiter, that the idea of writing the decline and fall of the city first started to my mind'" [Baldick, 120].

Leatherstocking Tales. A sequence of five *novels by the American novelist James Fenimore Cooper (1789-1851): *The Deerslayer*, *The Last of the Mohicans*, *The Pathfinder*, *The Pioneer* and *The Prairie*. The novels are set in the early 'frontier' period of American history. The collective title, Leatherstocking Tales, was taken from the name of the common central *character or the *protagonist of all the five novels, Natty Bumppo, who is variously called Leatherstocking, Deerslayer, Hawkeye and Pathfinder.

lebensraum [from German *lebensraum*, space to live and develop in or 'life space']. A person's environment, as it affects him mentally, psychologically or sociologically.

legend. Legends are *stories about saints or miracles (originally) or incredible heroes or their astonishing deeds—stories that lie somewhere between *myths and historical facts. According to *The Concise Oxford Dictionary of Literary Terms*, a legend is "a story or group of stories handed down through popular oral tradition, usually consisting of an exaggerated or unreliable account of some actually or possibly historical person—of a saint, monarch, or popular hero. Legends are sometimes distinguished from myths in that they concern human beings rather than gods, and sometimes in that they have some sort of historical basis whereas myths do not" [Baldick, 121]. Some of the legends are about Faust, the Flying Dutchman, the Wandering Jew, Hamlet, Beowulf, Robin Hood, Jasonik (the Czeck Robin Hood), Rommel, etc. Geoffrey Chaucer's (c. 1343/4-1400) *The Legend of Good Women* comprises a group of stories about Cleopatra, Thibe, Dido, Medea, Lucrece, Ariadne, Philomela, etc.

leitmotif, leitmotiv [from German *leit*, leading, and French *motif*, a theme, a subject, or German *Motiv*, motive, motif, theme]. The terms, literally, mean 'leading motive or theme'. As a critical term *leitmotif* or *leitmotiv* signifies a recurring *theme in a creative literary work, or a frequently repeated phrase, image, *symbol or *situation that is associated with a theme, so that a repetition of the phrase, etc. recalls to mind the theme immediately. For instance, the repeated use of the images of rings and arches in D.H. Lawrence's (1885-1930) *The rainbow* suggests sexuality and so the ring or the arch is a *leitmotif*. In E.M. Forster's (1879-1970) *A Passage to India*, the frequent descriptions of the rugged geography of India and her inhospitable flora and fauna, throughout the *novel, are varied *leitmotifs*, suggestive of her subdued but enduring hostile animus towards the Britishers. The term *leitmotiv* was given currency by Richard Wagner (1813-83), the German composer and poet. He used leitmotiv "to denote the practice (...) of using brief musical phrases to represent particular characters, ideas, or situations in an opera. The phrase is repeated whenever the person, situation, etc. re-enters the action, and so a web of musical cross-references is built up" [Ayto, 181].

linear plot. A *plot that strictly follows chronological order of *episodes or *actions from start to finish without any recourse to *flashbacks or *flashforwards.

lingo. A loosely colloquial term, used either humorously or contemptuously, for a strange and unintelligible language or *slang or jargon, which may, or may not, be a foreign tongue or a hybrid *patois.

lipogram [from Greek *leipein,* to leave, and gramma, a letter]. A quizzically done literary work (generally in verse) in which the writer has deliberately avoided the use of a particular letter of the alphabet, usually a vowel; for instance, Alonso Herrera wrote a sequence of five novellas "each eschewing a different vowel.... [and] Ernest Wright managed a 50,000-word novel, *Gadsby* (1939), without using *e*" [Baldick, 123].

lisible [from French *lisible*, legible, readable, decipherable]. A term introduced for critical discourse by Roland Barthes (1915-80) in his book *S/Z* (1970). It is one of the paired terms: *lisible* and **scriptable* [from French *scriptable*, writeable, which is from Latin *scriptum*, writing]. Barthes classified texts into two groups: *lisible* texts or *readerly texts and *scriptable* texts or *writerly texts. The *lisible* text is one which can be understood or experienced with little interpretative effort. On the other hand, the writerly text is one which is so complex, and sometimes so opaque, that an understanding of it requires an amount of effort on the part of the reader. Further, the meaning of the *lisible* text is fixed and dependent on established literary tradition shared by the writer and the reader; but the meaning of the *scriptable* text is not fixed and does not depend on established literary tradition shared by the writer and the reader—its meaning depends on the play of collusion or co-operation between the writer and the reader: the two jointly make out the meaning. The meaning of the *lisible* text is 'final', unalterable, and 'correct' but that of the *scriptable* text is ever-changing, depending on the co-operative interplay between the writer and the reader. Jeremy Hawthorn writes: "Barthes uses the terms to distinguish between traditional literary works such as the classical novel, with their reliance upon conventions shared by writer and reader and their resultant (partial) fixity or closure of meaning, and those works produced especially in the twentieth century which violate such conventions and thus force the reader to work to produce a meaning or meanings which are inevitably other than final or 'correct'" [Hawthorn, 288].

literalism. The term denotes a propensity of interpreting a text according to the literal meaning or the primary meaning of the words, phrases and sentences of it, ignoring their possible figurative meanings.

literariness. The term signifies that quality or a sum of qualities which makes a written work a literary work. Critics are not unanimous as to what actually invests a written work with literariness. There are, in fact, various theories about the literariness of a literary work. According to the theory of Russian Formalism, for one, literariness is "the sum of special linguistic and formal properties that distinguish literary texts from non-literary texts" [Baldick, 123].

literary forgery. See *plagiarism.

litterateur [from French *litterateur*, a literary man]. The word is used both in its normal sense and sometimes in its rather pejorative sense. Normally, it denotes a literary man, a writer or critic, or one who is occupied with literature. Pejoratively, it denotes a pretentious writer or one who engages in literary works in a superficial way or dilettantishly. Also see *literati.

literati [from Latin *litera*, letter]. The term signifies educated men or men of letters, collectively. Sometimes, it bears a disparaging suggestion of being 'fashionable' or superficial in literature. The term is plural and its singular form is literatus. Also see **litterateur*.

literature. Broadly, a rather vague umbrella term that refers to any written or printed works and even oral compositions, both fictional (*narrative, dramatic and poetic) and non-fictional (historical, philosophical, critical, scientific, biographical, etc.). Restrictively, the term denotes any *poetry, drama, and fiction having *high-value* or *aesthetic value*, and 'intended for the public or of interest to the public (and, therefore, private letters and dairies are excluded)', and, for the reason of those, deserving preservation (and, so, newspapers are excluded). In its restrictive sense, the term must be distinguished from *paraliterature or *subliterature that are *literose, or spuriously or pretentiously literary, such as *detective novel and story, *spy novel and story, *science fiction, *fantasy writing, *popular novel or *pulp novel, *pornography, chindren's adventure story, etc.

literature of escape. Literature (especially *fiction) that help imaginary escape from fearfully depressing situation, abiding horror, pounding anxiety, suffocating cares, aching uncertainty, etc. by providing pleasant excitement through presentations of magnetically attracting ideal situations. "Well-known examples from the First World War are: H.E. Hervey's *Cagebirds*; H.G. Durnford's *The Tunnellers of Holzminden*; *Escapers All* by various contributors; and *The Escaping Club*. Probably the most famous from the Second World war is *The Wooden Horse* (1949) by Eric Williams" [Cuddon, 473].

literature of sensibility. The word 'sensibility' signifies sensitiveness or the quality of being emotionally conscious or of being easily affected. Sensibility refers to a person's *sensuous* and *emotional*, as opposed to intellectual, modes of experience, or an *overriding affective and emotional responsiveness*. Literature of sensibility denotes that kind of literature that is flushed with heightened affective and emotional responsiveness. Such literature prevailed in England particularly in the 18th century. The hair-trigger responsiveness to another person's pain which was in vogue in England in the 18th century was a reaction against the overemphasis on rationalism in the previous century. The overdoze of sentiment and emotion in the literature of the 18th century is obvious in the poetry of the period as well as in that century's drama of sensibility or sentimental comedies, such as Richard Steele's (1672-1729) *The Conscious Lovers* and Richard Cumberland's (1732-1811) *The West Indian*.

The excess of sentiment is also to be found in such *novels as Samuel Richardson's (1689-1761) *Pamela* and *Clarissa Harlowe*; Laurence Sterne's (1713-68) *Tristram Shandy* and *A Sentimental Journey*; Henry Brooke's (1703-83) *The Fool of Quality*; Oliver Goldsmith's (?1730-74) sole novel *The Vicar of Wakefield*; and, of course, Henry Mackenzie's (1745-1831) *The Man of Feeling*. The excess of sentimentality was also to be found in the 18th century French and German literature; for example in Jean-Jacques Rousseau's (1712-78) *Julie, or the New Heloise* and Johann Goethe's (1749-1832) *The Sorrows of Young Werther*. In the beginning of the 19th century, the decline of the literature of sensibility was evident. Jane Austen (1775-1817) in her novel *Sense and Sensibility* and *Northanger Abbey*, lambasted the excess of sentimentality in her contemporary novels as Mary Wollstonecraft or Mary Shelley (1797-1851), the novelist, and Hannah More (1745-1833), the dramatist, bitterly criticized their contemporary novelists' trading in uncontrolled sentiment.

literature of the absurd ['absurd' from Latin *ab*, from, and *surdus*, deaf, out of fashion, not to the purpose]. 'Absurd' in this term means that which is 'opposed to reason', 'meaningless' or 'ridiculous'. The term 'literature of the absurd' denotes that kind of literary works which 'attempt to depict the universal meaninglessness'. Literature of the absurd "tends to discard analysis of motivation of characters and, as far as possible, all formal structures because both motivation and formal structure suggest order, and the suggestion of order in literature of the absurd would undermine its thematic premise" [Lemon, 119]. The roots of literature of the absurd may be traced in *existentialism (of Sartre and Camus), *expressionism, *surrealism, and in the works of James Joyce (1882-1941) and Franz Kafka (1883-1924). The movement of literature of the absurd began in France (where existentialism took its birth) soon after the horrors of the Second World War. It repudiated the traditional belief in man as a rational being and in the orderliness and intelligibility of the world and the social structure. It believed that human life as well as the world were chancy-chancy, so that no amount of heroism could fructify human aspirations, and that human beings were doomed to suffer *anguish* (pain of the mind). It, in brief, believed that life was, as the French playwright Eugene Ionesco (b. 1912) said, a 'tragic farce'. The writers of the literature of the absurd include: the dramatists Ionesco, Harold Pinter (b. 1930), Edward Albee (b. 1928); the novelists Kafka (1883-

1924), Joseph Heller (b. 1923), Thomas Pynchon (b. 1937) and Gunter Grass (b. 1927); and the playwright-novelist Samuel Beckett (b. 1906). The literature of the absurd, generally, is simultaneously comic, brutal, horrifying, anti-heroic, irrational, fragmentary, and, above all, post-modernist. Also see *absurd, the.

literose. Affectedly or spuriously literary.

livre a clef [from French *livre*, book; *a*, with; and *clef*, key]. The term literally means 'book (in the sense of *novel) with a key' and is synonymous with the term **roman a clef* ('*roman*' from French *roman*, novel). *Livre a clef* is a kind of novel or *fiction in which *characters (not all) are real persons in disguise (with a different name, occupation, habitation, etc.). The partial similarity between the real person and the fictionalised character works as the 'key' (of recognition or discovery). Examples of *livre a clef* are: Thomas Love Peacock's (1785-1866) *Nightmare Abbey*, which contains caricatures of Coleridge, Byron and Shelley; Benjamin Disraeli's (1804-81) *Venetia*, which points to many biographical details about Byron and Shelley; and Aldous Huxley's (1894-1963) *Point Counter Point*, in which the personalities of D.H. Lawrence, Oswald Mosley and Middleton Murry are thinly disguised. Somerset Maugham (1874-1965) also wrote a number of *livres a clef* and thereby earned some criticisms for not being able to adequately camouflage his targeted real persons.

local colour. The word 'colour' in the term 'local colour' does not mean dye, hue, paint, tinge, etc. but the peculiar distinguishing qualities of the communal life of a certain geographical region. By 'local colour' is meant the unique customs, manners, habits, mores, music, ethos, speech variety, folklore, etc. of the people of a certain region or locality as well as the environment of that region or locality. Writers sometimes depict the local colour in *novels or *fictions in order to give authenticity to their narratives and make them all the more interesting. Such novels or fictions are also called 'local colour writing' and their authors are sometimes called 'local colourists'. One of the most famous local colourists is Mark Twain (1835-1910). Some other local colourists or local colour writers are: (all Americans) Joel Chandler Harris (1848-1908), Kate Chopin (1851-1904), Sarah Orne Jewett (1849-1909), Bret Harte (1836-1902) and George Washington Cable (1844-1925); and (the French) Emile Zola (1840-1902) and (the English) Thomas Hardy (1840-1928). Local colour novel or fiction must be distinguished from the *regional novel or fiction, because "The regional novel emphasizes the setting, speech, and social structure and customs of a particular locality, not merely as local colour, but as *important conditions affecting the temperament of the characters and their ways of thinking, feeling, and interacting*" (emphasis added) [Abrams, 194]. Writers give their* narratives local colour not only for making them seem more authentic and making them more interesting but also as a decorative. The term 'local colour', unlike the term regional novel or 'regional fiction', is sometimes used pejoratively.

locale. The scene of some *event.

logocentrism [from Greek *logos*, word, and *kentron*, a sharp point]. A central term in Jacques Derrida's (b. 1930) theory of *deconstruction, sometimes used interchangeably with the term *phonocentrism. Derrida reminds us that the partial origin or source of the term logocentrism is the Greek word *logos* which means *word* and *truth*, besides reason and law. He says that according to logocentrism truth is the word or expression of an original, central and absolute *cause* or *origin* which is the transcendental signified—a God-Word or something like that—that exists beyond everything of the whole universe. To take an example from religion, according to Christianity, the meaning or truth of everything is ultimately to be derived from the Christian concept of God or from His Words or *Logos*, because God is the Centre (or *Presence) of the universe (such is the structure or 'construction' which Derrida's deconstruction strives to nullify, to de-construct). (In the Authorised Version of the Bible, we read: 'In the beginning was the Word, and the Word was with God, and the Word was God': John 1:1.) "Logocentrism refers to systems of thought or habits of mind which are reliant upon what Derrida, following Heidegger, terms the metaphysics of PRESENCE—that is, a belief in an extra-systemic validating prence or CENTRE which underwrites and fixes linguistic meaning but is itself beyond scrutiny or challenge" [Hawthorn, 193-94].

logodaedalus [from Greek *logos*, word, and *Daidalos*, the Greek mythical artisan-inventor]. The term literally means 'word-artisan-inventor'. Logodaedalus is an artificier in words, such as a poet. Logodaedaly is verbal legerdemain.

longueur [from French *longueur*, length, slowness]. The term denotes a tedious passage, for example, of a book, or prolixity, or a prolonged scene in a literary work.

Lost Generation, lost generation. Gertrude Stein's (1874-1946) term for the Expatriates of the 1920s (not those of the earlier 19th century who migrated from America to Europe and settled in London) who settled in Paris or London, such as (all novelists) Ernest Hemingway (1898-1961), Dos Passos (1896-1970), F. Scott Fitzgerald (1896-1940), Katherine Anne Porter (b. 1890); (both poets) Ezra Pound (b. 1885) and T.S. Eliot (1888-1965); and the novelist-poet Gertrude Stein herself. The lost generation generated the spirit of bohemianism, liberalism and radicalism, but, nevertheless, the period of the lost generation was highly productive for American creative writings and letters. "The phrase [lost generation] suggests the sense of alienation and philosophical uncertainty which has often been felt to be the defining characteristic of much American writing of the [nineteen] twenties; it also suggests the awareness of being a generation which existed among many of the writers of the period, and their sense that in a period of rapid change and uncertainty they had lost touch with the attitudes and norms of their parents. The generation was alienated, separated, lost (though all one needed do to find them was to go to Paris [or to London]" [Mottram, *et al*, 160]. The climate of the lost generation period is best evoked in such narrative works as Hemingway's *The Sun Also Rises* and *A Moveable Feast* and Fitzgerald's *Tender is the Night*.

low mimetic. See *high mimetic.

lyrical novel. A kind of *novel which verges on the *romance and "is characterized by a poetic use of language, often subordinating action, characterization, and verisimilitude to mood and setting" [Lemon, 7]. An example of the lyrical novel is William Henry Hudson's (1841-1922) *Green Mansions*.

M

Mabinogion. A collection of ancient Welsh *tales translated into English by Lady Charlotte Elizabeth Guest (b. 1929) to which she gave the incorrect title of *Mabinogion* (plural of *Mabinogi*, meaning 'instruction for young bards').

magic realism. The term, some believe, was first used by Franz Roh in 1925, and since 1955 it is increasingly being used to describe the post-Second World War Latin American *fiction. The term signifies the oxymoron of the real on the one hand and the magical on the other, and is used to describe the strange, uncanny, eerie, and dreamlike, but usually not the fantastic. It is a relative of, but not identical with, the *marvelous. Some say that the term originated out of the Cuban novelist Alejo Carpentier's (b. 1904) rhetorical question: 'What is the story of Latin America if not a chronicle of the marvelous in the real?' The term was first technically used as a literary definition by the American critic Alastair Reid who referred it 'to the large body of spectacular, fantastic fiction produced in South American countries after World War II.' "The genre [of magic-realistic fiction] is characterized by the juxtaposition of apparently reliable, realistic reportage and extravagant fantasy: [for instance,] Marquez's [Gabriel Garcia Marquez (b. 1927)] novel will at one moment narrate the building of a new banana-processing plant, at another describe a woman visibly ascending to heaven. While there is a certain inscrutable playfulness to magic realism (Marquez is recorded as proposing that 'you can get people to believe anything if you tell it convincingly enough'), its method was first conceived, more importantly, as a response to the nature of South American reality. In countries previously ruled despotically as colonies and subsequently negotiating independence with no long-established institutions or freedoms, the fact that informations can easily be manipulated or even commandeered by power groups makes *truth a far more provisional, relative entity—relativism which magic realism both mimics and exploits through its own merging of realism and fantasy*. Indeed, the genre's further assumption...is that *truth is best viewed as a communal, collaborative construct, rather than as residing in the integrity of individual perceptions, whose authority tends merely to that of caprice and rumour. Such emphasis, implying the limitation of individual responsibility and the quixotic unpredictability of fate, makes magic realism an essentially comic genre*" (emphases added) [Ousby, 584]. Also see **stracitta*.

Some of the outstanding features of the magic-realistic fictions are: juxtaposition or mingling of the realistic, *fantastic or bizarre; skilful time shifts; convoluted and even labyrinthine *narratives; fragmented *plots; accommodation of dreams, *myths and *fairy tales; expressionistic and surrealistic descriptions; suggestions of the inexplicable; and a tendency to shock, surprise or horrify. A classic example of the magic-realistic fiction is G.G. Marquez's

One Hundred Years of Solitude, in which the real and the fictional story, the documented and the dreamt, about the Buendia family is presented. Besides Marquez, the other exponents of magic realism are: the Cuban novelist Alejo Carpentier, the Mexican novelist Carlos Fuentes (b. 1929), the Czech novelist Milan Kundera (b.1929), the Italian novelist Italo Calvino (b. 1923), Indo-Anglian novelist Rushdie (b.1947), English novelist Angela Carter (b. 1940), German novelist Gunter Grass (b.1927), etc. And some of such fictions are: Kundera's *The Book of Laughter and Forgetting*, Grass's *The Tin Drum*, Carter's *Nights at the Circus* and Rushdie's *Midnight's Children* and *The Satanic Verses*. Also see *marvelous, the.

mannerism. A rather vague term that denotes the highly individualised and distinctive style of a writer or of a literary period. The distinctive peculiarities of an individual writer include such things as highly ornate language, strange or uncommon syntax, elaborate period, latinate language (as of Milton: 1608-74), far-fetched similes (as of Raymond Chandler: 1888-1959), etc. The *baroque style was a mannerism of the period from the late 16th to the 18th century. The term is sometimes used pejoratively, but Milton's and Ernest Hemingway's (1898-1961) mannerisms are appreciable.

maqama. An Arabic term for a picaresque *story in rhymed prose.

Marchen. See *fairy tale.

marivaudage. The term derives from the name of the French playwright and novelist Pierre Marivaux (1688-1763) and refers to his manner of writing, which is often affected by being strained, over-elegant, prolix, too nice, and subtle to a fault. Marivaudage is usually a derogatory or depreciative term, but, nevertheless, the two French playwrights-novelists Alfred Mussel (1810-57) and Jean Giraudoux (1882-1944) used the style of marivaudage effectively.

marvellous, the [(U.S. spelling 'marvelous') from Latin *mirabilis*, wonderful, improbable, altogether beyond belief]. The term refers to a kind of *fiction in which *episodes and *actions occur in an extravagantly imagined world, with supernatural and magical elements, a world that is presented in such a way that those supernatural and magical elements seem but natural. Fictions that fall within the category of the marvellous are: *fairy tales, many *fantasies and *romances, most *science fictions, etc. The marvellous must be distinguished from *magic realism, for while in the latter reliable and realistic elements are juxtaposed with supernatural and magical ones, in the former the supernatural and magical elements are presented in an extravagantly imagined setting with no realistic elements juxtaposed. R.R. Tolkein's (1892-1973) *The Lord of the Rings*, with a hob hero, is a classic example of the marvellous. The marvellous should also be differentiated from the *uncanny. In the uncanny, the supernaturals and the disturbing strangenesses are justified or explained as due to psychological causes, but in the marvellous these are justified or explained as magical. Also see *fantasy.

Marxist literary theory. It is grounded on the dialectical and historical materialism and the politico-economic theory of Karl Marx and Friedrich Engels, though there is no adequate and systematic treatment of aesthetic matters in their works. However, some of the principal convictions in the Marxist literary theory are the following: (i) literary art is a specific part of the 'superstructure' (non-material) of the society, that ultimately depends on (and is partially regulated by) the politico-economic (material) base of the society; (ii) it is emphasized that art is not totally and mechanically determined by social factors (by the politico-economic base of the society) and though there is a dialectical reciprocity between the two sometimes art itself may become a determining factor of society; (iii) the 'principle of uneven development' states that social development and artistic achievement do not necessarily go hand in hand: a higher social development, for instance, is not necessarily a precondition of higher artistic achievement; and (iv) the attitude revealed in *realism is the only authentic artistic attitude. After Marx and Engels, their literary theory was elaborated, and revised, by many of their followers, such as Lenin, Trosky, Lukacs, Plekhanov, Lunacharsky, Gramsci and Caudwell.

meaning and significance. Generally the two words, 'meaning' and 'significance', are used interchangeably, but the American critic E.D. Hirsch used the word significance as a technical term and thus differentiated between the two. In his *Validity in Interpretation*, Hirsch wrote: "*Meaning* is that which is represented by a text; it is what the author meant by his use of a particular sign sequence; it is what the signs represent. *Significance*, on the other hand, names a relationship between that meaning and a person, or a conception, or a situation, or indeed anything imaginable" [Hawthorn, 203]. "Meaning, that is to say, is what the work says in its own created context; *significance* is the meaning of that meaning in a wider context.... Thus the *meaning* of Shakespeare's Sonnet 138 (...) is all that it reveals of the emotional and cognitive complications in the relationship of an older man and unfaithful younger woman, plus the tonal effect of the inversion of the conventional use of the sonnet for love poetry. If, however, the reader were to take the persona of Shakespeare himself, and be primarily interested in what the sonnet revealed to his love life—as *his*—then he would be concerned with the poem's *significance*" (emphases added) [Rodway, 186]. Meaning is the province of *intrinsic criticism, significance that of *metacriticism.

mechanism. A rather loose term that generally signifies the structure of a literary work, or the relationship of its parts to the whole of it. It also refers to the way the *design or *plot of a literary work.

mekane [from Greek *mechane*, contrivance]. A crane-like machine or contrivance used in classical Greek theatre for lowering actors from the top into the play area, the actors (*characters) being supposed to be coming from heaven.

memoir novel. A form of *novel written from the *first-person point of view and feigning to be a true memoir or autobiography. It was in vogue in the 18th century and contributed to the birth of the modern novel. Daniel Defoe's (1660-1731) *Moll Flanders* and *Robinson Crusoe*, Oliver Goldsmith's (?1730-74) *The Vicar of Wakefield*, Tobias Smollett's (1721-71) *Roderick Random*, Henry Mackenzie's (1745-1831) *The Man of Feeling* and John Cleland's (1709-89) *Memoir of a Woman of Pleasure* and *Funny Hill* are examples of the memoir novel.

merde, mystique de la [from French *merde*, excrement or shit; *mystique*, mystery; *de*, of; *la*, there, or the]. The term literally means 'mystery of the excrement or shit', but as a technical or critical term it denotes a writer's preoccupation with such things as sex and money or with the muddier and bloodier aspects of life. Such modern novelists as James Joyce (1882-1941), Ernest Hemingway (1898-1961) and William Burroughs (b. 1914) have sometimes exploited *mystique de la merde* for desired effects.

metacriticism. Literally, the term means 'after criticism', but as a critical term it denotes a 'criticism of criticism' or that criticism whose subject matter is criticism. Metacriticism "attempts to analyse and categorize examples of critical practice and to establish generally applicable principles for it. In contemporary usage the term is often replaced by *literary theory*, although this can have a rather wider meaning" [Hawthorn, 207]. Also see *extrinsic criticism, *intrinsic criticism.

metafiction. The term was popularised by Robert Scholes and is often used as a synonym of *surfiction. It denotes that kind of *novel that flouts the convention of *realism and *foreground "the role of the author and reader in inventing and receiving the fiction" [Abrams, 196]. Metafiction is "fiction about fiction...that openly comments on its own fictional status. In a weak sense, many modern novels about novelists having problems writing their novels may be called metafictional.... The most celebrated case is Sterne's *Tristram Shandy* (1713-1768) which makes a continuous joke of its own digressive form" [Baldick, 133]. Jeremy Hawthorn, in his *A Glossary of Contemporary Literary Theory*, writes that "*Metafiction*, is, literally, fiction about fiction. To a certain extent the term overlaps with *metanarrative* because any work of fiction which contains a metanarrative will contain a metafictional element. It [metafiction] is generally used to indicate fiction which includes any *self-referential element*" [Hawthorn, 208]. The 'play within a play' in *Hamlet*, for instance, has a self-referential element, and so the play may be said to be a metafictional work. Also see *metanarrative.

metanarrative. The term literally means 'a narrative about a narrative'. "A *metanarrative* can (...) be either a narrative which talks about other, embedded narratives, or a narrative which refers to itself and to its own narrative procedures" [*ibid*.]. Also see *narrative, *embedded narrative, *metafiction.

miles gloriosus. The term was taken from the title of a play, *Miles gloriosus* (*The Boastful Soldier*), by the Roman dramatist Titus Plautus (c. 254-184 B.C.) in which the hero is a braggart captain whose "foolish bombast and the cynical effusiveness of his toady, exaggerated to the point of caricature, enliven a force in which he is ingeniously fooled by his mistress and her young lover" [Dudley and Lang, 137]. Miles gloriosus is the epithet for one who resembles such a *character. Also see *alazon, *braggadochio, *rodomontade.

mimesis. See *diegesis.

mise-en-abyme [from French *mise*, placing, putting; *en*, in, into; *abyme*, abyss]. Literally, the term means 'putting into the abyss' or 'thrown into the abyss'. It refers to the "recurring internal duplication of images of an artistic whole, such that an infinite series of images disappearing into invisibility is produced—similar to what one witnesses if one looks at one's reflection between two facing mirrors" [Hawthorn, 210]. The 'recurring internal duplication of images' (the *abyme* or abyss) occurs, for instance, in Andre Gide's (1869-1951) *novel *Les faux-monnayeurs* (*The Counterfeiters*) in which one of the *characters, Edouard, is writing the novel *Les Faux-monnayeurs* (the secondary novel) which very much resembles the (original or primary) novel in which he is a character. In Edouard's novel, there is endless reduplication of the material of the original or primary novel (the *abyme*). The *Chinese-box-like technique of mise-en-abyme is a favoured technique not infrequently adopted by post-modernist novelists, like Italo Calvino (b.1923) and such others.

mise-en-scene. [from French *mise*, placing, putting; *en*, in, into; *scene*, scene, stage, scenery]. The term literally means 'placement on stage or scene'. It denotes the total environment of a play or the total arrangement of the sets, props, costumes, blocking, etc. in staging of a play. It also denotes "the 'physical and psychological context in which an event takes place'" [Ayto, 199].

Mobius strip narrative. See *short-circuit, short-circuit narrative.

mode. A term rather loosely used as a general synonym for *form, 'kind' or 'type'. Recently it has entered into critical vocabulary, where it roughly signifies the 'medium' or 'channel of communication' of a text. Mode is associated with method, manner and *style, and refers to the general aspect of a work. As a critical term it is now specifically used in the narrative theory to refer to a work's mood, tone, type and kind. For instance, narrative poetry is in the narrative mode which is different from the mode of a *science fiction or of a *horror story. The modal (adj. of mode) aspects of literary works may be fictional or non-fictional; realistic or fantastic; mimetic, metaphoric, factual, abstract or rhetorical; tragic, comic, or tragic-comic; mythic or romantic; etc.

modernism. A general, non-specific and comprehensive term for a movement (or tendency) in literary productions prevalent roughly between the two World Wars (1914-18 and 1939-45), featuring radical break with the traditional literary *modes, *style, concepts and subject-matters; a credo for experimentation in all the literary elements and *forms; a doubt about the legitimacy of religion, morality and the prevailing social organization; a craze for *advent-grade*-ism and the motto of 'make it new' (Ezra Pound: b. 1885); introduction into literary *oeuvres* the effects of drugs, dreams and automatic writing; inclusion of previously forbidden subject-matters; a sense of 'alienation'; and an unexampled rapidity of change. Modernism was influenced by *Dadaism, imagism, vorticism, *futurism, *symbolism, *impressionism, *expressionism, *existentialism and *stream-of-consciousness technique. It was also influenced by such thinkers as Sigmund Freud, Karl Marx, Friedrich Nietzsch and James G. Frazer (*The Golden Bough*).

Some critics say that the inception of modernism may be traced far back beyond the outbreak of the First World War to the 1890s. In any case, however, the high tide of modernism showed itself since 1922, the year in which came out James Joyce's (1882-1941) *Ulysses*, Virginia Woolf's (1882-1941) *Jacob's Room* and T.S. Eliot's (1888-1965) *The Waste Land*. The sense of modernism grew when the moral basis, and the sedate coherence of thought processes in the Western civilisation were irreversibly shattered by the great shock of the First World War, bringing in a radically new **Weltanschauung* and sensibility which, the creative writers felt, the traditional literary modes were inadequate to give expression to, and the post-War harsh and dissonant reality, they thought, needed a new mode of creation—the modern mode, which allows (or, rather, requires) repetition of expressions, denial of normal punctuation, conscious control, freakishness, the technique of silence, etc. Among the notable (proximal and distant) harbingers of modernism are: (all novelists) Marcel Proust (1877-1922), Thomas Mann (1875-1955), Andre Gide (1869-1951), Franz Kafka (1883-1924) and William

Faulkner (1825-79), Dorothy Richardson (1873-1957), James Joyce, Virginia Woolf and Gertrude Stein (1874-1946); (all poets) Stephane Mallarme (1842-98), Rainer Maria Rilke (1875-1926), William Carlos Williams (1883-1963), Wallace Stevens (1879-1955), Marianne Moore (1887-1972), Ezra Pound, T.S. Eliot and W.B. Yeats (1865-1939); and (all dramatists) August Strindberg (1849-1912), Luigi Pirandello (1867-1936), Bertolt Brecht (1898-1956) and Eugene O'Neill (1888-1953). Also see *postmodernism.

modern period. The modern period has not been clearly identified as there are varied opinions about it. However, generally the period is thought to be extended from the breaking out of the First World War (1914) to the cessation of the Second World War (1945). The literature of the period showed some specific features (see *modernism) which were absent earlier in literature and which continued to remain in, or shaded into, the *post-modern period. Some of the notable novelists of the modern period are: Ford Madox Ford (1873-1939), D.H. Lawrence (1885-1930), James Joyce (1882-1941), Virginia Woolf (1882-1941), Wyndham Lewis (1882-1957), Aldous Huxley (1894-1963), E.M. Forster (1879-1970), Evelyn Waugh (1903-66), Anthony Powell (b. 1905), Christopher Isherwood (b. 1904), George Orwell (pseudo. of Eric Blair: 1903-50), Graham Greene (b. 1904), Samuel Beckett (b. 1906), David Jones (b. 1895), Elizabeth Bowen (b. 1899), Jean Rhys (1894-1979), Joseph Conrad (born Teodor Konrad Korzenioski: 1857-1924), William Faulkner (1897-1962), Joyce Cary (1888-1957), Scott Fitzgerald (1896-1940), *et al.*

moment. A term closely similar to, or identical with, the term *epiphany. Moment is 'a sudden spiritual manifestation', as James Joyce (1882-1941) says in his *A Portrait of the Artist as a Young Man*. P.B. Shelley (1792-1822) calls epiphany 'moment', as W. Wordsworth (1770-1850) calls it 'sports of time' and Thomas De Quincey (1785-1859) 'involutes'. Virginia Woolf (1882-1941) also believed in the phenomenon of 'moment'. Jeremy Hawthorn writes: "A Woolfian [adj. of Woolf] moment typically involved the sensation of time pausing, of a number of human and /or non-human factors coming together in a unity which was unique but which also had the power to 'speak' an interior truth or set of inner truths, both of the participants and components and to the observer. This observer of the Woolfian moment will thus simultaneously discover something fundamental about that which is observed and, at the same time, about him, or herself, something profound, complete, and of visionary interest" [Hawthorn, 219]. Also see **duende*, *inspiration.

money novel. See *economic novel, which is synonymous with *business novel.

monologue. An extended speech or written *narrative by one person only, directed either to some other person or persons, or to self or to no one (alone), as distinct from dialogue in which verbal or written communication involves at least two persons. Example of monologue (or monologic poem) may be found in Robert Browning's (1812-89) *My Last Duchess*. See also *interior monologue, *monologic novel, *dialogic novel, *stream of consciousness.

monologic novel. See *dialogic novel, dialogical novel.

montage [from French *montage*, assembling]. A device of assembling and piecing together elements from different sources and creating a new whole or producing an *effect or *atmosphere, in which case, normally, "the origin of the component parts is clearly discernible" [*op. cit.*, 220]. In the film industry, the term refers to the technique of showing brief pictures or impressions in quick succession with a view to producing a desired atmosphere.

moral. The term bears a range of disparate meanings: it means ethical, or something 'supported by evidence of reason or probability' and not by demonstration; or any practical reason, lesson, instruction or advice (not necessarily ethical) to be learnt from a literary work in which it is implicitly stated, generally and briefly at the end of the work.

motif. A basic, recurrant and conspicuous idea, image, *pattern, *incident or *situation in a work of literature, music or folklore that highlights the *theme or a part of it. The *quest* (eternal quest} is a motif in many works of literature, such as Homer's (c. 8th century B.C.) *Iliad*, Sir Thomas Malory's (1405-1471) *Le Morte Darthur*, Robert Browning's (1812-89) poem "Child Roland to the Dark Tower Came" and James Joyce's (1882-1941) *Ulysses*. In folklore, the kiss that awakens the sleeping beauty is a motif, and in Joyce's *A Portrait of the Artist as a Young Man* the flight of birds is a motif in so far as it suggests the freedom of the *protagonist Stephen Daedalus.

motivation. It refers to the objective or reason behind the actions of a *character in a play or *narrative.

mystery fiction, mystery novel, mystery story. A kind of *novel or *short story that first introduces a catastrophic mystery about, for instance, a murder and then shows the solution of that mystery by unveiling the 'who, why and how' of it. The detective fictions of Sir Arthur Conan Doyle (1859-1930) and the short stories of Edgar Allan Poe (1809-49) may be called mystery fictions or novels and mystery stories respectively. Some other mystery stories are to be found in the novels of E.T.A. Hoffman (1776-1822) and in the Gothic romances of Horace Walpole (1717-97) and Ann Radcliffe (1764-1823). Also see *Gothic novel, Gothic romance.

myth [from Greek *mythos*, story, plot]. A kind of rudimentary *story, with a supernatural being as its *protagonist, which is believed to have explained otherwise unexplained phenomena, such as the creation (Christian myth), human destiny, miracles, etc. Myths are generally anonymous, fabricated with high imagination, generally handed down orally, and mostly believed to be true (particularly in the primitive societies). The stories of Pan, Cupid, Psyche, Nemesis, Clotho, Lachasis, Atropos, etc. are myths. The myth of Er in Plato's *The Republic* (Bk X)—a personal myth of his—is a classic example. All nations of the world have their own store-houses of myths. In addition, some creative writers are adding to those store-houses their personal myths. Such writers are called mythopoeic ('poeic' from Greek *poieein*, to make). P.B. Shelley (1792-1822), William Blake (1757-1827), Herman Melville (1819-91), etc. are mythopoeic writers. Aristotle, in *Poetics*, however, used the term to denote the bare story of a play or its *plot. The term is also sometimes employed loosely to mean belief or faith, such as 'the American myth of progress', 'the American success myth', William Faulkner's (1828-79) myth of Yoknapatawpha County, etc. Myth should be differentiated from *legend and *folk tale. If the protagonist of a story is a supernatural being, it is a myth; if a human being, it is a legend; and if the story concerns a supernatural being but is not part of a systematic mythology, it is a folk tale. Myths are not only things of the past, but are alive even to-day, for, as T.S. Eliot (1888-1965) in *Murder in the Cathedral* says, 'human beings/Cannot bear very much reality'. And, for this reason, some modern writers have very successfully utilized myths or mythical elements in their works. Instances of such writers are: T.S. Eliot (*The Waste Land*), James Joyce (1882-1941: *Ulysses* and *Finnegans Wake*) and Eugene O'Neill (1888-1953: *Mourning Becomes Electra*).

N

narratee. The 'target' to whom a *narrator recounts his *narrative. This is simple; but the concept of narrator is not so simple, for the reader or listener is not always the narratee; even the narrator himself may be the narratee, if he directs his narrative to himself. Jeremy Hawthorn writes: "A narratee is not just the individual by whom a narrative is received; there has to be some evidence that the narrative is actually intended for a particular goal for it to count as the (or a) narratee. This leads Prince [Gerald prince, *A Dictionary of Narratology* (1988)] to argue that the narratee must be inscribed in the text. He argues that there is a difference between a narratee and both the reader and the implied reader. In the final section of James Joyce's *Ulysses* therefore, if we follow Prince on this matter, the narratee is Molly Bloom herself (she aims her comments at herself), but the implied reader is rather a person who can, for example, pick up the classical analogies contained in the text of *Ulysses* as a whole, with the real reader being anyone who actually reads the novel" [Hawthorn, 224]. Further, writes Hawthorn, "Narratees may be single or multiple, personified or non-personified. Thus in a complex work such a Joseph Conrad's *Heart of Darkness*, those sitting and listening to Marlow's account are the narratees of his narrative, but they are not the narratees of the frame narrative. Translating all this into a less technical form, we can say that whereas Marlow talks to certain personified individuals who are characters within the novel, the anonymous frame narratior directs his (or her) comments to an unpersonified, non-specific and somewhat diffuse narratee who exists within the novel as narratee and nothing else. "One should add that, of course, a well-defined narratee exerts considerable influence on the formation of the implied reader as well as on the attitudes and behaviour of the real reader" [*ibid*.]. Also see *implied reader, *frame story.

narration. The *act* or *process* of recounting an *event or a series of related events, as distinct from description, commentary, and dialogue. Sometimes the term is used interchangeably with the term *narrative.

narration, grammar of. The term refers to the special application of (general linguistic) grammar in cases of fictional *narratives, where normal grammatical rules are slightly violated or where understanding requires a special attention. M.H. Abrams writes that the grammar of narration is "The analysis of special grammatical usages that are characteristic of fictional narratives.... One focus of such analysis is the special play of deictics—that is, of words such as 'now', 'then', 'here', 'there', 'today', 'last month', personal pronouns and certain verbs—whose reference depends on the particular speaker and his or her position in the place and time. In many narratives, usually in a way not explicitly noted by the reader, the reference of such terms constantly shift or merge, as the narration moves from the narrator, by whom the events are told in the past tense (e.g., then and there), to a character in the narration, for whom the action is present (e.g., here and now). Another notable grammatical usage has been called free indirect discourse (equivalent to the French 'style indirect libre'), or 'represented speech or thought'. These terms refer to the way, in many narratives, that the reports of what a character says and thinks shift in pronouns, adverbs, tense, and grammatical mode, as we move—or sometimes hover—between the direct narrated reproductions of these events as they occur to the character and the indirect representation of such events by the narrator. Thus, a direct representation, 'He thought, "I will see her home now, and may then stop at my mother's,"' might shift, in an 'indirect representation,' to 'He thought that he would see her home and then may he stop at his mother's.' In a 'free indirect representation' the sentence might change to 'He would see her home then, and might afterward stop at his mother's'" [Abrams, 172]. Also see *deixis, *free indirect style, free indirect discourse.

narrative. As a noun, the term denotes a true or fictitious *event or an interconnected series of events recounted by a narrator(s) to a *narratee(s). In this sense, the term has a wide range of things to refer to: *novels, *epics, *short stories, biographies, diaries, *travelogues, etc. but not descriptions, commentaries, dramas or dialogues. As an adjective, it means the quality of being narrated or recounted. Aristotle used the term in the sense of a 'work with a plot' (e.g., epic poetry, tragedy, comedy). Also see *narration.

narrative hook. It is "a statement, incident, or whatever, calculated to create in the reader or the spectator an overwhelming desire to find out what will happen next" [Lemon, 41].

narrative level. The term was given currency by Monika Fludernik in her book *Towards a 'Natural' Narratology* (1996: Routledge: London). Her alternative term is 'realms of existence'. The *events that are the raw material of a *narrative may be thought to exist at least three levels or planes: chronological level (here events exist in chronological succession), causal level (here events exist as causally interconnected) and artistic level (here events are ordered artistically). Or, the narrative may be said to exist at the level of *story or at the level of *plot [Hawthorn, 226].

narrative situation. The term was introduced by Mieke Bal in 1993 in order to refer to the relationship of a *narrator to his *narrative: does the narrator exist within the world of the *story and is the narrative focalized through him? Jeremy Hawthorn writes that "narrative situation has nothing to do with whether the narrative is ostensibly delivered in Paris or Rome, or whether the narrator narrates in a sitting or standing position, but is defined according to the narrator's relationship to the narrative and the story. From this perspective the narrative situation in Joseph Conrad's *Heart of Darkness* and Woody Allen's film *Broadway Danny Rose* have certain striking similarities, even though the setting, story, and action of the two works have precious little in common" [*ibid.*].

narrative structure. The form or shape of the organisation or arrangement of the *events in a *narrative or the shape of a narrative's or *story's 'trajectory'. "Every story is projected from a state of rest by a force of some kind in an arc of rising tension until it reaches the apogee where it begins to fall towards a point of impact.

This trajectory represents the 'unity of action', proclaimed by Aristotle to be the essential principle of tragedy, but also applicable to related genres such as the epic" [Fowler, 2001, 158]. This trajectory is the narrative structure.

narrative voice. The term denotes no 'voice' but the *person* who 'speaks' or relates *events in a *story. The person may be the *narrator who represents the author (the *third-person narrative: where he is called *implied author or *omniscient narrator) or the person who is a *character (the *first-person narrator). In a *narrative, there may be some other narrative voices if some other persons participate in the *narration of the narrative, through dialogue or by taking over the act of narration from the 'first-person' or the 'third-person', from time to time.

"The concept of narrative voice can become problematic in 'indirect' modes of speech presentation. In indirect speech and *free indirect speech the voice is predominantly the (third person) narrator's, but the style may be coloured by the voice of the character whose words are being reported. Compare:

> *direct speech* He said, 'I'll cough up the cash tomorrow.'
>
> *indirect speech* He said (that) he would cough up the cash the next day.
>
> *free indirect speech* He would *cough up* the cash *tomorrow*.

In the free indirect style (without the reporting clause *He said*), although the main voice is the narrator's, the perspective is predominantly the character's" [McArthur, 1094].

narratology. The term was introduced by Tzvetan Todorov and denotes the subject that deals with the theory, discourse and critique of *narrative and *narration. In a wider sense, narratology is "'...a multi-disciplinary study of narrative which incorporates the insights of many other critical discourses that involve narrative forms of representation', and (that) today narratology 'studies the narrative aspects of many literary and non-literary genres and discourses which need not be defined as strictly narrative, such as lyrical poems, film, drama, history, advertisements'" [Hawthorn, 226-27].

narrator. There is little consensus among critics as to the exact definition or meaning of the term. Simply, narrator is one who narrates a *story—who is the presenter of the story. The term is used by various critics with different meanings: 'the one who narrates', 'a person who narrates', 'the narrative agent', 'the linguistic subject, a function and not a person, which expresses itself in the language that constitutes the text', etc. Monika Fludernik reserves the term for " 'those instances of subjective language that imply a *speaking* subject: the personal pronoun *I*, addresses to the narratee, metanarrative commentary and evaluation'" [Hawthorn, 227]. According to Wayne Booth, narrator may be of three types: *implied narrator, *dramatised narrator, and *undramatised narrator. The narrator sometimes may be identifiable and sometimes not, and in the later case the *narrative may be called 'narratorless narrative'. A narrator may be of two kinds: *personified narrator* and *un- or non-personified narrator*. Again, a narrator may be overt or covert. The term *covert narrator* is used in those cases of narratives "in which a telling is delivered from a non-personified and non-intrusive source which does not address a narratee" [*ibid.*]. In the dramatology, narrator denotes a "character outside the action of a play who explains or comments on events. In effect, such a person is the modern equivalent of the chorus in Greek drama" [Mobley, 98].

naturalism. The extreme form of *realism in literature that is informed by the post-Darwinian biology of the nineteenth century. It was also influenced by the French positivist Auguste Comte's (1798-1857) application of scientific ideas, laws and methods in the study of social phenomena and by another French positivist Adolphe Taine's (1828-93) 'application of deterministic theories to literature'. It believes "that a human being exists entirely in the order of nature and does not have a soul nor any mode of participating in a religious or spiritual world beyond the natural world; and therefore, that such a being is merely a higher-order animal whose character and behaviour are entirely determined by two kinds of forces, heredity and environment" [Abrams, 261]. It was a sort of movement in literature initiated by the famous Goncourt brothers: Edmond Goncourt (1822-96) and Jules Goncourt (1830-70). They wrote 'in collaboration' two **roman documentaires*, *Saeur Philomene* and *Germinie Lacerteux*, which may be said to show the path to naturalism in literature. For the former, they investigated hospital life from inside to very accurately describe the hospital situation, and for the latter 'they made a study of one of their own servants who had served them faithfully for years while leading unknown to them a life of debauchery revealed only after her death from consumption' with the purpose of drawing a similar character. The Goncourt Brothers' influence on the naturalistic *novels of Emile Zola (1840-1902) was enormous, which is shown particularly by his *Therese Raquin* and *Germinal*. Some other naturalistic novelsists are: Alphonse Daudel (1840-97), Gerhart Hauptmann (1862-1946), Maxim Gorky (1868-1936) and such others.

The naturalistic novel is distinguished for its accurate, scientific portrayal of minutiae of life and the reality, which is only less accurate than photographs. The naturalistic vision of man tends to be subjective, somber, morose, and the naturalistic novel generally shows the seamier side of life—the life of impoverishment, underprivilege, ugliness and diseases. In depicting the details of life, the naturalistic novel is not *selective*, like the realistic novel, but is inclusive. Zola is regarded as the high priest of naturalism. His novels are scientific, pathological, physiological, only pretty little less so than the terms actually suggests. His novel *L'assommoir* is held to be the harbinger of naturalism in literature. His influence is discernible in the works of such novelists as George Augustus Moore (1852-1933), George Gissing (1857-1903), Guy de Maupassant (1850-93), Leo Tolstoy (1828-1910), Maxim Gorky, Theodor Dreiser (1871-1945) and Frank Norris (1870-1902).

negritude. The term literally means negro-ness or negro-ism. It denotes the cultural movement, launched by black students in Paris in 1932, aimed at achieving negro identity and asserting the traditional African cultural values within the white culture. "Its principal elements are nostalgia for traditional African society, and elevation of emotion, intuition and spontaneous social interaction over the rationalistic Hellenism of the white man's forms of government" [Scruton, 319]. The Nigerian dramatist and poet Wole Soyinka (b. 1934) criticized the movement's limited aim of only establishing the identity of the negros: 'the tiger does not proclaim his tigritude—he pounces'.

neo-realism. The term denotes the revival of *realism in fictional works, especially *novels and *short stories, in Italy in the 1940s and 1950s. In the forefront of the neo-realistic movement were the novelists Carlo Levi (1902-75), Elio Vittorini (1908-66), Cesare Pavese (1908-50), Beppe Fenoglio (1922-63), Alberto Moravia (b. 1907) and Italo Calvino (1923-85). Neo-realistic fictions of Italy especially describe the lives of the down-trodden in the contemporary society. Parallelly with the Italian neo-realistic literary movement was the Italian neo-realistic cinematographic movement, led by Roberto Rosselini and Vittorio de Sica. The term now is used for any revival of realism in any literarture of any period. The stress of the neo-realistic movement in fiction is laid on faithful, minute description of the reality and the real, even though disagreeable. Also see *verism, *verismo.

nested narrative. Same as *embedded narrative, *Chinese Box narrative.

new criticism. A kind of movement for an altogether different mode of literary *criticism that was launched in America in the 1920s and was influential till the 1960s. It was aimed particularly to the criticism of poetry 'concentrating on the verbal complexities and ambiguities of short poems considered self-sufficient objects without attention to their origins or effects'; it was, however, not much successful in the fields of dramatic and narrative works. The term 'new criticism' was taken from the title of the critic and poet John Crowe Ransom's (b. 1888) book *The New Criticism* (1941). The assumptions of new criticism may be summarised as follows: " 'New Criticism' can be broadly characterized by its emphasis on the *autonomy* of a given literary work; it has made its purpose the 'close reading' of a single text, regarding biographical material, information about the writer's ideas, the work's reception, etc., as secondary. A work of art is a concrete whole, a concrete in itself, an unparaphrasable entity. It is also a *verbal* experience, a pattern of language working—unlike, say, science or discursive prose—by concentration, irony and ambiguity. The distinctiveness of literature lies in its capacity to be simultaneously particular and universal; hence it has a clear function (virtually an anti-scientific one) and great educational value in training responsiveness" [Bradbury, 192]. These assumptions derived mostly from the literary criticisms of Ezra Pound (b. 1885) and T.S. Eliot (1888-1965). Some of the leading New Critics are: John Crowe Ransom, Allan Tate (b. 1899) and Yvor Winters (1900-68)—all poets as well.

Newgate fiction. A kind of crime and underworld *fiction in which criminals are glamorously portrayed 'in a dangerously sympathetic manner'. The writers of Newgate fictions (novels) generally took their materials from real-life criminal cases. Writers of Newgate fictions include: Edward Bulwar Lytton (1803-73) and William Harrison Ainsworth (1805-82).

new historicism. Not a revival of earlier humanism but a new mode of literary study that developed in the early 1980s and is opposed to *Russian formalism or, simply, *formalism, as well as to *deconstruction and *New Criticism. According to new historicism, literature is not trans-historical or merely formal but contextual, and that literature is somehow linked to the economic, social, cultural and political conditions of its contemporary era. "In an oft-quoted phrase, Louis Montrose described the new historicism as a 'reciprocal concern with the historicity of texts and the texuality of history.' That is, history is conceived not to be a set of fixed, objective facts but, like the literature with which it interacts, a text which itself needs to be interpreted. Any text, on the other hand, is conceived as a discourse which, although it may seem to present, or reflect, an external reality, in fact consists of what are called representations—that is, verbal formations which are the 'ideological products' or 'cultural contructs' of the historical conditions specific to an era" [Abrams, 183-84].

new humanism. See *humanism.

Newspeak. A sort of simplified artificial telegraphic 'language' which may be said to have been invented by George Orwell (1903—50) in his *novel *Nineteen Eighty Four*. It intended to avoid ambiguities and shades of meaning and do away with irregular verbs, for instance, it used *stealed* for *stole* of the 'Oldspeak' or normal grammar. Affixes were randomly used: *unthink*, *ungood*, *goodwise*, *crimethink*, etc. In that novel, Newspeak was the official language of Oceania. However, the term now denotes misleading (especially political) *jargon and words modelled on the Newspeak words, such as *nukespeak*, *teenspeak*, etc.

nihilism. The term derives from the Russian novelist Ivan Turgenev's (1818-83) *Fathers and Sons* where one of the central characters, Bazarov, is politically an extreme radical "believing in nothing save science, materialism, revolution, and (in the abstract) the people" [Flew, 249]. The term now denotes any mindless destructive tendency, particularly in the political field.

Noble Prizes. The great Prizes established under the will of the Swidish chemist Alfred Bernhard Noble (1833-96) who invented dynamite. The Prizes, originally five in number, are awarded each year (there are breaks), since 1901, by the Noble Committee, to individuals who have made the greatest contributions in the fields of physics, chemistry, physiology or medicine, literature, and peace (promotion of fraternity among nations). Later on, another Prize for contribution in the field of economics has been founded (not with the original Noble fund).

Some of the novelists (who may, additionally, be poets and/or dramatists) who have received the coveted Noble Prize are: Bjornstjerne Bjornson (Norwegian: received in 1903), Rudyard Kipling (English: 1907), Paul Heyse (German: 1910), Gerhart Hauptmann (German: 1912), Rabindranath Tagore (Indian: 1913), Romain Rolland (French: 1915), Knut Hamsun (Norwegan: 1920), *Grazia Deledda (Italian: 1926), *Sigrid Undset (Norwegan: 1928), Thomas Mann (German: 1929), Sinclair Lewis (American: 1930), John Galsworthy (British: 1932), Ivan Alekseyevich Bunin (Russian: 1933), Luigi Pirandello (Italian: 1934), *Pearl S. Buck (American: 1938), Johannes V. Jensen (Danish: 1944), Hermann Hesse (German: 1946), Adre Gide (French: 1947), William Faulkner (American: 1949), Francois Mauriac (French: 1952), Ernest Hemingway (American: 1954), Albert Camus (French: 1957), Boris Pasternak (Russian: 1958), Ivo Andric (Serbian: 1961), John Steinbeck (American: 1962), Jean-Paul Sartre (French: 1964), Mikhail Sholokhov (Russian: 1965), Samuel Beckett (Irish: 1969), Alexander Solzhenitsyn (Russian: 1970), Patrick White (Australian: 1973), Saul Bellow (American: 1976), Gabriel Garcia Marquez (Colombian: 1982), William Golding (British: 1983), Claude Simon (French: 1985), Wole Soyinka (Nigerian: 1986), Naguib Mahfouz (Egyptian: 1988), Camilo Jose Cela (Spanish: 1989), *Nadine Gordimer (South African: 1991), *Toni Morrison (Nigerian: 1993), and Jose Saramago (Portugal: 1998). (*=female)

noble savage. The (concept of the) ideal primitive man with his natural goodness, dignity and nobility, uncorrupted by the evils of civilisation: "The romantic conception of man as enjoying a natural and noble existence until civilization makes him a slave to unnatural wants and seduces him from his original freedom. The theme was elaborated in Rousseau's *Discours sur l'origine de l'inequalite parmi les homes* (1755), where he maintained that only the uncorruted savage is in possession of real virtue" [Flew, 249]. Classic examples of the noble savage are to be found in *Paradise Lost*, Bk IV (in the image of Adam and Eve in Eden):

> Two of far nobler shape erect and tall,
> Godlike erect, with native honour clad
> In naked majesty seemed lords of all,
> And worthy seemed, for their looks divine
> The image of their glorious maker shone,
> Truth, wisdom, sanctitude severe and pure.

The idea of the noble savage may also be found in Montaigne's (1533-92) essay (trans.) *Of Cannibals*; in John Dryden's (1631-1700) play *The Conquest of Granada* (pt I: I, i); in Aphra Behn's (1640-89) *Oroonoko* (the 'fair rose i' the state'); in Rousseau's (1712-78) *Emile* and in the *character of Quequeg in Harman Melville's (1819-91) *Moby Dick*.

nom de plume [from French *nom*, name; *de*, of; and *plume*, feather]. The term literally means 'name of feather' but figuratively denotes a pseudonym or assumed name of a writer. It is synonymous with *pen-name. Some *noms de plume* are: Lewis Carroll (that of Charles Lutwidge Dodgson: 1832-98), George Eliot (of Marian, or Mary Ann, Evans: (1819-80), Boz (of Charles Dickens: 1812-70), Mary Westmacott (of Dame Agatha Christie: 1890-1976), and O (liver) Henry (of William Sydney Porter: 1862-1910).

non-fiction novel. One of the 20th century variant of *historical novel which "one of its innovators, Truman Capote [1924-84], named non-fiction novel. This uses a variety of novelistic techniques, such as deviations from the temporal sequence of events and descriptions of a participant's state of mind, to give a graphic rendering of recent people and happenings, and is based not only on historical records but often on personal interviews with the chief agents. Truman Capote's *In Cold Blood* (1965) and Norman Mailer's [b. 1923] *The Executioner's Song* (1979) are instances of this mode; both offer a detailed rendering of the life, personality, and actions of murders based on a sustained series of prison interviews with the protagonists themselves" [Abrams, 194].

nouveau roman [from French *nouveau*, new, and *roman*, novel]. The term literally means 'new novel'. It denotes a kind of *novel introduced principally by the French novelist Alain Robbe-Grillet (b. 1922) in about 1955. The *nouveau roman* rejects the traditional novelistic principles or features, such as sequential *plot, analysis of motives of *characters, incidents or *episodes, etc. The basic principles of the *nouveau roman* are to be found in Robbe-Grillet's collection of essays *Pour un nouveau roman* where he argued for "a neutral registering of sensations and things rather than an interpretation of events or a study of characters" [Baldick, 151]. According to him "reality cannot be moulded according to man's desires for it exists outside him with an objective 'thereness'.... he emphasizes man's distance from physical reality, denying him the emotional comfort of describing the world in anthropomorphic terms" [Thorlby, 658]. Consequently, he believed, the *narrative or *nouveau roman* has to be existentialist and absurd. Examples of the *nouveau roman* are: Robbe-Grillet's own *La Jalousie* and Nathalie Sarraute's (date of birth not available) *Le planetarium*. Sarraute's *Tropismes* is generally considered the first *nouveau roman*. Also see *anti-novel, **nouvelle vague*.

nouvelle [[from French *nouvelle*, news, short story]. The term generally denotes *short story or *novel.

nouvelle vague [from French *nouvelle*, news, short story, novel, and *vague*, wave, billow]. The term, literally, means 'novel wave'. It denotes a kind of *novel "which abandoned traditional sequential narrative technique in favour of a more abstract approach based on the reactions of an individual character to events and stimuli" [Ayto, 214]. The term is "Particularly applied to experimental work in the cinema...and then to experimental novels (for instance, works by Alain Robbe-Grillet, Michel Butor, Nathalie Sarraute, Allan Burns and B.S. Johnson) and also to playwrights like Harold Pinter, Samuel Beckett, Eugene Ionesco, Arthur Adamov, Jean Genet, N.F. Simpson and Ann Jellico" [Cuddon, 560].

novel. A most difficult term to define assuringly, for it has been used for so very different kinds of works. In the 14th century, for instance, collections of Italian or French *stories, such as the Italian Boccaccio's (?1313-75) *Decameron* were known as 'novels' and in the 17th century romances of illicit love were called *romans* (novels). A French critic attempted to define novel as a 'fiction in prose of certain extent'. But here the term 'fiction' is not appropriate, as, for instance, there are *factions which are also generally called novels; the term 'prose' is, again, not appropriate, because, for example, Vikram Seth (b. 1952) has his *The Golden Gate, a Novel in Verse*; and the phrase 'of a certain extent' is muddling, for the 'extent' is not ascertained. However, of the novel "we may hazard that it is a form of story or prose narrative containing characters, action and incident, and, perhaps, a plot" [Cuddon, 561]. The history of novel is only a matter of guessing or belief. "The absolute origins of the genre are obscure, but it seems clear that in the time of the XIIth Dynasty Middle Kingdom (c. 1200 BC). Egyptians were writing fiction of a kind which one would describe as a novel today, for instance, *The Princess of Backstraw*, *The Predestined Prince*, and *Sinube*. From classical times other works of fiction have come down to us: notably *The Milesian Tales* (2nd c. B.C.), *Daphnis and Chloe* (2nd c. A.D.) by Longus, *The Golden Ass* (2nd c. A.D.) by Apuleius, and the *Satyricon* (1st c. A.D.) of Petronius Arbiter. "But it is not until towards the end of the first millennium that we find work more recognizably like the novel we have become accustomed to in the last 200-odd years. These works are in Japanese" [*op. cit.*, 562]. Long after, since then, the **novella* or a kind of *short story developed in Italy which may be taken to be the prototype of the modern novel—the *novella* whose examples Boccaccio's collection of short stories or *novelle*, *Decameron*, till to-day bears.

There are various kinds of novel, such as *picaresque novel, *epistolary novel, *historical novel, *regional novel, **roman a these*, **Bildungsroman*, **roman a clef*, **roman-fleuve*, *non-fiction novel, *epic novel, *detective novel, *experimental novel, *documentary novel, *slice-of-life novel, action novel (see *novel of action), adventure novel (see *novel of adventure), biographical novel (see *novel, biographical), condition-of-England novel (see *novel, condition-of-England), fabulative historical novel (see *novel, fabulative historical), *drama-novel or dramatic novel, *comic novel, *confessional novel, *autobiographical novel, *novel of character, *novel-in-dialogue, *novel-in-verse, *memoir novel, *novel of doctrine, *novel of ideas, *novel of manners, *novel of plot, *novel of sensation, *novel of sensibility or *sentimental novel, *involuted novel or *self-reflexive novel, *sensation novel, *novel of sail, *realistic novel, *social novel, *symbolic novel or *symbolist novel, *novel of ratiocination, *well-made novel, etc., etc. (see some of them under particular headings, such as *dime novel, *poem novel, etc.).

novel, autobiographical. See *autobiographical novel.

novel, biographical. A kind of novel based on the biography of a person. It is sometimes called '*vie romancee*' "in which the line between critical biography and narrative art is hard to draw" [Thorlby, 522]. Andre Maurois (1885-1967) was a master of *vie romancee* with his masterpieces *Ariel ou la vie de Shelley* and *Promethee ou la vie de Balzac*.

novel, comic. See *comic novel.

novel, condition of England. A kind of novel that deals with the contemporary socio-economic condition of England. Benjamin Disraeli's (1804-81) *Sybil, or, The Two Nations* is an example [Ousby, 904].

novel, confessional. See *confessional novel.

novel, dialogic; novel, dialogical. See*dialogic novel, dialogical novel.

novel, dramatic. See *drama-novel, dramatic novel.

novel, epic. See *epic novel.

novelese. The term refers to the worn out and hackneyed catchy phrases and expressions that some second-rate novelists tend to employ, particularly to draw reader's attention. H. W. Fowler in his *A Dictionary of Modern English Usage* writes about the term: "What is (here) meant by *novelese* is the set phrases that the young writer [of the novel] remembers to have had his emotions stirred by in the days when he was reading novels instead of writing them, and relies upon to affect his own readers in turn. The phrases have had some wear and tear since he was first struck by them, and the emotional value of such things depreciates quickly. Influences that 'have come into' somebody's 'life', tempted ones who 'will not do this thing', fallen ones 'more sinned against than sinning', unfortunates 'hoping against hope', strong silent men, living deaths, that supreme moment, demoniacal glee, demonic energy, diabolical malignity, and devilish ingenuity, magnetic personalities and sinister machinations, utter abandon and pathetic indifference, innocent guile and serpentine charm, all these and hundreds of the like phrases, which thrilled our own youth, will not thrill but bore those on whom we sanguinely try the same experiment. The emotions may be sempiternal; the stimuli to which they will react lose their power with use, and must be varied" [Fowler, 1996, 387]. The term is generally used pejoratively.

novelette [from French *nouvelette*, short novel]. A kind of trivial middle-length *novel, somewhat between the expansiveness of the *novel proper and the briefness of the *short story, often deliberately infused with thrill or sentimentality, and therefore more commonly than not the term *novelette* is used pejoratively. *Novelette* usually deals with popular love stories. In Germany, the *novelette* is called **novella*. The term is sometimes used synonymously with **novella*. The American novelist Anais Nin's (1903-77) *The Winter of Artifice* is a collection of three *novelettes*.

novel, fabulative historical. A kind of *novel that "interweaves history with frenzied, even fantastic, events" [Abrams, 194]. For instance, John Barth's (b. 1930) novel *The Sot-Weed Factor* and Thomas Pynchon's (b. 1937) novel *Gravity's Rainbow*.

novel-in-verse. A normal *novel, its medium being verse instead of prose. The genre "seems to have arisen during the Romantic period in response to the new success of the prose novel" [Cuddon, 966]. Earlier examples of the novel-in-verse are: Goethe's (1749-1832) *Hermann und Dorothea*, Pushkin's (1799-1837) *Eugene Onegin*, E.B. Browning's (1806-61) semi-autobiographical *Aurora Leigh*, Robert Browning's (1812-89) *The Ring and the Book*, etc. Modern instances are: Derek Walcott's (b. 1930) *Omeros*, Vikram Seth's (b. 1952) *The Golden Gate*, Philip Toynbee's (b. 1916) *Pantaloon or The Vatediction* and *Two Brothers*, etc. The term is synonymous with *poem-novel and *verse novel.

novelisation. The conversion of plays, motion pictures, historical events or episodes, narrative poems, *folk tales, etc. into *novels.

novella [from Italian *novella*, a little new thing]. Earlier, the term was applied to short *narratives, such as Boccaccio's (?1313-75) *Decameron*, but now it generally denotes a short prose *fiction in length between the *short story and the *novel. Examples are: Henry James's (1843-1916) *The Turn of the Screw*, Joseph Conrad's (1857-1924) *Heart of Darkness* and Ivo Andric's (b. 1893) *The Vizier's Elephant*, *Anika's Times* and *Zeko*. Also see **novelette*, **Novelle*, **novellat*.

novellat [perhaps from Italian *novella,* a little new thing]. "A form of folk tale of the Semitic tradition which is of a particular time and place. It lacks universality (...) and thus differs from the chimerat (...)" [Cuddon, 601]. Also see **novella*, *chimerat.

novelle [from German *Novelle*, novel, long short story]. "Basically, the *novelle* is a fictional narrative of indeterminate length (a few pages to two or three hundred), restricted to a single event, situation or conflict, which produces an element of suspense and leads to an unexpected turning point (*Wendepunkt*) so that the conclusion surprises even while it is a logical outcome" [Cuddon, 600]. The term is sometimes used for long short story (as distinct from *short story and *novel). Examples of the *Novelle* are: Leo Tolstoy's (1828-1910) *The Cossacks* and *The Death of Ivan Ilyich*, Aldous Huxley's (1894-1963) *Two or Three Graces* and Ernest Hemingway's (1898-1961) *The Old Man and the Sea*.

novel, memoir. See *memoir novel.

novel, non-fiction. See *non-fiction novel.

novel of action. A kind of *novel where narration of *actions or incidents are relatively predominating compared with characterisation, dialogues, *plot, etc. It is also called *novel of incident or *novel of adventure. Novel of action "is usually an action-filled story involving fast guns, rustling, claim-jumping, range wars, etc." [Lemon, 12]. Also see *novel of character.

novel of adventure. See *novel of action.

novel of character. A kind of *novel in which *characters, rather than *plot, *incident, or *event, description of (human) nature, etc. are in the main focus of the novelist. Edwin Muir, in his *The Structure of the Novel*, writes: "The novel of character,..., is concerned immediately only with outside show of reality, and it implies beneath, not something corresponding to that, but something relatively incongruous with it. The novel of character brings out the contrast between appearance and reality, between people as they present themselves to society and as they [really] are" [Muir, 46-47]. "The distinction between the novel of incident and the novel of character cannot be drawn sharply; but in the novel of incident the greater interest is in what the *protagonist* will do next and on how the story will turn out; in the novel of character, it is on the protagonist's motives for what he or she does, and on how the protagonist as a person will turn out" [Abrams, 191]. Also see *novel of plot, *novel of incident.

novel of doctrine. A kind of *novel whose principal purpose is to propound, prove, support or propagate a particular social, political, ethical or religious ideology. It is also called novel of purpose and is not different from the *thesis novel. Ernest Baker, in his *The History of the English Novel*, writes: "The novel of purpose is the converse of the regular novel; if it were purposive fiction and nothing else, doctrine would be enforced and illustrated in it by an invented version of reality" [Baker, vol. V, 228]. Examples of the novel of doctrine are: Robert Bage's (1728-1801) *Mount Henneth*, *Barham Downs*, *James Wallace*, *Man As He Is* and *Hermsprong, or, Man As He Is Not* (in which he tries to establish the importance of physical fitness, female education, socio-economic equality, etc.); Thomas Holcroft's (1745-1809) *Alwyn, or, the Gentleman Comedian* and *Hugh Trevor* (in both the writer pleads for a revolutionary idealism); William Godwin's (1756-1836) *Caleb Williams* (in which the writer propounds his fanatically intellectual social ideology); etc. Also see *novel of ideas.

novel of ideas. A sub-genre of *novel in which the principal objective is to propound some definite idea or ideas generally through debate, conversation, etc., and in which such things as *plot, *narrative, characterisation play minor parts. This kind of novel may best be exemplified with Aldous Huxley's (1894-1963) *Crome Yellow*, *Antic Hay* (in both Huxley explains his ideas of good and evil), *Brave New World* (in which he exposes the evil of scientific totalitarianism) and *Island* (which 'invokes a Utopian community with a new spiritual perspective and reflects Huxley's own search for an extension of awareness'). Also see *novel of doctrine.

novel of incident. See *novel of character.

novel of manners. A realistic *novel that (like the play of manners) foregrounds or highlights the customs, behaviour, ways of thinking, habits, value system, etc. of a particular social class.

novel of plot. A sub-genre of *novel in which the construction of *plot predominates over characterization, narration, description, dialogues, etc. A negative instance though, the novels of so brilliant a novelist as Charles Dickens (1812-70) are not novels of plot. Ernest Baker writes: "Dickens was well aware as anyone of his besetting sin, clumsiness and carelessness in spinning his plots" [Baker, VII, 279]. Also see *novel of character, *well-made novel.

novel of sensation. A kind of *novel whose deliberate purpose is to stimulate the sense organs and provide thrill or fear for enjoyment. It was in vogue for some time since the 1860s. It deals with improbable, melodramatic and lurid matters. Examples of the novel of sensation are: Mrs Clive's (1801-73) *Paul Ferroll* and *Why Paul Ferroll Killed His Wife*, Mrs Henry Wood's (1814-87) *East Lynne*, Mary Elizabeth Braddon's (1835-1915) *Lady Audley's Secret*, and Wilkie Collins's (1824-89) *The Woman in White*. Also see

*Gothic novel, *detective novel, detective story.

novel of sensibility. This category of *novel falls within the range of the *literature of sensibility. The term is synonymous with *sentimental novel, because both the categories of novel aim at arousing the sensibility or sentiment of the reader and the result in most cases is his shading tears. Examples of the novel of sensibility are: Goethe's (1749-1832) *The Sorrows of Young Werther*, Samuel Richardson's (1689-1761) *Pamela, or Virtue Rewarded* and Laurence Sterne's (1713-68) *The Life and Opinions of Tristram Shandy*. The novel of sensibility or the *sentimental novel had a vogue in the latter part of the eighteenth century.

novel of sentiment. Same as *sentimental novel.

novel of the soil. A category of *novel "whose main theme is the struggle of human beings against the natural forces of the earth [soil]" [Cuddon, 602]. Its pessimistic philosophy is **lacrimae rerum* (literally, 'tears of things'), that is, 'sorrow is part of the scheme of things' and that man is doomed to fight a ceaseless but futile battle against his fate. Examples of the novel of the soil are: Ellen Glasgow's (1874-1945) *Barren Ground*, Erskine Caldwell's (1903-87) *Tobacco Road* and *God's Little Acre*, Patrick White's (1912-90) *The Tree of Man* and John Steinbeck's (1902-68) *The Grapes of Wrath*.

O

objective correlative. The term was apparently invented by the American painter Washington Allston about 1840 and was popularised by T.S. Eliot (1888-1965) through his famous essay on *Hamlet*, where he had slightly modified the meaning of it given by Allston. In that essay, Eliot wrote: "'The only way of expressing emotion in the form of art is by finding an "objective correlative"; in other words, a set of objects, a situation, a chain of events which shall be the formula of that *particular* emotion; such that when the external facts, which must terminate in sensory experience, are given, the emotion is immediately evoked'" [Cuddon, 605]. What Eliot wrote is enough to explain objective correlative. According to Eliot, Lady Macbeth's sleep-walking speech, for instance, has an objective correlative but Hamlet's extremely moribund state of mind does not betray any objective correlative in the circumstances in which we find him; his emotion spills over the facts. The point of objective correlative arises particularly in case of poetry and plays, but it may also arise in the case of *novels.

objet d' art [from French *objet*, object; *d'*, of; *art*, art, artificiality]. The term literally means 'object of art'. But, now the French term somehow has come to signify an object that is "alluring [in the prejorative sense] or faintly ridiculous according to one's point of view: 'the various little tables, loaded with "object of art" (as Mrs Gibson delighted to call them) with which the drawing room was crowded' (Elizabeth Gaskell, *Wives and Daughters*, 1866)" [Ayto, 217].

obscenity. In literature, obscenity signifies the use of language that refers to sex or excrement or is otherwise indecent and repulsive. In England, "The Obscenity Publication Act 1957 prohibited publication of obscene matter but did not define 'obscene', although it provided a test of obscenity, namely, the tendency to corrupt and deprave those likely to come in contact with material in question" [Scruton, 330]. Nevertheless, obscenity has yet remained a matter of debate. D.H. Lawrence's (1885-1930) *Lady Chatterley's Lover* was privately published in 1928 in Florence, in London, due to the fear of the charge of obscenity. After the 1957 Act, Lawrence was sued for obscenity but was exonerated by the court and only in 1960 an unexpurgated edition of *Lady Chatterley's Lover* was published in England.

officialese. A style of polysyllabic, pedantic and pompous language common in official usages. The term is pejorative in literature. Also see *journalese, *novelese.

O. Henry ending. A very surprising turn in concluding a *story, like in the *short stories of O. Henry (1862-1910). Also see *trick ending, *twist ending.

old wives' tale. An extremely unrealistic, quixotic, low-grade, gossipy *story, generally having superstitious elements, such as might be told by old women.

omniscient narrator. See *point of view.

omniscient point of view. See *point of view.

open novel. See *closed novel.

open text. See *closed text.

opsis [from Greek *opsis*, scene, spectacle]. A particularly "visible or picturable setting in any work of literature" [Abrams, 285].

optional reader. See *ideal reader.

oral literature. A rather nonsensical or 'preposterous' 20th century critical term (nonsensical or 'preposterous term, because, by definition, literature must be written, not oral) in vogue till date. *The Oxford Companion to the English Language* writes about the term: "A term in literary criticism for forms of oral art in societies with little or no recourse to writing that nonetheless have the same qualities as literary texts. Strictly speaking, the elements of the term are incompatible, because literature is fundamentally the outcome of writing and not of speech, but it is widely used and has proved convenient on the assumption that *literature* is an artistic enterprise whose nature is not confined to writing and print despite the fact that these are the main vehicles" [McArthur, 730]. Also see *orature.

orature. Jeremy Hawthorn defines the term thus: "a body of works of art transmitted in oral rather than written form and stored in memory rather than in writing, along with the conventions and techniques associated with oral transmission and memorial storage" [Hawthorn, 247]. Orature is sometimes used interchangeably with *oral literature, but perhaps orature is more appropriate than oral literature because the word literature (from Latin *litera*, a letter) suggests the presence of written or printed letters.

organicism. The term refers to the theory that likens a literary work with a living being or organism and insists that the parts of a literary work must be integrated, must be connected each to each, like the parts or members of an organism. It holds up the belief that like an organism, a literary work has a definite form or shape and, therefore, also insists that like an organism naturally grows to its full or complete form a literary work must develop 'naturally' and not mechanically—its form must not be superimposed. Organicism, further, insists that the whole of a literary work is *more* than the mere sum of its parts.

orientalism [from Latin *orientis*, to rise (of the sun)]. The word 'orient' refers to the countries of the East, or the Asiatic countries, and the word 'orientalism' ordinarily refers to the special characteristics and customs of the people of the East or Orient, as 'invented' or discovered by Europe and the West. Thus, for instance, Stendhal (1783-1842) noticed the Orient's 'stinking egoism'; Victor Hugo (1802-85) in his *Les Orientales*, saw the Oriental to be 'exotic, languorous and barbaric'; and some other writers of Europe 'imagined' the Orient to be only romantic, legendary, or mythic. And, as far as literature is concerned, orientalism usually used to refer to the *discourse of the West about the East and also the attitude of the West towards the East. But Edward Said, in his notable contribution *Orientalism* (1978), gave a new meaning to the word orientalism. "Said's development of the term attempts to draw out its concealed political allegiances—the fact that Orientalists were complicit with imperialism and that they effectively provided Europe with 'one of its deepest and most recurring images of the Other" [Hawthorn, 248]. To the Westerners, says Said, the Orientals are the inferior Other over whom the Westerners' political and military colonialism was justified. The Westerners' unchanging, repetitious knowledge or, rather 'vision', of the Orientals is that the latter are backward and stagnant in terms of civilisation, technology, intellectual achievement and, worse of all, that the latter suffer from 'weakness of character, sexual excess, dishonesty and cruelty', an excess of romanticism, and dreaminess. The most unfortunate thing is that the Westerners would not change this knowledge of theirs about the Orientals, i.e. they would not embrace openness to the Orientals. *This is the essence of orientalism*. Said writes: "'Orientalism staked its existence, not upon its openness, its receptivity to the Orient, but rather on its internal repetitious consistency about its constitutive will-to-power over the Orient'" [Simons, 272]. Also see *Other.

oriental novel, oriental tale. A kind of *fiction with exotic, extravagant, and improbable *tales or *stories having ideally virtuous heroes confronting extremely wicked adversaries; supernatural and magical elements freely strewn throughout; and, especially, having 'Eastern' or 'Near Eastern' settings (for which reason such *novels and tales are so called). These were in considerable vogue in the whole of the 18th century and in the early part of the 19th, chiefly for their entertaining aspect. Examples are: (Dr) Samuel Johnson's (1709-84) *The Prince of Abyssinia, A Tale* (later on entitled *Rasselas*) and William Beckford's (1759-1844) novel *Vathek* (both the stories are Arabian in origin). Also see *Gothic novel.

Other, other. Jeremy Hawthorn, in his *A Glossary of Contemporary Literary Theory*, explains the term thus: "To characterize a person, group, or institution as 'other' is to place them outside the system of normality or convention to which one belongs.... If members of a given racial group are collectively seen as other, then how they are treated is irrelevant to what humanity demands—because they are other. What lies behind use of this term is the perception that when we divide up reality into separate components these are typically seen in a sort of figure/ground manner, with one component representing a norm and other components representing divergences from this norm" [Hawthorn, 248]. The activity or process of treating a person, group, or institution is referred to by the verb form 'othering'. Also see *centre.

otiose [from Latin *otiosus / otium*, leisure]. Literally, the term means 'unoccupied', 'functionless' or 'superfluous'. As a critical term it denotes a style that is verbose, superfluous, idle, inefficient or useless. Also see **outré*.

outré [from French *outré*, beyond, further]. The term denotes something that is "extreme or excessive, especially in going beyond the bounds of conventional taste or propriety, or simply in being eccentrically odd" [Ayto, 222]. Also see *otiose.

outsider. The term owes its origination proximally to Colin Wilson's (b. 1931) non-fiction *The Outsider* (1956) and a little distantly to Albert Camus's (1913-60) novel *L'etranger* (1942; trans. S. Gilbert, *The Outsider*, 1946). Camus wrote an Afterword for *L'etranger* which has a great bearance for the significance of the term 'outsider'. The Afterword begins thus: "A long time ago, I summed up *The Outsider* in a sentence which I realize is extremely paradoxical: 'In our society any man who doesn't cry at his mother's funeral is liable to be condemned to death'. I simply meant that the hero of the book is condemned because he doesn't play the *game*. In this sense he is an *outsider to the society in which he lives, wandering on the fringe, on the outskirts of life, solitary and sensual*. And for this reason some readers have been tempted to regard him as a *reject*."(emphases added).The *game* in the above quotation refers to the rules (of game) of the society which everyone of the society must adhere to. In the case of *The Outsider* (*L'etranger*), the hero does not conform to the rules of game—does not demonstrate his grief at the death of his mother—and so he is condemned to death.

In his book *Mysteries*, Colin Wilson says that the outsider shows a greater amount of imaginative capacity and mental discipline so that they "can produce a strange sense of widening horizons, of inner breathing-space" and that they "feel an instinctive loathing of the people who are absorbed in the trivial values of everyday life, and are impatient of the stupid, whose inner freedom is almost non-existent" [Wilson, 531]. The outsider is intellectually and morally 'outside' or different from the society in which he lives. In Wilson's view, he is a kind of 'superman' endowed with a sort of 'genius'. Wilson says that most artists, philosophers and saints are outsiders, such as Friedrich Nietzsche (1844-1900), Soren Kierkegaard (1813-55), Franz Kafka (1883-1924), T.E. Lawrence (1888-1935), Ernest Hemingway (1898-1961). Some literary *characters are also outsiders, for instance, the hero of Camus's *L'etranger*. Also see *superfluous man.

overt plot. See *covert plot.

P

pale face. The term and its antonym *redskin were popularised by the critic Philip Rahv in his *Image and Idea* (1949). He divided writers into two categories or groups—the pale face and the redskin—considering their attitude, style, subject-matters, etc. According to him, "'Palefaces' have cultured and patrician attitudes and write in a mannered style using symbolism and lofty themes. 'Redskins' write of frontier life, working men, the plebs, low life in cities, etc. and are more colloquial and naturalistic in style" [Cuddon, 630]. According to Rahv, for instances, Herman Melville (1819-91), Henry James (1843-1916) and John Updike (b. 1932) may be considered as 'palefaces' and Walt Whitman (1819-92), Mark Twain (1835-1910) and William Faulkner (1825-79) as 'redskins' while Saul Bellow (b. 1915) and Bernard Malamud (1914-86) should fall in between the two categories.

palimpsest text [*palimpsest* from Greek *palin*, again, and *psaein*, to rub]. The term ordinarily means 'a manuscript in which old writing has been rubbed out to make room for new'. As a critical term, it denotes a "A text in which hidden or repressed meanings can be found between lines or under the surface" [Hawthorn, 252].

parable [from Greek *parabole*, a placing alongside, comparison]. A brief and simple *story for illustrating (by comparison) a certain lesson or moral or doctrine. Examples of parable may be found in the forty parables of Jesus Christ in the Gospels. Parables may be in verse or in prose. Wilfred Owen's (1893-1918) 'The Parable of the Old Man and the Young' is in verse and John Steinbeck's (1902-68) *The Pearl* is a parable in prose. Typically, the *characters of the parable are human beings, and not animals, as in *fables.

paradigm, paradigm shift. Literally, the word 'paradigm' means an exemplar, but as a critical term it denotes a "set of beliefs which both enables and constraints research" [Hawthorn, 254]. Michel Foucault in *The Archaeology of Knowledge* says that Gregor Mendel's (1822-84) theory of heredity was not accepted at first because it was not *dans la Vrai* (within the true), because it was outside the bound of the paradigm, but when there was a paradigm shift, i.e. when there was adequate change in the paradigm, it was. Jeremy Hawthorn writes about the term paradigm shift: "The term has entered into literary-critical vocabulary in relation, very often, to arguments about the *canon (a work is only recognized as major when new literary paradigms allow it to be understood or appreciated), and in relation to arguments about interpretation (we interpret the evidence of a text differently when our literary paradigm change, just as the scientist reinterprets the evidence provided by an experiment when his or her scientific paradigms change" [*Ibid.*].

parataxis [from Greek *para*, beside, and *taxis*, arrangement]. The term literally means co-ordination. In grammar, for instance, it means arrangement of clauses or propositions *without* connectives. Some literary critics, however, use it to refer to the desired co-ordination of different narrative elements, which is violated by some experimental writers. Also see *anachronism.

paratext. Jeremy Hawthorn defines the term quoting Richard Macksey as "those liminal devices and conventions, both within the book (*peritext*) and outside it (*epitext*) that mediate the book to the reader: titles, subtitles, pseudonyms, forewords, dedications, epigraphs, prefaces, intertitles, notes, epilogues, and afterwords" [Hawthorn, 255].

parody. See *burlesque.

parole and language. See *language and parole.

passeisme [from French *passé*, past, vanished, faded, bad]. The term literally means the state of being past, faded; or the theory that is faded or bad. "When the Italian poet Filippo Marinetti proclaimed the doctrine of Futurism in his Paris manifesto of 1909, his targets were the traditional artistic aims and methods of the past, the stifling weight of academicism. He had no time for such outdated literary conventions as metre and syntax. He saw the future of art in power, speed, technology, mechanization. Regard for traditional values was scornfully dismissed with the French term *passeisme*, a derivative of *passé* 'dated'" [Ayto, 228]. Also see *Futurism.

pastiche [from Italian *pasta*, paste]. The term literally means a jumble, a pot-pourri. In literary discourse, it denotes a composition in which various elements (words, sentences, images,*style, manner, ideas, etc.) from different sources (of earlier or contemporary writers) are patched up, sometimes as a form of *parody. A good example is John Fowles's (b. 1926) *novel *The French Lieutenant's Women* which is partly a pastiche of great Victorian novelists. Pastiche is a derogatory term but is a feature of *postmodernist literature. Also see *collage.

pastoral. See *bucolic.

pataphysics. The term was invented by the French writer and dramatist Alfred Jarry (1873-1907) to denote what he called a 'science of imaginary solution', an anti-rational 'science' or metaphysics of nonsense and the absurd. Jarry's drama *Ubu Roi* demonstrates how pataphysics works. The concept of pataphysics immensely contributed to the birth of the Theatre of the Absurd. Besides Jarry, the other exponents of pataphysics were: the dramatist Eugene Ionesco (b. 1912) and the novelist Raymond Queneau (b. 1903).

pathetic fallacy. A term coined by the great art critic John Ruskin (1819-1900) to denote a *tendency* of writers to treat objects of nature as if they are humans.

pathos. The quality or capability of a literary work to arouse the emotions of pity, tenderness or sadness—the emotions being 'less terrible and exalted than those aroused by tragedy.' In *Hamlet*, the death of Ophelia is pathetic, not tragic. Also see *tragedy.

patois. See *dialect.

pattern. A difficult term to explain, more so because there are differences among some critics as to what the term actually signifies; E.M. Forster (1879-1970), for instance, sees the pattern of a *novel as a *geometrical shape*, but professor Arnold Kettle observes it as the *moral vision* of the writer in his particular book. Pattern may be understood as a design, plan or model. Pattern is a disposition of form, or a figure or design, repeated indefinitely. In this sense, we use the word 'pattern' in such a way as in the expressions: 'to fashion after a pattern', 'to make a pattern upon', etc.

But what is the pattern in a novel? Forster, in his *Aspects of the Novel*, says that pattern is that in a novel which 'appeals to our aesthetic sense'. He writes: "whereas the story appeals to our curiosity and the plot to our intelligence, the pattern appeals to our *aesthetic sense*, it causes us to see *the book as a whole*" (emphases added) [Forster, 152]. To illustrate his point, Forster says that the pattern of Anatole France's (1844-1924) *Thais* is that of an hourglass, because the two central *characters of the novel, at the end of it, change their initial statuses or positions as their initial situations change. Likewise, says he, the pattern of Percy Lubbock's (1879-1965) fictional *travelogue, *Roman Pictures*, is like a grand chain, because here the protagonist starts from one position or situation to another, and then to another, and so on, until he comes back to his initial position.

According to Kettle, pattern is intimately connected with life: "Pattern is the way life develops" [Kettle, I, 24]. He says that "pattern is something to be spread like marmalade on a given surface of life" [*op. cit.*, 15] and that "the good novel does not simply convey life; it says something about life. It reveals some kind of pattern in life" [*op. cit.*, 13]. And this pattern, says he, is the 'moral vision' of the writer: "the author starts with his pattern, his moral vision" [*op. cit.*, 16].

PEN. An international association of *P*oets, *P*laywrights, *E*ditors, *E*ssayists and *N*ovelists founded in 1921 by Mrs Dawson-Scott under the presidency of John Galsworthy (1867-1933). The principal purpose of the association is to promote co-operation among writers world-wide.

pen-name. An assumed name, also called *pseudonym, under which an author writes, chiefly for secrecy. Examples of pen-names are: George Eliot (pseudo. of Marian, or Mary Ann, Evans: 1819-80), Dr Seuss (Theodor Seuss Giesel: 1904-91), Ed McBain (Evan Hunter: b. 1926), Mark Twain (Samuel Langhorne Clemens: 1835-1910), Michael Angelo Titmarsh (William Makepeace Thackeray: 1811-63), etc. Perhaps, incidentally, the Danish philosopher Soren Kierkegaard (b. 1813) used the maximum number of pseudonyms, 14 in all: Victor Eremita, John the Silent, Constantine the Constant, John the Ladder, Anticlimax, Nicolaus Note-well, etc.

penny dreadful. A kind of cheap and popular thrilling, sensational and fearful adventure, crime or mystery *novel, *tale or serial sold at around one penny in the nineteenth century. It is also called *dime novel (particularly in America).

period novel. Edwin Muir, in his *Structure of Novel*, says that this kind of novel "does not try to show us human truth valid for all time; it is content with a society at a particular stage of transition, and characters which are only true in so far as they are representative of that society. It makes everything particular, relative and historical. It does not see life with the universalising imagination but with the busy, informing eye, aided by the theorizing intelligence" [Muir, 115]. In the period novel, the *chronicle hardly matters or not at all. Examples of this kind of *novel are: Arnold Bennett's (1867-1931) *Clayhanger* and John Galsworthy's (1867-1933) *The Forsyte Saga*. The bondage of the period novel to a certain period naturally degrades it.

periods of American literature. The divisions of the history of American literature are, briefly, shown below (of course they lack consensus among scholars) [Abrams, 204-10].

1607-1775. The **Colonial Period.** Philosophical, practical, historical and religious writings were scantily noticeable. In 1773, a collection of the poems of Phyllis Wheatley (c. 1753-84), an African slave girl, sold in Boston to John Wheatley, was published (when she was only around 20). This inaugurated black writings in America. The period from 1765 to 1790 is sometimes called the **Revolutionary Age.**

1775-1865. The **Early National Period.** The emergence of national imaginative literature. The first American comedy *The Contrast* by Royall Tyler (1757-1826) was published in 1787 and the first American novel by William Hill Brown (dates n. a.) *The Power of Sympathy* in 1789. The remarkable poets of this period include William Cullen Bryant (1794-1878) and Edgar Allan Poe (1809-49) and some of the front-ranking novelists of this period were Charles Brockden Brown (1771-1810), James Fenimore Cooper (1789-1851), Nathaniel Hawthorne (1804-64), Herman Melville (1819-91), Harriet Beecher Stowe (1811-96) and William Gilmore Simms (1806-70). The span from 1828 to 1865 is often identified as the Romantic Period in America and is sometimes called the *American Renaissance. The period also spans the Age of Transcendentalism.

1865-1914. The span from 1865 to 1900 is often called the Realistic Period. Two of the great poets of this period were: Walt Whitman (1819-92) and Emily Dickinson (1830-86). Notable dramatists of the period included: William Dean Howells (1837-1920), Henry James (1843-1916), etc. And some of the notable novelists of the period are: Mark Twain (1835-1910), William Dean Howells, Henry James, John De Forest (1826-1906), etc. It was in this period that we find a number of regional novelists and short-story writers, such as Mark Twain (on the Mississippi River region), Bret Harte (1836-1902) (on California), Sarah Orne Jewett (1849-1909) (on Maine), Mary Wilkins Freeman (1852-1930) (on Massachusetts), George W. Cable (1844-1925) and Kate Chopin (1851-1904) (both on Louisiana). The period, 1900-1914, is sometimes discriminated as the **Naturalistic Period**.

1914-1939. The period between the World Wars, which witnessed the great economic depression that began in 1929. It signaled the birth of modern literature and recorded the first recognition of American literature world wide. Important poets of this period include Edgar Lee Masters (1868-1950), Edwin Arlington Robinson (1869-1935), Robert Frost (1874-1963), Robinson Jeffers (1887-1962), Marianne Moore (b. 1887), T.S. Eliot (1888-1965), Edna Millay (1892-1950) and e. e. Cummings (1894-1962). The period produced the first great dramatist Eugene O'Neill (1888-1953). Among writers of prose *fiction of the period were Edith Wharton (1862-1937), Sinclair Lewis (1885-1951), Gertrude Stein (1874-1946), Sherwood Anderson (1876-1941), John Dos Passos (1896-1970), F. Scott Fitzgerald (1896-1940), William Faulkner (1897-1962), Ernest Hemingway (1898-1961), John Steinbeck (1902-68), etc. After the First World War disillusionment gripped across the country. In the 1920s, the pleasure-seeking flamboyant jazz culture and the ***Harlem Renaissance** rocked America.

It was in this period that some American writers left for London or Paris to seek 'for a richer literary and artistic milieu and a freer way of way'. They are collectively called the American expatriates or the **Lost Generation** (a term of Gertrude Stein). Some of them, later on, returned, others did not. The great economic depression of the period had sown the seed of radicalism in the minds of some writers in the 1930s and they include William Faulkner, John Dos Passos, Eugene O'Neill, etc.

1939-2000. This period was highly plethoric in germinating a number of strong literary currents or movements. Stalin's signing the Russo-German pact with Hitler in 1939 broke the illusion of communism and consequently literary radicalism of the 1930s in America gave way to freedom and humanism. The collapse of Russian communism and the dissolution of the Soviet Union intensified the urge for freedom and humanism. The ***New Criticism** fought out the conservative **Agrarians** of the South, who 'had championed a return from an industrial to an agricultural economy', and 'typified the prevailing critical tendency to isolate literature from the life of the author and from society and to conceive a work of literature, in formal terms, as an organic and autonomous entity'. Some of the New Critics are: T.S. Eliot, (1888-1965), Ezra Pound (b. 1885), Robert Penn Warren (b. 1905) and Cleanth Brooks (b. 1906). The New Criticism concentrated principally on poetry.

In the 1950s, which was the period of 'cultural conformity and complacency', a few literary movements were launched: the movement of the ***Beat Generation**, the movement of the Blake Mountain Poets, the movement of the New York Poets, etc. The 1950s saw the emergence of the literature of the *absurd and of confessional poetry. Likewise, the 1960s and 1970s saw the rise of counterculture marked by violent youthful protest against the prevailing culture and particularly by adoption of an attitude of extreme sexual candour. However, some of the prominent poets of the period were Marianne Moore, Robert Penn Warren, Theodore Roethke, Allen Ginsberg, Sylvia Plath, etc. and some of the dramatists were Thornton Wilder, Arthur Miller, Tennessee Williams, Edward Albee, etc. The writers of prose fictions of this period were Vladimir Nabokov (b. 1899; emigrated to America in 1940), Eudora Welty (b. 1909), Robert Penn Warren (b. 1905), Bernard Malamud (b. 1914), Saul Bellow (b. 1915), Norman Mailer (b. 1923), John Updike (b. 1932), Thomas Pynchon (b. 1937), John Barth (b. 1930), etc. The last phenomenon to emerge in the period is ***poststructuralism**. This was also the period when African-American literature began to emerge noticeably.

periods of English literature. One of the convenient ways of dividing the history of English literature chronologically into segments or periods is the following [Abrams, 210-17].

450-1066. The **Old English (or Anglo-Saxon) Period**. After the conversion of England in the seventh century, the level of culture and learning elevated, as a result of which poetry began to be popular side by side with some prose works. No drama, let alone *novel, came into sight.

1066-1500. The **Middle English Period**. Poetry continued to be put out but drama was not visible. Some prose *romances were produced, the most notable of which is Sir Thomas Malory's (d. 1471) *Le Morte Darthur*.

1500-1660. The **Renaissance** (or **Early Modern**) **Period**. This period may be divided into the **Elizabethan period** (1558-1603), the **Jacobean period** (1603-25), the **Caroline period** (1625-49) and the **Commonwealth period** (or the **Puritan Interregnum**) (1649-1660). Poetry and drama showed rapid and luxurious growth between 1500-1660 but yet no novel or any semblance of it was in view. Shakespeare was the brightest star of the

Elizabethan period besides Philip Sidney, Christopher Marlowe, Edmund Spenser, Ben Jonson, etc. The Jacobean period was adorned by John Donne, Ben Jonson, Francis Beaumont, John Webster, etc. The Caroline period produced such writers as John Milton, George Herbert, Sir Thomas Brown, etc. And the Commonwealth period saw the sad closure of public theatres (1642-1660) that sent the drama to the limbo for more than a decade.

1660-1785. The **Neoclassical Period**. This period may be divided into three 'sub periods': the **Restoration period** (1660-1700), the **Augustan period** (or the **Age of Pope**) (1700-1745) and the **Period of Sensibility** (or the **Age of Johnson**) (1745-85). Poetry and drama continued to entertain and instruct the people from 1660 through 1785, in the hands of such poets and dramatists as (in the Restoration period) Sir George Etherege, William Wycherley, William Congreve, John Dryden and Thomas Otway; (in the Augustan period) Alexander Pope; (in the period of Sensibility) Robert Burns, Dr Johnson and Oliver Goldsmith. Mrs Aphra (or Afra) Behn's (1640-89) *story, *Oroonoko or the Royal Slave*, published in 1688, (i.e., in the Restoration period) was truly an important precursor of the novel. In the Augustan period, Jonathan Swift (1667-1745) and Daniel Defoe (1660-1731) were the two most brilliant novelists. And in the period of Sensibility, Samuel Richardson (1689-1761), Henry Fielding (1707-54), Tobias Smollett (1721-71) and Laurence Sterne (1713-68) were great novelists.

1785-1830. The **Romantic Period**. This period is alternatively dated since 1789 (the outbreak of the French Revolution). Great poets adorned this period: William Blake, Lord Byron, P.B. Shelley, John Keats, etc. The vogue of drama virtually vanished; only a few dramas were produced. William Beckford (1759-1844), Mathew Gregory Lewis (1775-1818), William Godwin (1756-1836) and Mrs Anne Radcliffe (1764-1823) wrote excellent *Gothic *romances and notable novelists of the period were Jane Austen (1775-1817), Sir Walter Scott (1771-1832) and Mary (Wollstonecraft Godwin) Shelley (1797-1851).

1832-1901. The **Victorian period**. The beginning of this period is sometimes alternatively dated 1830 or 1837 (the accession of Queen Victoria; 1901 her death). For convenience of discussion, this period may be divided into: the period of the **Pre-Raphaelites** (1848-60) and the period of **Aestheticism and Decadence** (1880-1901). The Victorian period saw immense productions of excellent poetry and prose *fictions—drama still remaining in relative negligence. In the field of drama, a boost came in the shape of 1843 Theatre Regulation Act which marginalized the almost blanket ban on the theatre by the 1737 Licencing Act that forced Henry Fielding (1707-54) to leave drama and turn to novel. Yet, there appeared on the scene some worthy dramatists, such as Henry Arthur Jones (1851-1929), Arthur Wing Pinero (1859-1943), Oscar Wilde (1858-1900) and, of course, George Bernard Shaw (1856-1950). The Victorian period certainly produced a brilliant galaxy of poets: Alfred Lord Tennyson (1809-92), Robert Browning (1812-89), Elizabeth Barrett Browning (1806-61), Christina Rossetti (1830-94), Mathew Arnold (1822-88) and Gerard Manley Hopkins (1844-89)etc. Likewise, it also produced a good number of excellent novelists, such as Charlotte Bronte (1816-55), Emily Bronte (1818-48), Charles Dickens (1812-70), William Makepeace Thackeray (1811-63), George Meredith (1828-1909), Anthony

Trollope (1815-82), Thomas Hardy (1840-1928) and Samuel Butler (1835-1902). The two powerful literary movements of the Victorian period are *aestheticism and *decadence.

1901-14. The **Edwardian Period**. The period is so named after King Edward VII who reigned from 1901 (death of Queen Victoria) to 1910, and extends from 1901 to 1914 (beginning of World War I). Poets who flourished during this short period include Thomas Hardy (1840-1928), Alfred Noyes (1880-1958), W.B. Yeats (1865-1939) and Rudyard Kipling (1865-1936); noted dramatists who continued to write in this period include Henry Arthur Jones (1851-1929), Sir Arthur Pinero (1855-1934), Sir James Barrie (1860-1937), John Galsworthy (1867-1933) and G.B. Shaw (1856-1950; and the great novelists of this period include Thomas Hardy, Joseph Conrad (1857-1924), Ford Madox Ford (1873-1939), John Galsworthy, H.G. Wells (1866-1946), Rudyard Kipling and Henry James (1843-1916).

1910-36. The **Georgian Period**. It is clear from our account that this period overlaps the previous (Edwardian period) by four years, end to beginning. This period covers the whole span of the reign of King George V, i.e. from 1910 to 1936. The group of poets known as *Georgian poets* belong to this period— such minor ones as Rupert Brooke (1887-1915), Walter de la Mare (1873-1956), Ralph Hodgson (1871-1962), W.H. Davis (1871-1940) and John Masefield (1878-1967). Drama fell into relative indifference. The novelists of this period consist of E.M. Forster (1879-1970), Joseph Conrad, D.H. Lawrence (1885-1930), Ford Madox Ford, Aldous Huxley (1894-1963), Virginia Woolf (1882-1941), etc.

1914—. The **Modern Period**. [For the features and the novelists of this period see *modernism and *modern period.] Some of the important poets of this period are W.B. Yeats, Wilfred Owen, T.S. Eliot, W.H. Auden, Robert Graves, Dylan Thomas and Seamus Heaney, and some dramatists who flourished in this period are G.B. Shaw, Sean O'Casey, Noel Coward, Samuel Beckett, Harold Pinter, Caryll Churchill, Brendan Behan, Frank McGuinness and Tom Stoppard.

1945—. See *postmodernism.

peripeteia or peripety [from Greek *peri*, around, and *piptein*, to fall]. The term denotes a sudden change or reversal of the fortune of a (usually the chief) *character, or of his circumstances, in a drama, that brings in his tragic downfall (in a tragedy) or happily restores his former brighter fortune (in a comedy). Peripeteia or peripety is sometimes used synonymously with **coup de theatre* and may be applied, by extension, in the case of a *novel.

persiflage. A light, flippant, inconsequential talk or writing; or banter; or a non-serious manner of dealing with a *theme or subject-matter.

persona [from Greek *persona*, mask]. Originally, the term denoted an artificial template of a face worn by ancient Greek actors. Later on it came to denote a *character or assumed identity or fictive 'I' in a drama or poem or *novel. Marlow in Joseph Conrad's (1857-1924) *Heart of Darkness*, for instance, is a persona. The plural form of the term is personae.

perspective. See *focalisation and *point of view.

phallocentrism [from Greek *phallos*, penis]. A term of *feminist criticism, given currency chiefly by Julia Kristeva (b. 1941) and Helene Cixous (b. 1937), both of whom violently opposed the prevalent binary oppositions, such as male/female, masculine/feminine, in literary criticism and elsewhere. The term signifies a system (of society, culture, etc.) in which the phallus (the male genital organ) is held to be a *symbol and source of power. In a phallocentric *novel, such as those of Ernest Hemingway (1898-1961), male *characters, and not female ones, have the upper hand, particularly for their macho features, and there male characters generally hold female characters as their sex objects.

phantasy. Same as *fantasy.

pharmakos. "The character in an ironic fiction who has the role of a scapegoat or arbitrarily chosen victim" [Frye, 367].

phatic communion. A term introduced by the British-Polish anthropologist Malinowski "to refer to communication between people which is not intended to seek or convey information but has the social function of establishing or maintaining social contact" [Richards, 214]. Phatic communion is the "minimal communicative activity which has no obvious consequence save to inform all concerned that the channels are in good working condition for the transmission of more 'important' messages" [Hockett, 585]. When a telegrapher clicks his key for a little while just to draw the attention of the operator on the other end and tell him that the channel is in good working condition, he is in phatic communion with him. Examples of phatic communions are such expressions as *How are you?*, *Nice day, isn't it?*, etc. Phatic communion plays an important role in human social activities.

phenomenological criticism. Phenomenological is a branch of philosophy that was introduced by the German mathematician Edmund Husserl (1859-1938). Its objective is to map out the essential structure of consciousness that bestows meaning to our concrete experience or phenomenon, devoid of all inauthentic associations of meanings accrued to it through history. When we see a fountain pen, for instance, and call it a pen, we bestow the object pen the name or meaning of 'pen', as determined by our consciousness. But what are the basic features of a pen? This is a difficult question. Changes in the size, colour, etc. to certain limits will not make the pen look like something else; it will still be pen. What, then, determines the 'penness' of the different versions of the pen (as a result of the changes in the size, colour, etc.)? The answer must be: our consciousness, or, to be specific, the structure of our consciousness. Husserl's endeavour was to discover this structure of consciousness trans-subjectively.

Maurice Merleau-Ponty, and, especially, Roman Ingarden, Hans-Georg Gadamer, Hans Robert Jauss, etc. employed Husserl's trans-subjective method of enquiry in the field of literary criticism. Their objective was to investigate and understand the underlying nature and essence of a literary work and to get access to the author's consciousness in order to chart its structure during the time of composition of that piece of literary work. This is phenomenological criticism that was practised by the Geneva School of critics or the 'Critics of Consciousness'. "Geneva [School of] critics regard each work of literature as a fictional world that is created out of the *Lebenswelt* [life world] of its author and embodies the author's unique mode of consciousness. In its approach to literature as primarily subjective, this criticism is opposed to the objective approach of *formalism*, both in its European variety and in American *New Criticism*. Its roots instead go back through the nineteenth century to that type of romantic *expressive criticism* which regarded a literary work as the revelation of the personality of its author, and also proposed that the awareness of this personality is the chief aim and value of reading literature" [Abrams, 221]. Also see *formalism, *Russian formalism, *New Criticism, *expressionism.

phonocentrism. See *logocentrism.

picaresque novel [from Spanish *picaro*, rogue]. The Spanish *picaro*, from which the term is derived, is a rogue, an outcast, an *anti-hero (if he is the *protagonist in a *novel, or in a drama as in Dale Wasserman's *Man of La Mancha* and Roger Miller's *Big River*). A picaresque novel is one in which the protagonist is like a *picaro*. Usually its structure is episodic and it deals with low-life. Examples of the picaresque novel are: Spanish Mateo Aleman's (1547-?1614) *Guzman de Alfarache*, French Alain-Rene Lesage's (1668-1747) *Gil Blas*, Daniel Defoe's (1660-1731) *Robinson Crusoe*, Mark Twain's (1835-1910) *Adventures of Huckleberry Finn* and Henry Fielding's (1707-54) *Tom Jones* (partially).

pinchbeck writing. Pinchbeck is a yellow alloy that much simulates gold. It contains copper and much less zinc than brass. Figuratively, pinchbeck, as an adjective, means sham or false in taste. The term pinchbeck writing signifies a sort of writing that is sham or false in taste, or not genuine.

plagiarism. The term denotes a literary theft. A writer who does it, i.e. steals from another writer's works (ideas, *plots, thoughts, etc.) without the latter's consent or knowledge and publishes the stolen items as his own is called a plagiarist or plagiary. If plagiarism in any form or amount is to be depreciated is debatable, for even some famous writers have resorted to plagiarism. For instance, Edmund Spenser (?1552-99) freely borrowed from other epics for his epic poem *The Faerie Queene* and T.S. Eliot used many thoughts, images as well as expressions in a number of his poems, and even forcefully argued for such borrowings in his article 'Tradition and Individual Talent'. S.T. Coleridge (1772-1834) was also a great (creative) plagiarist [Lefebure, 13].

Plagiarism should be distinguished from *literary forgery. In literary forgery, a writer professes his own writing to have been done by some other writer. For instance, James Macpherson (1736-96) claimed that his epic poems, *Fingal: An Ancient Epic Poem*, *Temora: An Ancient Epic Poem* and *The Works of Ossian* (all the three were actually his own original creations), were merely his translations of the works of the 3rd century legendary warrior and bard Ossian (or Oisin). S.T. Coleridge (1772-1834) was also a great (creative) plagiarist.

***plaisir*.** See *jouissance.

plot. A term of highly varied status. As is generally understood, plot is a scheme or *pattern or arrangement of connected events running through a *novel or play. *The Concise Oxford Dictionary of Literary Terms* defines plot as "the *pattern of events and situations* in a narrative or dramatic work, as *selected* and *arranged* to emphasize relationships—usually of *cause and effect*—between incidents and to elicit a particular kind of interest in the reader or audience, such as surprise or suspense" (emphases added) [Baldick, 170]. The plot is a (a) pattern of events and situations (b) which are selected (c) and then arranged (d) to show the cause-and-effect relationships between them. And these four components of the plot distinguish it from the *story. The story is a chronological or sequential statement of imagined *events that we may construct from the plot of a *narrative or play (there, of course, are stories outside a narrative or play, indistinguishable from such a story). It may be noted here that E.M. Forster (1879-1970), in his *Aspects of the Novel*, laid the central emphasis on the causal relationship between events or incidents while differentiating plot from *story: "Let us define a plot. We have defined a story as a narrative of events arranged in their time-sequence. A plot is also a narrative of events, the emphasis falling on causality. "'The king died and then the queen died,' is a story. 'The king died, and the queen died of grief,' is a plot" [Sarker, 1084]. We may take another example of the grammar of plot (not Forster's): boy meets girl; boy loses girl; boy wins girl. Forster further tells us that the story requires of the reader the drive of 'curiosity'; the plot requires of him 'intelligence and memory also'.

The story may be taken to be the raw material of the plot. The plot is the skeleton, the story the sinews, guts, etc. The story is the texture, the plot the pattern, the design. In a narrative (a novel or short-story), of course, the two cannot be separated; the plot resides in the story. The same story may be displayed on different plots. The French poet and novelist Raymond Queneau (b. 1903), for instance, wrote 99 versions (plots) of the same story in his *Exercises in Style*. Aristotle called the plot *mythos*, which term is now rarely used. But Aristotle's *mythos* (which he conceived of only in the drama, narratives being non-existent then) or plot is more than arrangement of events, for "he assigned to plot the most important function in a drama, as a governing principle of development and coherence to which other elements (including character) must be subordinated" [Baldick, 171]. However, the plot may be firmly woven or loosely structured, and when the plot is absent, the narrative is episodic.

Is the plot (or, for that matter, the story) essential for the narrative? Modern novelists and critics answer in the negative. "Since the 1920s, a number of prose fiction and drama—building on the example of Laurence Sterne's *Tristram Shandy*, so early as 1759-67—have deliberately designed their works to frustrate the expectations of chronological order, coherence, reliable narration, and resolution that the reader or auditor has formed by habituation to traditional plots; some writers have even attempted to dispense altogether with a recognizable plot" [Abrams, 227]. The truth of this quotation is reinforced by the literature (novel, drama) of the *absurd, *modernism and *postmodernism. Also see *covert plot, *overt plot, *sub-plot.

plot types. There may be various types of *plots. However, Helen McNeil, in an essay (*Quarto*, May 1991), has spoken of five main types of plots of *fictions or *novels (interestingly, all based on types of heroines):

(i) *Pamissa type*: named after Samuel Richardson's (1689-1761) two novels, *Pamela*, and *Clarissa Harlowe*: 'a desirable but low-status heroine who has to resist the hero's advances until he has proposed marriage.'

(ii) *Cinderella type*: 'a fantasy of class and derivation of the governess plot found in Bronte's Jane Eyre (1847).'

(iii) *Rebecca type*: 'also a fantasy of class. The second wife or girlfriend is a quiet mousy type who has to live up to the sexual aggression of her predecessor.'

(iv) *Masquerade type*: 'the heroine finds herself in a situation where she pretends to be married/engaged to her social superior.'

(v) *Bartered Bride type*: 'the heroine is traded, usually by her father, to a man she hates but eventually comes to love and respect' [Hawthorn, 252].

plurisignation. A critical term that denotes the ability of a word, passage, etc. to carry with it more than one significations or meanings or levels of *meaning. Cognate terms are: *allegory, *allusion, ambiguity. Also see *four levels of meaning.

poem novel. Same as *verse novel, *novel-in-verse. Also see *poet novelists.

poetic justice. A term coined by the critic and historiographer Thomas Rymer (?1643-1713) in his *The Tragedies of the Last Age Consider'd and Examined by the Practice of the Ancients and by the Common Sense of All Ages*. It signifies a writer's dispensing of justice to different *characters by allocating happy or unhappy fates to them, being dictated only by the absolute moral principle or absolute moral sense and not by the laws or mores of different lands. Poetic justice occurs rather frequently in poetic, narrative or dramatic compositions (such justice is found rarely in real life). For instance, in Jane Austen's (1775-1817) *Pride and Prejudice* each one of the five Bennet daughters marries exactly the sort of man she justifiably deserves, in accordance with the degrees of their virtues or vices.

poet novelist. A writer who is a poet but chiefly a novelist, such as Henry James (1843-1916), James Joyce (1882-1941), Virginia Woolf (1882-1941), D.H. Lawrence (1885-1930), etc. Likewise, a writer who is a dramatist but chiefly a novelist is called a *dramatist novelist, such as Henry James, Henry Fielding (1707-54), etc. [G.B. Shaw (1856-1950) was a novelist dramatist].

point de capiton [from French *point*, point; *de*, of; and *capiton*, silk-flock, stuffing]. Literally, the term means 'point of stuffing' or 'quilting point'. The term was coined by the very influential psychoanalyst after Sigmund Freud, Jacques Lacan (b. 1901), to express his concept of 'quilting' which concept is utilized in literary criticism. Slavoj Zizek illustrates the concept of *point de caption* thus: "He [Zizek] is writing about a scene in Alfred Hitchcock's 1940 film *Foreign Correspondent*. In a scene from this film which is set in Holland, the hero notices that the arms of one of a number of windmills is rotating in a different direction from those of the others, Zizek comments: 'Here we have the effect of what Lacan calls the *point de capiton* (the quilting point) in its purest: a perfectly 'natural' and 'familiar' situation is denatured, becomes 'uncanny', loaded with horror and threatening possibilities, as soon as we add to it a small supplementary feature, a detail that 'does not belong,' that sticks out, is 'out of place,' does not make any sense within the frame of the idyllic scene'" [Hawthorn, 265].

pointillism, *pointillisme* [from French *pointille*, dotted, stippled]. The terms denote 'in printing, the use of separate dots of pure colour instead of mixed pigments' for obtaining a special effect not achievable otherwise. In literary criticism, the term can be employed to refer to the use of "tiny, even sub-liminal, effects which nevertheless contribute subtly to the poetic total" [Rodway, 183].

point of attack. The point or *moment in a play or *narrative at which the main *action starts or the *plot begins.

point of turning. The point or *moment of *climax or *crisis, in a play or *narrative, at which the *action or *plot takes a turn towards a different direction.

point of view. The term refers to the position of the *narrator in a *novel or narrative text from where he narrates his *story or describes the *characters. The matter of point of view is very important in *narratives. Percy Lubbock, in his *The Craft of Fiction* writes: "The whole intricate question of method, in the craft of fiction, I take to be governed by the question of the point of view—the question of the relation in which the narrator stands to story" [Lubbock, 251]. The term 'point of view' is synonymous with the terms 'account' and 'perspective'—'perspective' presently being more preferred. Thus the *first-person point of view in a story may also be called the first-person account or the *first-person perspective, and thus there may be second-person account or *second-person perspective and *third-person account or *third-person perspective. Again, a narrative done from the first-person point of view may also be called *first-person narrative, and thus there may also be *second-person narrative and *third-person narrative.

In the *first-person narrative, the *narrator is a character within the narrative, and he refers to himself as 'I'. He looks at the other characters from outside and sees only their *externals* (manners, movements and actions) and describes them as he does the situations—he cannot enter into their consciousnesses. He is 'only a fortuitious witness and auditor of the matters he relates'. Examples of the first-person narrators are: Ishmael in Herman Melville's (1819-91) *Moby-Dick*, Nick in F. Scott Fitzgerald's (1896-1940) *The Great Gatsby*, Marlow in Joseph Conrad's (1857-1924) *Heart of Darkness*, etc. In the second-person narrative, "the story gets told solely, or at least primarily, as an address by the narrator to someone he calls by the second-person pronoun 'you' [who is the *narratee]" [Abrams, 234]. "This second person may turn out to be a specific fictional character, or the reader of the story, or even the narrator himself , or not clearly or consistently the one or the other; and the story may unfold by shifting between telling the narratee what he or she is now doing, has done in the past, or will or is commanded to do in the future" [*loc. cit.*]. Examples of the second-person narratives are: Michel Butor's (b. 1926) *Second Thoughts*, Italo Calvino's (b. 1923) *If on a Winter's Night a Traveller*, etc.

The narrator of the third-person narrative may have two sorts of point of view: the *limited point of view* and the *omniscient point of view*. In both the cases, of course, he tells the story in the third person. In the case of his having the limited point of view, the narrator (unlike the narrator of the first-person narrative or the narrator of the second-person narrative) stays inside the confines of the consciousness of a single character or the consciousness of a *limited* number of characters, alternately, and describes his (or their) perceptions, thoughts, remembrances, feelings, etc. as an observer and reporter. The narrator, of course, is one character in the story. In Henry James's (1843-1916) *The Ambasadors*, for instance, Lambert Strether, the narrator, alternately frequents the consciousnesses of the other characters, like a **flaneur*, and describes them. This view of the narrator is called limited because he views only the inside of the consciousness of a character and not also the character's outside. In course of time, the limited point of view contributed to the development of the *stream-of-conscious method.

This limitation is not present in the omniscient narrator who "knows everything that needs to be known about the agents, actions, and events, and has privileged access to the characters' thoughts, feelings, and motives; also (that the narrator) is free to move at will in time and place, to shift from character to character, and to report (or conceal) their speech, doings, and states of consciousness" [*op. cit.*, 232]. He is omniscient because he is both inside and outside all the characters. Traditionally, his reports are trusted as *authoritative*. If he also comments and evaluates the characters' actions and motives, he is called the *intrusive narrator*. Most novels of the greatest novelists from Jane Austen (1775-1817) and Charles Dickens (1812-70) to Leo Tolstoy (1828-1910) and Thomas Hardy (1840-1928) have been written from the *omniscient point of view, i.e. the stories of those novels have been told by *omniscient narrators. Sometimes, novelists switch from one point of view to another, and this called *shifting of view-points*. Many modern writers have resorted to *multiple points of view*.

police procedural. The term denotes a *sub-genre of the *detective novel, detective story. "Police procedurals deal realistically with crime from the point of view of the police and how they solve crimes and catch criminals. The central figure is a professional police officer (such as Commander Gideon)" [Cuddon, 683]. Police procedurals have been popular in the USA and Britain. Major writers of this sub-genre in Britain have been John Creasey (1908-73) (who, under the pseudonym of J.J. Marric, wrote the Commander Gideon series of 21 police procedurals), Maurice Procter (1906-73), Michael Gilbert (b. 1912), Jonathan Ross (b. 1916), John Wainwright (b. 1921) etc. And the major authors of America are: Elizabeth Linnington (b. 1921), Ed McBain (b. 1926), etc. The term should not be confused with *crime fiction.

polyphonic novel ['polyphonic' from Greek *poly*, much, and *phone*, sound, voice]. The term literally means 'many-voiced' and was introduced into literary criticism by Mikhail Bakhtin (1895-1975) when he was about to identify the *novels of Fyodor Dostoevsky (1821-81) as 'many-voiced'. What Bakhtin writes about the novels of Dostoevsky will explain the term polyphonic novel: *"A plurality of independent and unmerged voices and consciousnesses, a genuine polyphony of fully valid voices is in fact the chief characteristic of Dostoevsky's novels*. What unfolds in his works is not a multitude of characters and fates in a single objective world, illuminated by a single authorial consciousness; rather a *plurality of consciousnesses, with equal rights and each with its own world*, combined but are not merged in the unity of the event" [Hawthorn, 266]. Also see *dialogic.

polyphonic prose ['polyphonic' from Greek *poly*, much, and *phone*, sound, voice]. A term coined by John Gould Fletcher (1886-1950). It refers to a kind of poetic prose (printed as prose) that betrays many of the attributes of verse, such as assonance, alliteration, tuneful rhythm, elaborate cadence, and even rhyme and return—the so called 'voices' of poetry. Polyphonic prose was first developed by the American poet Amy Lawrence Lowell (1874-1925). Lowell, of course, got the idea of polyphonic prose from the French poet Paul Fort (1872-1960).

popular novel. A loose term for a *novel with a wide readership, or a *best-seller novel. It often carries a slightly pejorative insinuation since a wide readership frequently includes a majority of common readers or since its authors have in most cases been mediocre. Some of the British writers of popular novels are: George Warwick Deeping (1877-1950; *Love among the Ruins*); Robert Howard Spring (1889-1965; *O Absalom*!); Dornford Yates (1885-1960; *Maiden Stakes*); etc.

pornography [from Greek *porne*, a whore, and *graphein*, to write, to draw]. The term literally means 'description or portrayal of prostitutes and prostitution'. In literary discourse, it denotes a writing that lays emphasis on sexual matters with the intention of only arousing sexual excitement. Pornographic writings are of two sorts: *erotica* and *exotica*. Erotica deals nakedly with normal heterosexual physical activities and exotica deals unabashedly with all sorts of deviationist sexual activities. Pornography should not be confused with eroticism, for eroticism utilises sexual impulse for spiritual or the other socially approvable purposes. "Lawrence [D.H. Lawrence (1885-1930)], for example, saw eroticism as an essential element in human relations and as a reassuring contrast to the sterility of the modern environment; the surrealists discovered in the erotic evidence of the central role of intuition and evidence of that reconciliation of opposites which was their chief aim" [Fowler, Roger, 189]. Indian Tantric religion also finds a portal to spirituality in eroticism. However, the matter of pornography in literature is debatable (recall the *case* in the High Court judgment of 1960 in favour of D.H. Lawrence's *Lady Chatterley's Lover*). Also see *erotic literature.

postcolonialism, postcolonial studies. Postcolonialism is a nebulous and difficult term, particularly because the meaning of the word 'colony' is a matter of debate, for once in the past even Britain and America, for instance, were colonies—the former of Rome, the latter of Britain. Likewise, there is also no agreed definition of the term 'post colonial studies'. However, what M.H. Abrams says in the following quotation may significantly explain the term 'postcolonial studies'. About the term he writes that it is "The critical analysis of the history, culture, literature, and modes of discourse that are specific to the former colonies of England, Spain, France, and other European imperial powers. These studies have focused especially on the Third World countries in Africa, Asia, the Caribean islands, and South America. Some scholars, however, extend the scope of such analyses also to the European discourse and cultural productions of such countries as Australia, Canada, and New Zealand, which achieved independence much earlier than the Third World countries. Postcolonial studies sometimes encompass also aspects of British literature in the eighteenth and nineteenth centuries, viewed through a perspective that reveals the extent to which the social and economic life represented in the literature was tacitly underwritten by colonial exploitation" [Abrams, 236].

The term 'postcolonialism' first got currency from the Palestinian-American Edward Said's influential book *Orientalism* (New York: Pantheon, 1978), though the concept of *orientalism can be discerned even in Joseph Conrad's (1857-1924) slim novel *Heart of Darkness* (1902). Conrad's *Heart of Darkness*, says Said in his *Culture and Imperialism*, masterfully betrays the attitude of the imperial Occident towards the people of the Orient, or, simply, the quintescence of Orientalism (i.e., the imperial West's sense of their superior and central culture as against the inferior culture of the Orient). Said writes in that book of his that the "imperial attitude, is, I believe, beautifully captured in the complicated and rich narrative form of Conrad's great novella *Heart of Darkness*"

[Rice, 372]. "1974, however, saw the beginning of the formal dissolution of the European colonial empires and the granting of independence after world-wide campaigns of anti-colonial resistance. The contemporary colonial situation begins, therefore, in 1947, though postcolonialism as a discourse and theoretical space is not named until 1978" [Rice, 360]. Postmodernialism does not denote a single object, or space for discourse, but two: "Like 'postmodernism', the term has come to refer both to a *condition* (here postcoloniality) and to the *discourses which theorise that condition*" (emphases added) [*loc. cit.*]. The postcolonial condition or postcoloniality refers to the zealous reactive attitude of the peoples of the earlier colonies towards the imposed culture of the imperialists over them, and an enthusiastic urge to promptly return to their native ancient cultures. On the other hand, 'the discourses which theorise that condition' refer to the imperialists' discourse (or scholarship) that treats the colonial cultures as the inferior cultural *Other, taking their own culture to be superior and to be the model that they think the colonial and cultural Other should emulate.

postmodernism. A rather vague, difficult and disputed term, especially regarding two questions about it: is postmodernism a new phenomenon or but a continuation and proliferation or furtherance of *modernism? And, if a new phenomenon, when actually did it begin? Regarding the first quiry, critics are divided between the two alternative answers contained in the question. And regarding the second quiry, too, they hold diverse opinions: some say postmodernism began since the conclusion of WWII, some others rather vaguely say that it came into being in the 1940s, and yet some others allow it to start in the 1950s. On the other hand, Jean-Francois Lyotard (1924-98), a philosopher of the Frankfurt School, has a somewhat queer theory. In his book *The Postmodern Condition*, Lyotard says that "*Post modern* would have to be understood according to the paradox of the future (*post*) anterior (*modo*)" [Rice, 337]. That is, according to him, postmodern is not 'after' (*post*) modern, but 'future' (*post*) modern(*modo*) or what has not yet happened or what is likely to happen.

Regarding the nature of the postmodern, Lyotard writes in the same book: "The postmodern would be that which, in the moderns puts forward the unpresentable in presentation itself; that which denies itself the solace of good forms, the consensus of a taste which would make it possible to share collectively the nostalgia for the unattainable; that which searches for new presentations; not in order to enjoy them but in order to import a stronger sense of the unpresentable. A postmodern artist or writer is in the position of a philosopher: the text he writes, the work he produces are not in principle governed by preestablished rules, and they cannot be judged according to a determining judgement, by applying familiar categories to the text or to the work. Those rules and categories are what the work of art itself is looking for. The artist and the writer, then, are working without rules in order to formulate the rules of what *will have been done*. Hence the fact that work and text have the characters of an *event*; hence also they always come too late for their author, or, what amounts to the same thing, their being put into work, their realization (*mise en oeuvre*) always begins too soon. Now we repeat *post modern* would have to be understood according to the paradox of the future (*post*) anterior (*modo*)" [*loc. cit.*]. The elements that make a literary work postmodern (a term of Frank Kermode) or that are the constituents of postmodernism have been listed by Malcolm Bradbury and James Farlane. They write about postmodernism: "The term is acquiring high currency now to talk about a compound of that art of chance or minimalization, that 'literature of silence', in which, as in Beckett or Borges, the idea of absurd creation, random method, parody or self-exhausting fictionality is paramount; of the new *chosisme*, which expands to include not only the *nouveau roman* in France but the non-fiction novel in Germany and the States, where facts, objects or historical events are placed in the context of questioning narrative; of multi-media forms, like the happening or the street theatre; and of anti-retionalistic anti-art of psychedelics, pornography, and revolutionary outrage" [Bradbury, 34].

The postmodern space or world is qualitatively different from the modern space, even if we admit that the former is a continuation of the latter, and so "where a modernist artist or writer would try to wrest a meaning from the world through myth, symbol or formal complexity, the postmodernist greets the absurd or meaningless confusion of contemporary existence with a certain numbed or flippant indifference, favouring self-consciously 'depthless' works of fabulation, pastiche, bricolage, or aleatory disconnection" [Baldich, 175]. The other features of the postmodernist literature include *magic realism, masochistic horror, neo-Gothic imagination, the influence of the Freudian and Jungian psychoanalyses, effect of the burgeoning *feminism, proximity to *post-structuralism, impact of the Marxist thoughts, *deconstruction and of some revolutionary theories of philosophy, some desired achievements of vigorous linguistic experiments, the influence of the uncertainty principle of Heisenbergian physics and William James's theory of *stream-of-consciousness, etc. Post-modernism, in brief, wants "to subvert the foundations of our accepted modes of thought and experience so as to reveal the meaninglessness of our existence and the underlying 'abyss,' or 'void,' or 'nothingness' on which any supposed security is conceived to be precariously suspended" [Abrams, 168-69]. As stated before, according to some, postmodernism carries some of the features of modernism to their extremes, but maintaining some difference from it all the same. Jeremy Hawthorn writes: "those modernist characteristics which may produce postmodernism when taken to their most extreme forms, would include the rejection of representation in favour of self-reference—especially of a 'playful' and non-serious, non-constructive sort; the willing, even relieved, rejection of artistic aura and of the sense of the work of art as organic whole (...); the substitution of confrontation and teasing of the reader for collaboration with him or her; the rejection of 'character' and 'plot' as meaningful or artistically defensible concepts or conventions; even the rejection of meaning itself as a hopeless delusion, a general belief that it is not worth trying to understand the world—or to believe that there is such a thing as 'the world' to be understood. Postmodernism takes the subjective idealism of modernism to the point of solipcism, but rejects the tragic and pessimistic elements in modernism in the conclusion that if one cannot prevent Rome burning then one might as well enjoy the fiddling that is left open to one" [Hawthorn, 216].

Some of the postmodernist writers are: Samuel Beckett (b. 1906), Vladimir Nabokov (b. 1899), Thomas Pynchon (b. 1937), Italo Calvino (b. 1923), William S.

Burroughs (b. 1914), Angela Carter (b. 1940), etc. (If, however, the matter of the period (1945 onwards) is ignored and only the features of postmodernistic literature is counted, such works as the fictions of Franz Kafka (1883-1924), Knut Hamsun's (1859-1952) *Hunger*, Ezra Pound's (b. 1885) 'Cantos' and Laurence Sterne's (1713-68) *Tristram Shandy* may as well be called postmodern.) Also see the *absurd, *anti-hero, *metafiction, *new novel, *anti-novel, *poststructuralism, *postmodern period, *modernism.

postmodern period. There is no agreed opinion about the beginning and the end of the period but generally the period is believed to begin after the conclusion of the WWII when the 'late capitalism' drastically changed the human condition, and, perhaps, the period still continues. For the features of this period see *postmodernism. Some of the notable novelists of this period are: Henry Green (pseudo. of Henry Vincent Yorke: b. 1905), George Orwell (pseudo. of Eric Blair: 1903-50), Ivy Compton-Burnett (1892-1969), Elizabeth Bowen (b. 1899), Samuel Beckett (b. 1906), Anthony Powell (b. 1905), Arthur St. John Evelyn Waugh (1903-66), William Golding (b. 1911), J.R.R. Tolkein (b. 1892), Kingsley Amis (b. 1922), Graham Greene (b. 1904), Brain-Moore (b. 1921) and Angela Carter (b. 1940). Also see *postmodernism.

poststructuralism. Based on Ferdinand de Saussure's *Course in General Linguistics* (1915), Claude Lavi-Strauss, in the 1950s launched structuralism that found a sort of *structure* (formation, pattern or texture) common among the language, kinship relations, mythology, religion, etc. of a given society, the structure depending on hierarchical and binary opposition (for instance, of food; savoury vs sour, permitted vs tabooed, to be taken simultaneously vs to be taken successively, etc.). Structuralism found *meaning*, in the fields of literature, social phenomena and human activities in the abstract codes or signs that govern every social activity. It rejected mimetic theory of literature (that says that literature is the mimicry or imitation of reality) and the expressive theory of literature (that says that literature expresses the emotion and imagination of the author) and treated a text merely as an objective structure which 'activates various [social] codes and conventions which are independent of the author, reader, and external reality'. It wanted, or rather 'pretended' to establish a 'scientific objectivity' that would provide more or less *fixed, stable, and universally valid meanings*.

Poststructuralism appeared in the 1970s as a reaction against structuralism's false assurance of this scientific attitude and success as regards meanings. It rejected the possibility of a text's fixed, stable meaning, and emphasised the indeterminacy of a text's meaning, denying the existence of any fixed abstract structure of codes or signs in any society. Poststructuralism got its basic ideas and continuous support from Jacques Darrida's *deconstruction. It developed parallelly with *postmodernism in literature and art. M.H. Abrams writes: "poststructuralists undertake to subvert the foundations of language in order to show that its seeming meaningfulness dissipates" [Abrams, 169].

The salient features of poststructuralist thought are, succinctly, the following:

(i) It rejected the structurality of *structuralism as well as the *logocentrism of Western thought. It denied any fixity of meaning and thus denies the traditional mode of thinking.

(ii) It discarded the traditional concept of the author or the human *subject*, in line with structuralism which "had already tended to divest the subject of operative initiative and control, evaluating the purposive human agent into a mere location, or 'space,' wherein the differential elements and codes of a systematic *langue* precipitate into a particular *parole*, or signifying product" [*op. cit.*, 239]. Poststructuralism decenters or diffuses the author—the subject.

(iii) Poststructuralism, like it did the author, also rarefied, dispersed the reader and the text. "The decentering or deletion of the author leaves the reader, or interpreter, as the focal figure in poststructural accounts of signifying practices. This figure, however, like the author, is stripped of the traditional attributes of purposiveness and initiative and converted into an impersonal process called 'reading'. What this reading engages is no longer called a literary 'work' (since this traditional term implies a purposive human maker of the product); instead, reading engages a 'text'— that is, a structure of signifiers regarded merely as a given for the reading process" [*op. cit.*, 240]. According to poststructuralism, the meaning of a text is never stable but shifts, varies, modifies, changes depending on the nature of the interplay between the different sorts of 'location' or 'space' that the 'reader' is and the collocation of signifiers that is the text.

(iv) The poststructuralists erased the boundary between a literary text or 'writing' and non-literary modes of signification, and subsumed the two under the name 'general text' or, simply, *discourse*. And, "they conceive of discourse as social parlance, or language-in-use, and consider it to be both the product and manifestation not of a timeless linguistic system, but of particular social conditions, class-structures, and power-relationships that alter in the course of history" [*op. cit.*, 241].

(v) Lastly, the poststructuralists believed that 'no text means what it seems to say, or what its writer intended to say.' They believed that the surface, manifest or overt meaning of a text is actually a 'disguise' or 'mask' of the underlying real meaning of it, the real meaning being distorted by the self-conflicting nature of language itself, the psychic compulsions of the writer, and the social power-structure, material realities of history, and such other things of the society and time in which the text was written, etc.

Poststructuralism had had an aggressive vogue during the 1970s and 1980s in the fields of linguistics and literary criticism, after which it, to an extent, lost its edge.

potboiler. A literary work or art work done merely to keep the pot boiling, i.e. to procure the bare necessities of life. A hack-work or literary drudgery. Also see *Grub Street, *hack, *kitsch.

povest [from Russian *povest*, fiction]. The term denotes a kind of Russian fictional narrative which deals with the facts of a single individual or incident in terse and compressed words and expressions. The *povest* is comparable with **Novelle*, **recit*. Alexander Pushkin's (1799-1837) *Povesti Belkin* (*povesti* is plural of *povest*) are notable examples of *povest*. In Bulgarian literature, *povest* refers to a long short-story.

practical criticism. A term that is almost synonymous with *new criticism and is derived from I.A. Richards's (1893-1979) book *Practical Criticism* (1929). The main objective of practical criticism is to analyse a poem quite objectively—"without any information about its authorship, date, or circumstances of composition" [Baldick, 176].

***preciosite*, preciosity** [*preciosite* from French *preciosite*, precious, preciosity, affected]. The two terms denote a sort of writing that is mannered and laboured in style as well as too refined in diction or language. The terms are frankly derogatory. Moliere (1622-73), in his *Les Precieuses*, bitterly satirised *preciosite*.

presence [from French *presence*, presence, appearance]. The present existence of the communicator is presence; his present non-existence is *absence. In speech, the speaker is present, i.e. in speech there is presence. In writing, on the other hand, the writer (in a sense the speaker) is absent, i.e. in writing there is absence. All these Ferdinand de Saussure discussed in *Course in General Linguistics* (1916), where he also privileged speech over writing. The presence is the *centre and the source of authenticity of the meaning of speech.

primitivism. The term denotes the belief that the life of the primitives in the natural setting was morally and eudaemonically better than the life in civilisation, unnaturalised, faked, corrupted and alloyed as the latter has been. Votaries of primitivism include: Rousseau (see *noble savage), William Wordsworth (1770-1850), Mark Twain (1835-1910), Ernest Hemingway (1898-1961), etc. They extolled the simplicity, honesty and goodness of the primitive 'untutored' man.

privilege. The word has lately acquired enhanced importance in literary criticism. "The verb *to privilege* and cognate noun and adjectival forms are frequently used by recent theorists to indicate a hierarchical structuring of causal factors. To privilege gender , for instance, in a consideration of class and gender in historical change, then, is to suggest that gender is more influential than class in historical causality" [Hawthorn, 278].

problem novel. A *novel that deals specifically with a particular problem; for instance, with the problem of education or with the problem of inter-caste marriage. For example, Thomas Hardy's (1840-1928) *Jude the Obscure* is a problem novel, for it deals with the 'deadly war waged between flesh and spirit'. Also see *propaganda novel, *sociological novel.

prochronism. The term denotes dating of an event before the right time, i.e. setting an event at a time when it did not happen, and only after that time did it do. Sometimes *fiction writers set their plots prochronistically. Mark Twain's (1835-1910) fiction *A Connecticut Yankee in King Arthur's Court* is an example of prochronistic fiction. Also see *anachronism.

Professorenroman [from German *Professoren*, professorship, and *Roman*, novel]. The term literally means 'professorship novel', but as a critical term it denotes a kind of *novel (generally historical novels or novels with academic subjects) that displays uncommon erudition but no appreciable re-creative *imagination—a kind of novel that is not accessable to the general reader.

projection character. The word 'projection' in this term has been borrowed from Sigmund Freud's psychoanalysis where it means "the process by which specific impulses, wishes, aspects of the self, or internal objects are imagined to be located in some object external to oneself" [Rycroft, 125-26]. The projective character is that *character into whom the author projects, casts, throws traits of his character or aspects of his own self. In Thomas Hardy's (1840-1928) *Jude the Obscure*, for instance, Jude Fawley is a projection character, in so far as Hardy has supposedly projected his own conflict between flesh and spirit into Jude.

prolepsis. Same as *flashforward.

proletarian novel. ['proletarian' from Latin *proletarius*, a citizen (in the ancient Rome) who belonged to the sixth and lowest class and who had to serve the state not with his property but with his offspring (*proles*)]. The term denotes a *novel whose *theme is based on the life of the working-class people, sometimes for propaganda purposes. A good example of the proletarian-novel is Walter Greenwood's (b. 1903) novel *Love on the Dole* which deals with the problems of unskilled workers and unemployment in the early 1930s. Also see *documentary novel, *thesis novel, *novel of doctrine, *propaganda novel.

prolixity. Use of periphrases, circumlocutions or long and wordy expressions while dwelling unnecessarily too long on particulars in writing or speaking.

prologue. The introductory section, and not the concluding section or *epilogue, of a literary work—a poem, a drama or, rarely, a *novel.

promythium. See *epimythium.

propaganda novel. A kind of *novel that intends to argue in favour of some ideology, principle or action. Upton Sinclair's (1878-1968) *The Jungle*, dealing with the meat-packing industry in Chicago, for instance, is a propaganda novel. Also see *thesis novel.

prophecy. Prophecy, as a critical term, has been introduced by E.M. Forster (1879-1970) through his critical book *Aspects of the Novel* (1927). He has not employed the term 'in the narrow sense of foretelling the future' but in a much wider sense. He writes in the same book: "Prophecy—in our sense—is a tone of voice. It may imply any of the faiths that have haunted humanity—Christianity, Buddhism, dualism, Satanism, or the mere raising of human love or hatred to such a power that their normal receptacles no longer contain them" [Forster, 129]. Forster says that the prophetic *character or the character with a prophetic vision is one who reaches out to the whole compass of humanity—he magnifies himself spiritually to an extent we cannot ordinarily conceive of, and he does this, as if, by melting himself into the whole of humanity through love and pity—the two that conjointly demand rejection of the lightness of humour as well as imbibing of maximal humanity. Ordinary men may recognise the prophet to be a laughing stock, a butt of satire, but the grave, who is impleted with pity for others, only will recognise the prophet's prophetic vision, hear his voice. Forster, for instance, calls Fyodor Dostoevsky (1821-1881) a prophetic novelist. Mitya, a character in Dostoevsky's *The Brother Karamazov*, is a prophetic character, because just before his execution (near the close of the *novel) 'felt that a passion of pity [for the poor poor folk standing before him in his imagination], such as he had never known before, was rising in his heart [so that] he wanted to cry'.

propriety. See *decorum.

prose rhythm. Like verse or poetry, good prose has also rhythm or what John Dryden (1631-1700) once called the 'other harmony of prose'. Good prose betrays reccurance of accents though not at regular intervals, like verse or poetry does, but, all the same, as in a good verse or poetry, in good prose also there is a constant flow of accent, the flow changing its pattern every now and then.

protagonist. See *hero, heroine.

provincialism. *The Oxford Companion to the English Language* defines the term thus: "A usually pejorative term for a lack of social and linguistic sophistication regarded as typical of provinces and provincials, and for a word or other usage that is not accepted in the capital or the main cultural centre(s) of a nation" [McArthur, 819]. Provincialism plays a great part in the dialogues of some *regional novels.

pseudonym. Same as *pen-name.

psychoanalytical criticism, psychological criticism. The objective of psychological criticism is to ascertain how far a work of literature expresses the (conscious) motives and the personality traits of its author. M.H. Abrams writes: "Psychological criticism deals with a work of literature primarily as an expression, in fictional form, of the state of mind and the structure of personality of the individual author" [Abrams, 247]. Psychological criticism upholds the expressive theory of literature or *expressionism in both art and literature as against the *mimetic theory of literature*, according to which art or literature only mimics the reality, or the *pragmatic theory of literature* which says that the principal aim of literature is to serve some practical need. Psychological criticism had its predominance in the early decades of the nineteenth century, though it is as old as Aristotle (384-322 B.C.) who in his *Poetics* psychologically explained the healthy effect of tragedy with the concept of *catharsis. In the early nineteenth century, when the surge of Romanticism was flushing the whole of England, psychological criticism, along with expressive theory of literature, ruled supreme. S.T. Coleridge in his celebrated *Biographia Literaria* (1817), for instance, psychologically explained the creative faculty in literature. "Psychological speculation in English criticism continues through the 'appreciative' but subtle essays of Swinburne and Peter, and into T.S. Eliot's major work on the relations between the writing of poetry and the presence of tradition" [Fowler, 193].

But the place of psychological criticism was not very long afterwards overtaken by psychoanalytical criticism—the sort of criticism that was built up on the foundation of the psychoanalytical theory of Sigmund Freud (1856-1939) and, later on, principally on that of Jacques Lacan (b. 1901). Freud's most important discovery was that most of human activities are controlled or influenced by the unconscious part of mind and that talking out the suppressed and repressed contents of the unconscious cures neurosis. Freud said that the contents of the unconscious (will, emotion, etc.) are ever struggling for coming out and appearing before the conscious part of the mind through *symbols (especially in dreams). Psychoanalytic or psychoanalytical criticism is also known as *Freudian criticism. "Broadly speaking, so-called Freudian Criticism or classical psychoanalytic criticism—which is often speculative—is concerned with the quest for and discovery of (and subsequent analysis of) connections between the artists (creators, artificers) themselves and what they create (novels, poems, paintings, sculptures, buildings, music, etc.). As far as literature is concerned it analyses characters 'invented' by authors, the language they use and what is known as 'Freudian imagery'. Thus in the Freudian method a literary character is treated as if a living human being; whereas, for example, in the method of Jacques Lacan literature is seen as a 'symptom' of the writer" [Cuddon, 332].

psychic distance, psychological distance. See *aesthetic distance.

psychological novel. A kind of *novel that is concerned less with the exploration of the externalities of the principal characters than with the exploration of their internal psychological (spiritual and emotional) states. The *theme or subject of such a novel is generally the conflict(s) between the internal aspects of its principal character(s). The psychological novel, is less interested in building up a *plot and describing actions of *characters than in analysing the characters themselves. As regards technique, the psychological novel often inclines towards the *stream-of-consciousness technique and the technique of *interior monologue. Examples of the psychological novel are Virginia Woolf's (1882-1941) *To the Lighthouse* (psychological conflict between Mr Ramsay and Mrs Ramsay or between male and female principles, worked up through stream of consciousness technique) and Fyodor Dostoevsky's (1821-81) *Crime and Punishment* (internal or psychological conflict of the protagonist expressed mainly through interior monologue). Also see *stream-of-consciousness novel.

puffery. The term refers to the sort of criticism in which an author is unjustly over praised or is puffed up in laudation ('to puff' is to blow).The term, however, is not derived from the verb 'to puff' but from the character, Mr Puff, in Richard Sheridan's (1751-1816) play *The Critic*, who is a bogus and verbose critic.

pulp fiction, pulp novel. Both are pejorative critical terms denoting third-rate, cheap *fictions or *novels printed on inexpensive paltry paper made out of wood pulp. During and before the First World War, pulp fictions were very popular, particularly in America,—fictions such as *detective stories, *horror stories, *science fictions, *sentimental romances, etc. Also see *shilling shocker, *penny dreadful.

punch line. The final sentence or conclusion of a humorous short *story or joke in which the meaning or point of the story or joke lies and which has an unexpected twist that has a more or less powerful impact (the 'punch' of the story or joke). An example of punch line is the following: "A Catholic known for his drinking asks his priest, 'Father, what's sciatica?' The priest, sensing an opportunity, describes sciatica as a foretaste of hell, specially visited on drunkards. 'Why do you ask?' he finishes, and the sinner replies (*punch line*), 'Because they're saying in the pub the Pope's got it.'" McArthur, 824].

pure novel. A term used by Andre Gide (1869-1951). The pure *novel is devoid of all the elements that are strictly not essential for a novel. Gide wrote: "I should like to strip the novel of every element that does not specifically belong to the novel. Just as photography in the past freed painting from its concern for a certain sort of accuracy, so the phonograph will eventually no doubt rid the novel of the kind of dialogue which is drawn from the life and which realists take so much pride in. Outward events, accidents, traumatisms, belong to the cinema. The novel should leave them to it. Even the descriptions of the characters do not seem to me properly to belong to the *genre*. No; this does not seem to me the business of the *pure* novel" [Ellmann, 127]. Also see *experimental novel.

purism. A rather derogatory term denoting excessively scrupulous observance of purity or correctness in language and *style generally adhered to, and professed by, precisionists and pedagogues. Also see *preciosite, preciosity.

purple passage, purple patch. A stretch of writing (in prose or verse) that stands out from its context by its hightened *style, due to liberal use of select diction, alliterations, assonances, rhyths, repetitions, metaphors and other rhetorical devices, colourful descriptions, etc. as well as a sudden picking up of tone and emotional intensity. An example of purple patch in verse may be found in Shakespeare's *Richard II* (II, i. 40ff) where John of Gaunt eulogises England:

> This royal throne of kings, this scept'red isle,
> This earth of majesty, this seat of Mars,
> This other Eden, demi-paradise....

And an instance of purple passage in prose is to be found in Walter Pater's description of *Mona Lisa* in his essay on Leonardo da Vinci in *The Renaissance* (1873). The term purple patch or purple passage, however, generally bears a pejorative undertone.

purport. Literally, the term means 'meaning conveyed; substance, gist, tenor'. But as a critical term, it is sometimes supposed to have a range of meanings: meaning, *mode, kind, internal intention of a work or the conscious intention of its author, etc. If the author of a work purported his work, for instance, to be didactic, the work's meaning, mode or kind is didactic; but not always, for sometimes there may be a discrepancy between the purport and the mode of a work, because there may be a discord or divergence between the conscious intention of the author (his purport) and his unconscious performance (his *implication* or his departure from that purport). "For instance, Milton's *Paradise Lost* certainly purports to be on God's side, indeed specifically to be justifying the ways of God to Man. And everything we know of Milton's life and opinions suggests that such a purport represents his conscious intention. Yet Blake held that he was on the Devil's side without knowing it, and Shelley thought he was deliberately attacking Christianity under the guise of defending it. And it is at least arguable that as a defeated rebel, cast (doubly) into darkness, Milton had a subconscious sympathy with Satan that caused a discrepancy (especially in the early books) between purport and mode—the discrepancy itself being the implication glimpsed in tone, mood, and matters of diction" [Rodway, 185].

putative author. An alleged author (not the real author) under whose name a work has been published, the real author, here, being the ghost author or *ghost writer.

Q

quattrocento [from Italian *Quattro*, four, and *cento*, hundred]. The term literally means 'four century or hundred', but Italians use the term for 'fourteen hundred or century'. The English numerical system is *ordinal* while the Italian numerical system is *cardinal* so the English 'fifteenth century' is Italian 'fourteenth century'; that is, *quattrocento* even in English will mean 'fifteenth century'. Consequently, *quattrocento* will refer to the Italian fine arts and literature of the *fifteenth century* and will refer to the early works of such great artists of the Italian Renaissance as Leonardo, Michelangelo, Raphael, Giorgione and Ariosto. In the same way, *seicento* (though in Italian means 'six hundred or century', in Italian actually means 'sixteen hundred or sixteen century') in English refers to the *seventeenth century* mode of Italian art and literature. The anglicized form of *seicento* is secento, and that of *seicentismo* is secentismo, i.e. the **Zeitgeist* or artistic and literary attitude of the seventeenth century Italy. Secentismo was a reaction against *classicism and was a counterpart of the *baroque. It favoured **preciosite*, flamboyance, stylistic conceits, the *taste for the bizarre and the extravagant, etc.

queer theory. The term "is often used to designate the combined area of gay and lesbian studies and criticism, as well as theoretical and critical writings concerning all modes of variance (such as cross-dressing) from the normative model of biological sex, gender identity, and sexual desires" [Abrams, 254].

quest narrative. "In Anne Cranny-Francis's definition, a linear narrative in which temporal sequence is taken to signify material causation. She uses this as the dominant structure in nineteenth- and twentieth-century Western writing, a structure which carries a particular ideological and political charge, for it privileges linear sequence rather than, say, seasonal cycles, and thus underwrites dominant discourses in our [Western] culture" [Hawthorn, 286]. "There are significant differences in the way in which heroes and heroines experience the quest in traditional (non-feminist) narrative. The hero is active in the quest, overcoming difficulties and aided by helpers, whereas the heroine is passive (is often the object of quest), has to endure suffering and humiliation, and rather than overcoming the world has to learn to adapt to its demands (as these are mediated by men)" [*loc. cit.*]. Also see *narrative.

quod semper quod ubique [from Latin *quod*, which; *semper*, always; and *ubique*, everywhere]. The Latin phrase literally means 'which always, which everywhere' and is held in all times and all places to be the hallmark of any great literature: great literature is that which is always and everywhere rated as such by general consensus or belief (*omnibus creditum*).

quotation title. The term denotes the title of a book that is actually a phrase quoted or borrowed (in toto or slightly modified) from an earlier work by a famous writer. The intention behind the quotation title is to evoke an association in the mind of the reader with that earlier work in order to provide him with a presumption about the essence of the present work. Examples are: E.M. Forster's (1879-1970) *Where Angels Fear to Tread* (taken from a line in Alexander Pope's *Essay on Criticism*: 'For fools rush where angels fear to tread'); W. Makepeace Thackeray's (1811-63) *Vanity Fair* (taken from the name of the town—Vanity—in which a fair was held by Beelzebub, Apollyon and Legion in John Bunyan's (1628-88) *The Pilgrim's Progress*); Ford Madox Ford's (1873-1936) *Ladies Whose Bright Eyes* [taken from John Milton's *L' Allegro* (1. 121)]; William Faulkner's (1897-1962) *The Sound and the Fury* [taken from Shakespeare's *Macbeth* (V, v, 27)]; Aldous Huxley's (1894-1963) *Eyeless in Gaza* [taken from John Milton's *Samson Agonistes* (l. 41)]; etc.

R

Rabelaisian. The term denotes the literary features of the French satirist, comic writer and author of *Pantagruel* and *Gargantua* Francois Rabelais (c. 1490-1553), particularly his ribald humour and fantastical and exuberant sort of imaginative writing.

raconteur [from French *raconteur*, to tell, relate or narrate]. The term denotes a teller of anecdotes (feminine form is *raconteuse*).

Rahmen [from German verb *rahmen*, to frame (a picture, etc.)]. The term literally means a 'frame', but as a critical term it signifies a *frame story. "There are two basic forms of frame story technique: the *zyklischer* or 'cyclic' and the *Einzelrahmen* or 'single frame'. The former combines a series of stories into a unified entity; the latter constitutes a self-contained story linked to the frame by a narrator" [Cuddon, 724]. Also see **Rahmenerzahlung*.

Rahmenerzahlung [from German *Rahmenerzahlung*, framework story, story within a story]. The term denotes a *frame story which contains either a single story within itself or multiple stories (more than a single story). Examples of *Rahmenerzahlung* are Ovid's (43 B.C.-17/18 A.D.) *Metamorphoses*, Boccaccio's (1313-75) *Decameron*, the anonymous *The Arabian Nights*, etc. Also see **Rahmen.*

raisoneur [from French *raisoneur*, one who reasons]. In drama, the *raisoneur* is a sort of *chorus character through whom the dramatist expresses his own views, for instance the waiter William, in G.B. Shaw's *You Never Can Tell*, who reasons that always it is the unexpected that happens and so you never can tell. The *raisoneur* of this sort is also present in *novel. The term is synonymous with *confidant.

rasa [from Sanskrit *rasa*, juice, flavours, feeling or emotion]. The term refers to the traditional Indian aesthetic theory according to which there are nine desirable feelings/emotions that we get from literature or art. These are: erotic, heroic, furious, piteous, comic, fearful, repulsive, marvelous, and peaceful.

ravissement [from French *ravissement*, rapture, to carry away by violence, to rape]. A term introduced by Ronald Barthes. Lynne Pearce (1997) says that it denotes those 'sexual/textual pleasures' which apply to "'the emotional field associated with that euphoric first connection between "self" and "other" in which the amorous subject (reader) is swept away on a tide of abandonment, joy and devotion to the loved object (text)'" [Hawthorn, 288]. Also see **plaisir*, **jouissance.*

readerly text. See **lisible*.

reader-response criticism, reader-response theory. This sort of criticism or theory came into being in the 1960s and first of all outright rejected the traditional view that the meaning of a text is ingrained there in the text itself, finished, complete, and the only task of the reader is to unearth it for his consumption; i.e. the reader-response criticism or theory rejected the text-oriented theories of meaning expounded by formalism and new criticism, and in their stead believed that the meaning of a text evolves out of the interaction between the text and the reader or out of the reading process. The 'real' text (not the printed matters of the so-called text) has no existence; it is born as soon as the reader reads the printed matters of the so-called text and so there is no meaning in the so-called text, or, rather, there is only a *potential* meaning. J.A. Cuddon writes: "fundamentally, a text, whatever it be (poem, short story, essay, scientific exposition), has no real existence until it is read. Its meaning is *in potentia*, so to speak. A reader completes its meaning by reading it. The reading is complementary; it *actualizes potential meaning*. Thus, the reader does not have, as has been traditionally thought and accepted, a passive role; on the contrary, the reader is an active agent in the creation of meaning. By applying codes and strategies the reader decodes the text" [Cuddon, 726]. The reader-response criticism or theory says that there is no 'correct' meaning of a text, because each individual reader understands or decodes the text in his own way depending on his personal expectations, experiences, etc. However, reader-response criticism or theory is only a general term for a number of critical theories, the most common factor among all of them being their emphasis on the stand that the meaning of a text only evolves out of the continual interactions between the text and the reader, decodings, expectations, modifications of decodings and expectations of the individual reader as he progresses with his reading, etc. being the determinants of the evolved meaning. Wolfgang Iser's *The Act of Reading* (1978) and Umberto Eco's *The Role of the Reader* (1979) are among the best works on reader-response criticism or theory.

realism. A philosophical and critical term that is 'exceptionally elastic' with a range of significations. Philosophically, it carries two fundamental meanings: in scholastic philosophy, it was a term contradictory to nominalism, signifying that universals have real existences; but in modern philosophy it is a term contradictory to idealism, professing that physical objects are quite independent of our perceptions, and that physical objects have real existences. In literature, on the other hand, realism denotes "a mode of writing that gives the impression of recording or 'reflecting' faithfully an actual way of life" [Baldick, 184]. Realism is thus far apart from idealization, from any tendency to beautify the reality when it is not beautiful (but when it is so, it may be portrayed thus). Of course, mystical or visionary writings may be treated as realistic only if we believe in supernatural beings, but yet, in that case, such writings should better be considered not as realistic but as super-realistic. "On the whole one tends to think of realism in terms of the everyday, the normal, the pragmatic. More crudely, it suggests jackets off, sleeves rolled-up, a 'no nonsense' approach." [Cuddon, 728]

Realism was generally the established tradition in the nineteenth century *novels of England, America, France and Russia, as is evident in the works of such writers as (of England) Jane Austen (1775-1817); George Eliot (1819-80); Anthony Trollope (1815-82); (of America) W.D. Howells (1837-1920); Henry James (1843-1916); (of France) Stendhal (1783-1842); George Sand (1804-76); Honore de Balzac (1799-1850); Gustav Flaubert (1821-80); (of Russia) Ivan Turgenev (1818-83) and Leo Tolstoy (1828-1910). Realism is to be observed also in the plays of the late nineteenth century and early twentieth century, particularly in those of Henrik Ibsen (1828-1906) and G.B. Shaw (1856-1950). Realism has generally always been the standard of film and television dramas. Also see *romanticism, *naturalism, *veritism, *social realism, *realistic novel.

realistic novel. A mode of *novel that faithfully reflects the actual way of life without any attempt at idealisation, or distortion (as in some modern experimental novels). The realistic novel may be said to be the novel proper. Also see *realism.

rear-mirrorism. The term has a suggestion to the rear-view mirror, i.e. the mirror that is fitted with a vehicle to show what is behind it. Rear-mirrorism signifies "the tendency of new media to be constrained by the limits of existing media when first introduced, and to take time to find their potentialities fully exploited" [Hawthorn, 294].

reception theory. A theory about how readers' responses change over a course of time. Apparently, it may seem similar to the *reader-response theory but while the reader-response theory focuses on the response of a *single reader* to a text at a *particular time*, the reception theory is concerned with altering responses, i.e. interpretations and evaluations, of the *general reading public* about a particular text or literature in general *over the course of time*. In fact, there is no particular theory called reception theory; the reception theory rather signifies "a branch of modern literary studies concerned with the ways in which literary works are received by readers" [Baldick, 185] or a "school of theory which is associated particularly with the University of Konstanz and the journal *Poetik and Hermeneutik* (published in 1964)" [Cuddon, 733]. One of the foremost theorists of the reception theory was Hans Robert Jauss.

rechauffe [from French *rechauffer*, to warm over, to heat up]. The term etymologically or literally means a heated-up dish or a dish made from reheated left-overs. But as a critical term *rechauffe* denotes a literary work that is actually a rehash or re-working of previously used materials. The term is obviously pejorative. Also see *pastiche, *collage.

***recherché*.** [from French *recherché*, search, quest, particular choice]. The term etymologically or literally means something that is carefully sought out. In the 18th and 19th centuries, in English the term was used to mean a refined or dainty dish, or exquisite clothes, but to-day, as an adjective, it means 'out-of-the-way, exotic, rare'.

recit [from French *recit*, story, narrative, yarn]. The *recit* has an intermediary position between the *novel and the **nouvelle*. Typically, the *recit* is a highly compressed *narrative around a single *theme with a very few heavily focused *characters. The *recit* is related by a self-effaced *narrator (one of the characters) in the first person without interfering into the progression of the narrative with a view to explaining the motives of the characters, passing judgments on their *actions, drawing a conclusion at the end, etc. Unlike in the novel, the *events in a *recit* "are depicted by an oblique, reflective and associative method" [Cuddon, 734]. The *recit* may be (and generally is) as short as the *nouvelle* but also may be as long as the novel of moderate length. It is mostly ironically structured. Examples of the *recit* are: Albert Camus's (1913-60) *La Chute* (*The Fall*), Samuel Beckett's (1906-89) *Malone Dies* and Andre Gide's (1869-1951) *L'immoraliste* (*The Immoralist*), *La* *symphonie pastorale* (*Two Symphonies*), *Isabelle*, *Robert*, *Genevieve*, *Thesee*, etc. Gide is considered as one of the notable writers of *recits*.

redaction. Editing or revising a work for publication.

redskin. See *pale face.

reflector, reflector character. The reflector or reflector *character is alternatively called the focaliser. For focaliser see *focalisation.

reflexive novel. The term denotes the kind or form of *novel that reflects, or turns back, upon itself, i.e. the kind of novel which is self-referential. The reflective novel tells us that its author or *narrator is writing a novel (a novel within another) which reflects, represents, manifests or expresses the novel proper (the outer novel). It is one "in which the author calls the reader's attention to the fact that he or she is writing (or has written) a novel" [Cuddon, 735]. Examples of the reflexive novel are: Laurence Sterne's (1713-68) *The Life and Opinions of Tristram Shandy, Gentleman* (in which Tristram attempts an autobiographical novel mimicking the main novel), Andre Gide's (1869-1951) *Les faux-monnayeurs* (in which the character, Edouard is writing a novel mimicking the main novel), etc. The reflexive novel, briefly, is self-referential or self-conscious.

refunctioning. Refunctioning (re-functioning) is using or appropriating a work of literature, at a date much later than the date of its production, for purposes other than that for which its author wrote it. Refunctioning "is a translation of the German term *Umfunktionierung*, which was used by certain left-wing German writers and critics of the 1930s (Bertolt Brecht and Walter Benjamin in particular) to suggest the way in which works of art and literature could be constantly put to diverse uses. Such writers rejected the view that literary works were 'timeless', stressing the historical conditions of their production and reception; but they also dismissed the notion that literary works belonged only to their historical moment, and that their meaning was 'exhausted' by what they meant to their contemporaries" [Fowler, 2001, 203]. An example of refunctioning is Bertolt Brecht's (1898-1956) "attempt to produce Shakespeare's politically conservative *Coriolanus* for socialist audiences and socialist political ends" [*op. cit.*, 204].

regional literature. A category of literature that emphatically and displayingly utilizes the manners, mores, moralities, habits, customs, thoughts, beliefs, dialects, dresses, social structures, etc. plus the historical background of the people of a certain geographical area as well as the topography, environment, etc. of that geographical area *not merely as *local colours but as important factors of the life of the people*. The regional novel, is an important part of regional literature.

regional novel. The regional *novel belongs to the *regional literature, for it carries with it the features of the regional literature in toto. Generally, a writer of the regional novel chooses a rural or provincial area for his *setting or *locale. Examples of the regional novel are: Thomas Hardy's (1840-1928) *'Wessex' novels; William Faulkner's (1825-79) *'Yoknapatawpha County' (in Mississippi) novels; Maria Edgeworth's (1767-1849) *Castle Rackrent*, *Belinda* and *The Absentee*; Arnold Bennett's (1867-1931) *Anna of the Five Towns*; etc. Some other regional novelists are: Lady Morgan (1776-1859), John Galt (1779-1839), Sir Walter Scott (1771-1832), etc. Interestingly, Stella Dorothea Gibbons (b. 1902) wrote a witty burlesque about the country life parodying the regional novel in her successful novel *Cold Comfort Farm*.

register. The term refers to the specific features of a particular kind of language belonging to a definite social situation or a particular profession or a certain way of life. *Longman Dictionary of Applied Linguistics* defines the term as "A speech variety used by a particular group of people, usually sharing the same occupation (e.g., doctors, lawyers) or the same interests (e.g., stamp collectors, baseball fans)." "A particular register often distinguishes itself from other registers by having a number of distinctive words, by using words or phrases in a particular way (e.g., in tennis deuce, love, tramlines, van), and sometimes by special grammatical constructions (e.g., legal language)" [Richards, 242]. Scientific language, i.e. the language used in expressing scientific concepts, for instance, is a particular register, and so are religious, journalistic, formal and such other languages are different registers.

relativism. In aesthetics, the theory that value judgement is subjective in nature, and that it may differ from person to person as well as from time to time. Relativism is opposed to *absolutism.

Renaissance [from Italian *rinascenza*, rebirth, or from French *renaissance*, rebirth]. The historical period to which the term is ascribed has never been clearly defined, but generally it is presumed to have begun in the later part of the 14th century and continued till the end of the 16th century, and perhaps even a little later. By the rebirth imputed to Renaissance is understood primarily the revival of interest in classical Greek and Roman literatures, conceiving them as glorious models of aesthetics for imitation and directions of human conduct, "but it quickly progressed from mere imitation of past glories to the expression of its own enlightened interest in exploration, science, nature, and man the individual" [Russell, 210]. In the Renaissance period, English poetry and drama achieved excellence, but it was barren of English *fiction. The great *Elizabethan period (Queen Elizabeth reigned: 1558-1603) of English literature falls within the range of Renaissance. Renaissance stressed both sense and sensibility.

replevin [from Old French *plevir*, to pledge]. The verbal form of the term is 'replevy' which, as a legal term, means 'to recover, or restore to the owner (goods distrained) upon pledge to try the right at law'. Replevin means replevying. As a literary term replevin "denotes an inquiry intended to secure for a writer recognition which has been denied" [Cuddon, 743].

resolution. The term generally refers to drama, but is sometimes also used as regards *fictions and *short stories. It denotes those *events which occur (in *Freytag's Triangle) between the *crisis or *climax and the *catastrophe. It may be said to be the outcome of the climax, and is synonymous with *falling action or *denouement.

Restoration period. The time frame from 1660, the year of the restoration of Charles II to the throne of England, to 1685, the year of his death and succession of King James II, or to 1700, the end of the century. Like the Elizabethan period or the *Renaissance period, the *Restoration period also witnessed huge production of dramas and was almost barren of novelists—the only notable fiction writer of this period was Samuel Butler (1835-1902), the author of *The Way of All Flesh*.

retrospection. Same as *analepsis, *cutback, *flashback, *switchback.

retroversion. Same as *retrospection.

rhetorical criticism. A kind of criticism which, *ceteris paribus*, differs from other sorts of criticism in that it concentrates on how and how far a work of literature is successful in imposing certain desired (rational or emotional) effects upon the reader. Briefly, the rhetorical criticism is interested chiefly in the mode of literary communication from the author to the reader. It began since the 1950s.

rhozzum. A term of unknown origin denoting a kind of short humorous *yarn about a gullible neighbour or local character.

risqué [from French *risqué*, risky, hazardous]. In literary criticism, the word is used in its rather narrower sense of 'on the verge of impropriety, especially in being sexually suggestive' [Ayto, 266].

rising action. See *Freytag's Triangle.

Ritter und Rauberroman [from German *Ritt*, ride (on a horse); *Ritter*, knight; *und*, and; *Rauber*, robber; and *Roman*, novel]. The term literally means 'knight and robber novel'. "As the term suggests, such novels were tales of adventure and daring-do; basically historical novels, which were elaborately contrived, melodramatic and sensational" [Cuddon, 756].

rhythm. The term literally means 'regular recurrence, especially of stress or long and short sounds' or 'a pattern of recurrence'. It generally applies to verse but there may be rhythm also in prose which is called *prose rhythm. In his *Aspects of the Novel*, E.M. Forster (1879-1970) has demonstrated that there is (sort of) rhythm even in the *novel. He has borrowed the term from music where it means repetition and variation, though in the novel the repetitions and variations are not so regular as in the music's 'diddidy dum'. He has illustrated the concept of rhythm showing that in Marcel Proust's (1871-1922) works there are instances of the 'diddidy dum' with variations. But it could be done with the help of his own novels. For example, "In *Where Angels Fear to Tread* we come across a few things which recur, but they recur with variations. Lilia marries for the second time but her second marriage is different from her first; Philip and Miss Abbott go to Italy twice, but their second journey brings for them quite different experiences; etc." [Sarker, 401].

Robinsonade. "The German term for stories which derived from Defoe's ever popular *The Life and Strange and Surprising Adventures of Robinson Crusoe* (1719). The first German translation appeared the following year and there were numerous imitations. Among the notable examples were Johann Schnebel's *Die Insel Felsenburg* (1731-43), Johann Campe's *Robinson der Jiingere* (1779-80) and Johann Wyss's *Der schweizerische Robinson* (1812-27)" [Cuddon, 756].

rococo [probably from French *rocaille* (pronounced rokay), rock-work]. The term literally means 'a style of architecture, decoration, and furniture-making prevailing in Louis XV's [1710-74] time, marked by ornamental details unrelated to structure, and unsymmetrical and broken curves, a freer development of the baroque.' In literary discourse, the term denotes a style of florid writing of the 18th century England that is distinguished by its lightness, gaity, elegance, gracefulness as well as flourishes of wit, imagination, verbal dexterity and twirling chicanery. Also see *baroque.

rogue literature. The kind of literature which deals with the underworld lives of criminals, near criminals and other condemnable people, such as thieves, cutpurses, beggars, vagrants, loafers, con-men, etc.—in short, the Autolycuses of this world. Examples of rogue literary works are: Robert Greene's (c. 1558-92) *A Notable Discovery of Coosnage*, Thomas Dekker's (c. 1570-1632) *Lanthorne and Candle-light* and Jean Genet's (b. 1910) *Journal du voleur* (*Thief's Journal*: 1964). Rogue literature enjoyed popularity in the 16th and 17th centuries.

roman [from French *roman* novel, romance; or from German *Roman*, novel]. Originally, the French word *roman* meant a common or ordinary language as opposed to Latin, but in course of time the word came to denote a *novel (or an extended work of *fiction). M.H. Abrams writes: "The term for the novel in most European languages is roman, which is derived from the medieval term, the romance. The English name for the form, on the other hand, is derived from the Italian novella (literally, 'a little new thing') which was a short tale in prose" [Abrams, 190]. Also see *romance, *novella, **roman a clef*, **roman de these*, **roman documentaire*, *romanesque, **roman-feuilleton*, **roman-fleuvre*, **roman noir*.

roman a clef. Same as **livre a clef*.

roman a tiroir [from French *roman*, novel; *a*, of; and *tiroir*, episode]. The term literally means 'novel of episode' or 'episodic novel'. *Roman a tiroir* denotes a *novel that comprises a series of very loosely connected *episodes and has no obvious common *theme or themes among those episodes. A noteworthy instance is Alain-Rene Lesage's (1668-1747) *picaresque novel *Gil Blas*.

Romance, romance, *romance* [from Spanish *romance* (pronounced approximately *ro-mahn-thay*, with the middle syllable stressed and the last very short), a particular language; or from French *romance*, love-song, melody, sentimental ballad; or from Latin *romanice*, in (popular) Roman language]. A confusing term having more than one meanings: (i) in Spanish, the term *romance* referred to the 'romance languages', such as vernacular French, Italian, Spanish, Rumanian, etc.; (ii) in French, the term *romance* meant and means love-song, melody or sentimental ballad; (iii) in English, the word Romance (cap. R) means what *romance* in Spanish means (see i); and (iv) in English, the word 'romance' (lower case 'r') means a tale of chivalry, originally in verse or any fictitious *narrative in prose or verse 'which passes beyond the limits of ordinary life'. However, in English, again, in its modern sense, the term romance denotes the type of *novel that is concerned not so much with analysis of *characters as with *actions, not so much with *legend as with *fiction, and not so much with understanding the actualities of life as with escaping life itself. In the 13th century all sorts of adventure *story written in verse were called romances. Gradually verse was replaced by prose, and romances continued to be in moderate demand. "In the 19th c. three very different novelists wrote a large number of works which can be variously classified as kinds of romance. They were Sir Walter Scott, Nathaniel Hawthorne and George Meredith" [Cuddon, 761]. Romances continued to be produced and consumed also in the 20th century, and Joseph Conrad (1857-1924) was perhaps the best 'romancer': "There is nothing airy or 'faery' about Conrad's novels but many would probably agree that Conrad was a supreme 'romancer', especially in *Lord Jim* (1900), *Romance* (1903) and *The Shadow Line* (1917). No one knew better than Conrad how to relate an extraordinary and improbable tale of adventure. He is an expert in dealing with the exotic, the remote and the extravagant" [*op. cit.*, 762]. In the 20th century also a few novelists attempted to reconcile romance and *realism; for instance H.G. Wells (1866-1946) in *Kipps*, *Tono-Bungay* and *The History of Mr Polly*.

***roman cycle*, roman cycle** [from French *roman*, novel, and *cycle*, cycle]. A series of loosely connected *novels with a central *hero, where each novel in the series is self-contained and independent (as in the sonnet cycle). A good example of the roman cycle is Georges Duhamel's (1884-1966) *Vie et Adventures de Salavin*. The **roman-fleuve* and the *saga novel are kins of the roman cycle.

roman de these [from French *roman*, novel; *de*, of; and *these*, thesis]. The term literally means 'novel of thesis' or 'thesis novel', and as a critical term also it means the same thing. *Roman de these* denotes a kind of *novel in which certain proposition or didascalic position regarding morality, philosophy, politics, etc. is put forward and attempts are made to prove it right. Examples are: Harriet Beecher Stowe's (1811-96) *Uncle Tom's Cabin* which powerfully argued against slavery and Jean-Paul Sartre's (b. 1905) *La nausea* (*Nausea*) which attempts to establish his existentialist philosophy.

roman documentaire [from French *roman*, novel, and *documentaire*, documentary]. The term literally means 'documentary novel'. *Roman documentaire* is a form of realistic, if not naturalistic, *fiction or *novel in which facts are researched and even minute details are painstakingly recorded as if in a document. This form of fiction was invented in the 1860s by the two German brothers—Edmond Goncourt (1822-96) and Jules Goncourt (1830-70). Examples of this form of fiction are the Goncourt Brothers' (they always co-authored their fictions) *Saeur Philomene*, in which they studied and recorded the hospital life from inside, and *Germinie Lacerteux*, in which "they made a study of one of their servants who had served them faithfully for years while leading unknown to them a life of debauchery revealed only after her death from consumption" [Thorlby, 322].

romanesque [from French *Romanesque*, romantic, imaginary, fabulous]. Romanesque (cap. R), as an adjective means "of the transition from Roman to Gothic architecture, characterised by round arches and vaults" [Davidson, 863]. But as a critical adjectival term Romanesque (lower case 'r') signifies fanciful or fabulous literary works, and only rarely the qualities of *romance.

roman-feuilleton [from French *roman*, novel, and *feuille* (pronunciation: faey), leaf, sheet (of paper), or *feuilleton* (pronounciation: fae-to), serial story]. See **feuilleton*.

roman-fleuve [from French *roman* novel, and *fleuve* (pronunciation: floev), river]. The term literally means 'stream novel' (or 'stream of novels). In literary discourse, the term denotes "a novel or a series of novels, that in a broad sweep of narrative tells the story of a character or set of characters (such as the members of a family) over an extended period of time" [Ayto, 267]. The genre of *roman-fleuve* had its vogue in France during the first four decades of the 20th century, where Emile Gaboriau (1832-73) was the first practitioner of this genre, beginning with his series of *detective stories (or rather *police procedurals) centering on the character, policeman Lecoq, the forerunner of the Sherlock Holmes *fictions. In England, two of the practitioners were Anthony Trollope (1815-82), with his 'Palliser' *novels, and John Galsworthy (1867-1933), with his sequence of novels *The forsyte Saga*. Also see **roman cycle*, *saga novel.

roman noir [from French *roman*, novel, and *noir*, black, dark, gloomy, wicked]. The term literally means 'black, dark, gloomy or wicked novel', but actually it was used in France first as synonymous with *Gothic novel. Now, of course, by *roman noir* is meant *thriller (or thrilling *novel) containing sensational crimes, violence, etc.

roman policier [from French *roman*, novel, and *policier*, of the police]. The term literally means 'novel of the police'. However, in literary-critical discourse, it is the French equivalent of the English term *detective novel or detective story.

Romantic fallacy. See *biographical fallacy.

Romanticism, romanticism. A vogue and variously defined term; so variously defined that in his *The Decline and Fall of the Romantic Ideal* (1984), F.L. Lucas counted 11,396 definitions of it. "In *Classic, Romantic and Modern* (1961) Barzun cites examples of synonymous usage for *romantic* which show that it is perhaps the most remarkable example of a term which can mean many things according to personal and individual needs. Barzun gives: 'attractive', 'bombastic', 'conservative', 'emotional', 'exuberant', 'fanciful', 'formless', 'futile', 'heroic', 'irrational', 'materialistic', 'mysterious', 'nordic', 'ornamental', 'realistic', 'stupid', 'unreal', and 'unselfish'. To which one might add: 'adventurous', 'daring', 'extraordinary', 'gallant', 'melodramatic', 'passionate', and 'wild'" [Cuddon, 767-68]. All these point to the correctness of Lucas. It is because of the nebularity of the term that the American scholar A.O. Lovejoy once said that the word 'romantic' means nothing at all. And yet, in literary discourse, 'it still appears to be as potentially sustaining as a twist of pemmican.'

Romanticism (or the Romantic movement) is generally believed to have been first founded (or launched) in Germany in the 18th century chiefly by the two Schlegel poet brothers Augustus (1767-1845) and Friedrich (1772-1829), the poet Novalis (1772-1801) and the poet Ludwig Tieck (1773-1853). Of course, "many hold the theory that it was in Britain that the romantic movement really started" [*op. cit.*, 769]. It is very difficult to make an inventory of the features of Romanticism, for the term is at once sweeping and slippery, yet a short-list of them might consist of the following: (i) individualism, (ii) increased sensibility, (iii) sentimentality, (iv) hightened imagination, (v) greater interest in Nature, (vi) added importance given to beauty, (vii) emphasis on natural religion, (viii) a tendency to exalt natural genius or originality, (ix) emphasis on spontaneity of thought and expression, and (x) a reverence for the cult of the Noble Savage. Romanticism rejected the earlier neo-classicism and the ordered rationalism of the *Enlightenment as mechanical and artificial. Though poetry initiated the Romantic movement, the contributions of *novel and Shakespearean drama in that movement cannot be ignored. "The novel is particularly important in tracing the history of romanticism. Especially the following works: Richardson's *Pamela* (1740), *Clarissa Harlowe* (1747), and *Sir Charles Grandison* (1754); Goldsmith's *The Vicar of Wakefield* (1766); Sterne's *Sentimental Journey* (1768); Henry Mackenzie's *The Man of Feeling* (1771); Henry Brooke's *Juliet Grenville; or the History of the Human Heart* (1774). On the continent three major works of fiction are a counterpart—namely: Prevost's *manon Lescaut* (1735), Rousseau's *La Nouvelle Heloise* (1761) and Goethe's *Die Leiden des jungen Werthers* (1774). One should add that the Gothic novel and a considerable revival of Shakespeare's plays round about the middle of the 18th c. also contributed to the movement subsequently known as 'romantic'" [*ibid*]. In England, there was no Romantic movement as such (in fact there was no literary movement whatsoever worth the name) but it was there all right in the first half of the 19th century, and was associated with the poets S.T. Coleridge (1772-1834), William Wordsworth (1770-1850) John Keats (1795-1821), Lord Byron (1788-1824) and P.B. Shelley (1792-1822). Also see *Romantic period, Romantic revival.

romantic novel. A vague term, it generally signifies a kind of *novel that, like the romantic comedy, is distinguished for its emphasis on love and *action rather than *character analysis or anything else. Also see *romance, *Romanticism.

Romantic period, Romantic revival. The time span or the tenure of the Romantic movement or *Romanticism. No time frame has been ascertained of the beginning and the end of the Romantic period. In England, the Romantic period is generally assumed to have begun with the publication of William Wordsworth's (1770-1850) *Lyrical Ballads with a Few Other Poems* in 1798 and ended in the year of the death of Sir Walter Scott (1771-1832). But the other opinion is that it began sometime before 1798 and ended only with the death of William Wordsworth. The notable novelists (of England) of the Romantic period were: Walter Scott and Jane Austen (1775-1817), and, if we believe the period to have ceased in 1850, Charles Dickens (1812-70) and Benjamin Disraeli (1804-81). Monica Dickens (b. 1915) was a minor novelist of the extended Romantic period with her *Mariana* and *The Fancy*.

round character. See *developing character.

Royal Literary Fund. A benevolent society founded in 1790, in England, to help authors and their dependants, its fund depending on donations. Some of its beneficiaries were: S.T. Coleridge, Thomas Love Peacock, James Joyce (1882-1941), D.H. Lawrence (1885-1930) and Dylan Thomas.

rural novel. A kind of *novel whose *setting is *pastoral, rural, agrarian or arcadian and its *characters are mostly countrymen, rustics, peasants, yokels, etc. speaking colloquially and demonstrating simplicity and honesty. Writers of the rural novel should include Mary Webb (1881-1927) and Thomas Hardy (1840-1928).

Ruritania. A fictitious land, like *Utopia, in Anthony Hope's (1863-1933) 'Ruritanian' novel *The Prisoner of Zenda*.

Russian Formalism. In a piece of literature, there are two fundamental things: *content* or subject-matter (or substance or raw-material) and **form,* *structure or pattern (or shape or mould). A bare *yarn is a content, a raw-material; a *short story (or a **novelette*) that is created out of it is this content plus a certain definite form. It is the form that determines a literary work's uniqueness, identity, or its *genre or *sub-genre. *Formalism, in its most general sense, focuses exclusively on the formal quality of a literary work, ignoring altogether the content or substance, and meaning, of it either in literary practice or in literary evaluation. Extreme insistence on formalism is considered derogatory. Though there are different approaches to formalism, it more frequently and specifically refers to Russian formalism.

Russian formalism flourished in Russia from 1915 to 1929, but during the dictatorship of Stalin (1924—53) it was forced to shift its centre to Prague where it sustained in the 1930s. Russian formalism is a school of literary theory and analysis that is distinguished by: (i) its emphasis on *literariness, "i.e. the sum of 'devices' that distinguish literary language from ordinary language" [Baldick, 196]; (ii) its disregard of the content (or substance or raw-material) of a literary work; (iii) its ignoring of the *meaning or significance of a piece of literature; (iv) its insistence on *defamiliarisation (i.e., it does not want to see literature as a 'reflection' of the reality or world; instead, it urges literature to de-familiarise the reality or world to us); (v) its accentuating the distinction between *plot or **sjuzet* and *story or **fibula*; (vi) its stressing on *foregrounding; and, most importantly, (vii) its emphatically accentuating the form of a literary work, which, it believes, bestows the work its *beauty*. Mikhail Bakhtin, Jan Mukarovsky (of Czechoslovakia), Roman Jakobson, Boris Eikhenbaum and Shklovsky were among the prominent Russian formalists (Bakhtin and Mukarovsky adhered to their slightly different versions of the Russian formalism). In the 1930s, Russian formalism spread from Prague to the United States.

S

saga novel ['Saga' from Norse *saga*, a prose *tale]. Saga is 'a prose tale of the deeds of Icelandic or Norwegian heroes in the old literature of Iceland' or 'a body of legend about some subject', for instance the *Volsunga saga* or the *Njals saga*. In English, the saga novel denotes the *novel that deals with 'any long family story spanning two or more generations', for example, D.H. Lawrence's (1885-1930) *The Rainbow* and John Galsworthy's (1867-1933) *Forsyte Saga*. Also see **roman-fleuvre*, **romancycle*.

Samizdat [from Russian *sam*, self, and *izdatelstvo*, publisher]. The term literally means 'self-publisher', but as a technical one it "denotes the system of illegal underground publishing carried on in the USSR and other Eastern European countries during the years of Communist sway, when only material that was ideologically pure was allowed to be put out..... It began to be widely used in English in the mid-1960s. Also sporadically employed in English is the derivative *samizdatchik* 'someone who writes or publishes samizdat material'" [Ayto, 272]. The novels of Alexander Solzhenitsyn (b. 1918) and articles by Andrei Sakharov were, for instance, considered by the Soviet authorities of the 1960s and 1970s as *samizdat* materials.

Sapir-Whorf hypothesis. The hypothesis of the two American linguisticians, Edward Sapir and Benjamin Lee Whorf. They studied the American Hopi Indians in the 1930s and arrived at this hypothesis. The hypothesis denotes "The belief that any language will fundamentally and inevidently condition the way that those who have it as their mother tongue will perceive social and material world" [Hawthorn, 309].

sarcasm. A bitter sneer or biting remark in scorn or contempt, often but not necessarily ironical, with a view to hurt one's feeling or giving him pain, but never designed to correct his fault or vice as in *satire. Also see *sardonic, the; *irony; *humours; *wit.

sardonic, the. A scornful, heartless, bitter, forced, unmirthful and hollow *laugh* (or attitude) at some person or thing. The sardonic is to be distinguished from the *cynic or cynical which signifies a dog-like ('cynic' or 'cynical' from Greek *kynikos*, meaning dog-like), sneering attitude with disinclination to recognise or believe in goodness or selflessness. Also see *sarcasm.

satire. Essentially a criticism of folly or vice through ridicule or scorn, the objective or aim being the correction or forsaking of the folly or vice. "The satirist is a kind of self-appointed guardian of standards, ideals and truth; of moral as well as aesthetic values. He is a man (women satirists are *very* rare) who talks it upon himself to correct, censure and ridicule the follies and vices of society [and of individuals within society] and thus to bring contempt and derision upon aberrations from a desirable and civilized norm" [Cuddon, 780]. Satire has always been a staple in English literature from the 16th to the 19th century, and it reached its highest level of excellence in the prose *fictions of Jonathan Swift (1667-1745) as in the verse of Alexander Pope (1688-1744). Some of the novelists of the 20th century who produced satiric fictions are: Aldous Huxley (1894-1963: his early *novels, for instance. *Antic Hay*), Evelyn Waugh (1903-66: *Vile Bodies*, *Black Mischief*, *A handful of Dust*, *The Loved One*, etc.) and George Orwell (1903-50: *Animal Farm* and *Nineteen Eighty-Four*). Also see *sarcasm.

Scapino. A *zanni or clown servant of the commedia, crafty, liar, given to scampering and a ladies' man. Also see *Scaramuccia.

Scaramouche, Scaramuccia. A commedia *character in the form of a braggart soldier or a clown servant and given to wine and women. Also see *Scapino.

scatology [from Greek *skatos*, dung]. Literally, study of, or interest in, excrement; figuratively, obscene or bawdy literature. Also see *obscenity.

scene. The place of actual occurrence or *action in a *story. The term generally refers to drama. "In the study of narrative works, 'scene' is (also) the name given to a 'dramatic' method of narration that presents events at roughly the same pace as that at which they are supposed to be occurring, i.e. usually in detail and with substantial use of dialogue" [Baldick, 199]. Also see *setting.

scene a faire [from French *scene*, scene; *a*, of; and *faire*, to do, to suit]. "The scene of crucial confrontation between two adversaries whose meeting or recognition has been delayed. In the well-made play it is the prelude to the denouement" [Ousby, 819]. It is the scene that the audience anticipates and demands—it is an obligatory scene. For instance, in *Hamlet*, the scene of the meeting between Hamlet and his mother is the *scene a faire*. Such a scene is of necessity intensely emotional. Similar scenes are also found in *novels.

Schauerroman [from German *Schauer*, shower, or from German *Schauder*, shudder (from horror); and *Roman*, novel]. The term denotes what in English is called *Gothic novel or *horror story, because like these, it is also spine-chilling and produces shudder.

Schelmenroman [from German *Schelmen* which is from *Schelm*, rogue, and *roman*, novel]. The term denotes what in English is called *picaresque novel.

Schlusselroman [from German *Schlussel*, key, and *roman*, novel]. A German term for *key novel or **roman a clef*.

schmaltz [from German *schmaltz* which is the plural form of *Schmalz*, sentiment (*schmaltzy*, sentimental)]. Sentimental material or treatment of material in a tender, emotional or sentimental way.

Schwank [from German *Schwank*, prank, farce, comical tale]. A German term for an *anecdote or a *tale that is deliberately done in a simple, light or comical mode.

schwarmerei [from German *schwarm*, craze, crush, enthusiasm]. The term signifies zeal or enthusiasm for religion, ideology, etc. but more recently it refers to irrational 'sexual infatuation' or crush, for instance, that of a schoolgirl for another or her teacher: "It's true we weren't allowed to schwarm' says Amanda of her school in Joyce Cary's [1888-1957] *The Moonlighti* (1946)" [Ayto, 277].

science fantasy. See *science fiction.

science fiction. The term denotes "a popular modern branch of prose fiction that explores the probable consequences of some improbable or impossible transformation of the basic conditions of human (or intelligent non-human) existence"

[Baldick, 200]. It is a kind of *fantasy or *romance that banks upon some utopia (or dystopia) and deals with seemingly scientific imaginative vagaries with a view to providing a sort of intellectual enjoyment. The term "was first used, it seems, in 1851,..., in William Wilson's *A Little Earnest Book upon a Great Old Subject*" [Cuddon, 791], but "was first given general currency by Hugo Gernsback, editor of the American magazine *Amazing Stories* from 1926 onwards" [Baldick, 200]. Mary Shelley's (1797-1851) *Frankenstein, or the Modern Prometheus* is generally supposed to be the first science fiction.

In the second half of the 19th century, the science fiction began to be popular, and some writers, such as Jules Verne (1828-1905), produced a number of science fictions. Since then, this genre enjoyed stunning popularity across the 20th century, thanks to the arrival of paperback editions. Some of the notable writers of science fictions in the 20th century were: H.G. Wells (1866-1946: *The Time Machine*, *The Wonderful Visit*, *The Island of Dr Moreau*, *The War of the Worlds*, *First Man in the Moon*, etc.); Edgar Rice Burroughs (1875-1950: *Tarzan of the Apes*, *A Princess of Mars*, *A Fighting Man of Mars*, *Pellucidar*, *The Pirate of Venus*, *Lost on Venus*, etc.); Edgar Wallace (1875-1932: *Crimson Circle*, *Green Archer*, *The Day of Uniting*, etc.); etc. By the 1920s, dystopian science fictions replaced the earlier utopian ones. Some of the dystopian science fiction writers of the 20th century were: George Orwell (1903-50: *Nineteen Eighty-Four*); Aldous Huxley (1894-1963: *Brave New World*); Evelyn Waugh (1903-66: *Love Among the Ruins*); Antony Burgess (b. 1917: *A Clockwork Orange* and *The Wanting Seed*); etc.

The two terms science fiction and *science fantasy are not very different from one another, and sometimes, leniently, they are used interchangeably, but, strictly speaking, there is a thin watershade between them. M.H. Abrams writes: "These terms encompass novels and short stories that represent an imagined reality that is radically different in its nature and functioning from the world of our ordinary experience. Often the setting is another planet, or this earth projected into the future, or an imagined parallel universe. The two terms are not sharply discriminated, but by and large science fiction is applied to those narratives in which—unlike in pure fantasy—*an explicit attempt is made to render plausible the fictional world by reference to known or imagined scientific principles, or to a projected advance in technology, or to a drastic change in the organization of society*" [Abrams, 278-79].

sci-fi. A form of abbreviation of *science fiction. Also see *SF.

scriptable. See **lisible*.

second-person narrative. See *point of view.

second-person perspective. See *point of view.

second-person point of view. See *point of view.

seicentismo. See **quattrocento*.

seicento. See **quattrocento*.

self-reflexive novel. A mode of *novel that incorporates within itself references to the process and status, from time to time, of its own growth and development, i.e. a novel "which incorporates into its narration reference to the process of composing the fictional story itself" [Abrams, 235]. The term may be illustrated with the help of Andre Gide's (1869-1951) novel *The Counterfeiters* which is apparently "the diary of a novelist who is writing a novel [to be called *The Counterfeiters*] about a novelist who is keeping a diary about the novel he is writing" [*loc. cit.*]. An early instance of this mode of novel is Laurence Sterne's (1713-68) *Tristram Shandy*, and this mode flourished in the modern or postmodern 20th century. Vladimir Nabokov (1899-1977) was an accomplished writer of self-reflexive novels (witness his *Pale Fire*). The self-reflexive novel is also called *involuted novel. Also see *Chinese Box narrative, *framed narrative, *nested narrative, *embedded narrative.

send-up. 'To send up' means 'to make fun of (somebody)' but a send-up is a play, film, *novel, etc. in which somebody or something is made a fun of. For instance, "...William Blake's fragment *An Island in the Moon*, which he wrote c. 1784-85, [is] a kind of 'send-up' of cultural and scientific pretensions" [Cuddon, 100].

sensation novel. See *novel of sensation.

sensibility. The term denotes the capacity, readiness and delicacy of feeling or emotion. It refers to emotionalism as opposed to rationalism, and is a relative term of sentimentalism and *romanticism. The *novel in which sensibility is rather rampant is called *novel of sensibility.

sentimental novel. A form of *novel, also called *novel of sentiment or *novel of sensibility, that was, like the sentimental comedy, much popular in the 18th century England as well as in Europe. Rampant and intense emotionality, arising chiefly out of distress of the virtuous and morally upright, is the cardinal feature of the sentimental novel (which, of course, usually concludes by showing that the virtuous and morally upright is ultimately justly rewarded). A classic example of sentimental novel (and, perhaps, the first such in England) is Samuel Richardson's (1689-1761) *Pamela, or Virtue Rewarded* that shows the virtuous teenage maidservant Pamela Andrews, the heroine, withstanding all the lustful aggressions of Mr B. and consequently being rewarded when Mr B. submits to her and proposes marriage. Some other notable sentimental novels are: Oliver Goldsmith's (1730-74) *The Vicar of Wakefield*, Henry Mackenzie's (1745-1831) *The Man of Feeling*, Maria Edgeworth's (1767-1849) *Castle Rackrent*, Henry Brooke's (1703-83) *The Fool of Quality*, Laurence Sterne's (1713-68) *A Sentimental Journey*, Jean-Jacques Rousseau's (1712-78) *La Nouvelle Heloise*, and J.W. von Goethe's (1749-1832) *The Sorrows of Young Werther*. Also see *novel of sensibility.

sequence of novels. An alternative term is 'group of *novels'. A number of novels, one following the other, their connecting link running through a common *theme, *setting or *background, or a central *character, and sometimes bearing a group name (in most case not given by the writer). Examples are: John Galsworthy's (1867-1933) *Forsyte Saga*; Margaret Laurence's (1928-87) 'Manawaka' novels; Upton Sinclair's (1878-1968) *World's End* (eleven novels); Sir C.P. Snow's (1905-80) *Strangers and Brothers* (eleven novels); Doris Lessing's (b. 1919) 'Martha Quest novels' entitled *Children of Violence* (four novels); Durrell Lawrence's (1912-90) *Alexandria Quartet* (four novels); James Fenimore Cooper's (1789-1851) *Leatherstocking Tales* (five novels); Thomas Hardy's (1840-1928) 'Wessex novels'; Anthony Trollope's (1815-82) 'Barselshire novels'; Emile Zola's (1840-1902) *Les Rougon-Macquart* (twenty novels) and K.R. Narayan's (b.1907) 'Malgudi novels'. Also see *serial novel.

serial novel. A *novel originally serialised in a periodical regularly from time to time in instalments or parts and then separately published in a volume or volumes. Because of its fragmented nature, or of its lack of monolithic form, it usually needs a *narrative hook at the end of each instalment in order to arouse the audience's or the reader's interest in the next issue of the periodical to continue reading the novel. As the serial novel runs a number of instalments over a long period (say, from 6 months to one year or more), to keep the reader's memory ever fresh, its *characters usually have descriptive names (e.g., Mr Donothing, Mr Wayward, Mrs Peawit, etc.) and easily identifiable characteristics. Many of Charles Dickens' (1812-70) novels were first serialised; for example, *Bleak House* (20 monthly parts: (1852-53), *Hard Times* (serialised in *Household Words*: 1 April to 12 August 1854), *Little Dorrit* (20 monthly parts: 1855-56) and *A Tale of Two Cities* (serialised in 8 monthly parts in *All the Year Round*). James Joyce's (1882-1941) *A Portrait of the Artist as a Young Man* was also at first serialised in the *Egoist* in 1914-15.

setting. The term refers to the space (or locale), the time (or period), and the form (or quality, way, or characteristics) of life (including its social, moral, economic, religious and emotional conditions) in which the sequence of *actions of a whole narrative work or a particular action of an *episode or *scene of it takes place.This means that setting may be of two sorts: an overall setting of a whole *narrative and a particular setting of a particular episode or scene. M.H. Abrams writes that "The overall setting of a narrative or dramatic work is the general locale, historical time, and social circumstances in which its action occurs; the setting of a single episode or scene within such a work is the particular physical location in which it takes place" [Abrams, 284]. The medieval Scotland and its way of life, for instance, is the overall setting of *Macbeth* and the setting of scene iii of Act I of the play, where Macbeth and Banquo meet the witches, is the blasted heath and its eerie milieu of witchery. Again, the overall setting of James Joyce's (1882-1941) *Ulysses* is the way of life in Dublin particularly on June 16, 1904, and the setting of its opening scene is the environment in the Martello Tower, overlooking Dublin Bay, on the same date, early in the morning when Stephen takes his breakfast. Also see *atmosphere, *background.

S & F. 'S & F' is the abbreviation of 'Shopping and Fucking', and denotes a category of romantic fiction that deliberately indulges in sexual debauchery. The S & F "usually written by and for women, is distinguished by its shamelessly explicit descriptions of expensive clothes, jewellery, perfumes, cars, and other accessories of the very rich, naming actual brand names ['Shopping']: several sexual encounters are also described in graphic detail ['Fucking']. The genre established itself in the 1980s, following the huge commercial success of Judith Krantz's *Scruples* (1978)" [Baldick, 197].

SF. A form of abbreviation of *science fiction. Also see *Sci-fi.

shaggy dog story. Colloquially, the phrase means 'a groaner'. In literary critical discourse, the term denotes 'a whimsically extravagant story humorous from its length and the inconsequence of its endings.' It is "An improbable kind of yarn, often long and spun out, which, as a rule, does *not* have a witty or surprise ending; but comes, rather, to a deflating and quasi-humorous conclusion" [Cuddon, 813]. The staggering story of a bee in Sydney aspiring to be a ballet dancer and through lots of hazards ultimately achieving its dream may serve as an instance. Also, "In fiction, Joseph Heller's [b. 1923] digressive and crazily funny novel *Catch-22* (1961) might be taken as an example" [*loc. Cit.*].

shilling shocker. A cheap (suggested by the word 'shilling' which was a coin worth the value of 12 old pence) adventure, horror or detective *novel or *story, like the *dime novel, the *penny dreadful or the *pulp novel, or *fiction, that was popular in the second half of the nineteenth century.

shmaltz [from Yiddish *shmaltz*, literally 'melted fat, dripping', which is from German *schmaltz*, sentiment]. The term (in the metaphorical sense of the Yiddish word *shmaltz*) means 'unctuous sentimentality in writing, music, art, etc.' [Ayto, 282]. Also see **schmaltz.*

short-circuit, short-circuit narrative. "In narrative theory the deliberate and pointed mixing of narrative levels, or the flouting of conventions appertaining to narrative levels. Much postmodernist fiction indulges frequently in such short-circuiting, as when an author speaks in his own extra-fictional voice about one of his or her created characters. "The terms *short-circuit narrative*, or alternatively *Mobius strip narrative*, are used to describe a narrative that forms a seamless circuit, so that one can join it at any point and continue to go round, and round, in an endless loop" [Hawthorn, 321].

short fiction Roger Fowler's *A Dictionary of Modern Critical Terms* defines the term thus: "Probably the most ancient of all literary forms , the term covers everything from the fable, folk-tale or fairy-story, to such sophisticated and highly-developed structures as the German *Novelle*, via the stories of the *Decameron* and Cerventes's *Exemplary Tales*" [Fowler, Roger, 220-21].

short novel. A 'middle distance' *novel, shorter than an usual novel but longer than a *short story. E.M. Forster (1879-1970) said about the general length of a novel that it would be a book of roughly 200 pages and that one could have finished it in a train journey, and this can suggest the general maximal length of a short novel. A short story, again, may be as long as, if not more than, say, Somerset Maugham's (1874-1965) 'The Alien Corn' or Fyodor Dostoyevsky's (1821-81) 'White Nights' or D.H. Lawrence's (1885-1930) 'The Fox' (about 30,000 words), and this may suggest the shortest general length of a short novel. But however short a short novel may be, it must be different from a short story, for whereas a short story 'concentrate on a single event with one or two characters', a novel (short or long) deals with a *plot (more than one *events) and maintains sustained explorations of a couple of *characters. Examples of the short novel are: Joseph Conrad's (1857-1924) *The Heart of Darkness* and Aldous Huxley's (1894-1963) *Two or Three Graces*. The short novel is sometimes called long short story or **novella*.

short short story. A prose fiction "which is a slightly elaborated anecdote of perhaps five hundred words" [Abrams, 287]. Also see *story, *short story.

short story. A difficult term to define or explain, particularly due to the perplexing variety of meanings attached to the words 'story' and 'short' in it. In any case, however, a **story* that is *short* is not necessarily a short story. Let us first try to understand the story. *The Oxford Companion to the English Language* defines the story thus: "A narrative, spoken or written, *in prose or in verse*, true or fictitious, related so as to inform, entertain, or instruct the listener or reader. A story has a *structure* that may be more or less formal, unfolds *a sequence of events* and descriptions (even when devices like flashbacks alter the flow of time), and concerns one or more characters in one or more settings" (emphases added) [McArthur, 987]. *The Concise Oxford Dictionary of Literary Terms* defines the story, on the other hand, thus: "*in the everyday sense*, any narrative or tale recounting a *series of events*. In modern narratology, however, the term refers more specifically to the *sequence of imagined events* that *we construct from* the actual arrangement of a narrative (or dramatic) *plot*" (emphases added) [Baldick, 211]. Further, according to the *Russian formalists, the story is the **fabula* that can be extrapolated from the *plot of a *novel. Also see *short short story.

Now, the short story. The said *Oxford Companion* defines the short story as "A fictional narrative brief enough to be transmitted at a single hearing or reading" [McArthur, 933]. It may be supposed here that the said *Oxford Companion* differentiates the short story from the *novel (and other fictional *narratives) only (and, perhaps, inadequately) on the parameter of length. But the said *Oxford Dictionary* explains the short story "as a fictional prose tale of no specified length, but too short to be published as a volume on its own,.... [and] will *normally concentrate on a single event* with only one or two characters, more economically than a novel's sustained exploration of social background" [Baldick, 204]. To summarise: (i) the short story comprises only a single event while the story and the novel includes a series of events, and this differentiates the short story from the story and the novel; and (ii) the short story is much shorter than the novel, and this, further, distinguishes the short story from the novel.

Is there any *plot in the story? No. E.M. Forster (1879-1970) in his *Aspects of the Novel* writes: "Let us define a plot. We have defined a story as a narrative of *events arranged in their time-sequence*. A *plot is also a narrative of events*, the emphasis falling on *causality*. 'The king died, and then the queen died,' is a story 'The king died, and then the queen died of grief', is a plot" (emphases added) [Forster, 93]. So, there is no plot in a story. But is there a plot in a short story? If, according to the said *Oxford Dictionary*, the short story 'normally concentrate on a single event', then there can be no plot in it, but if it is not a normal short story and it contains more than one event, then there can be one. Also see *event.

showing and telling. These two are the primary narrative techniques. M.H. Abrams writes: "In showing (also called 'the dramatic method'), the author simply presents the characters talking and acting and leaves the reader to infer the motives and dispositions that lie behind what they say and do. The author may show not only external speech and actions, but also a character's inner thoughts, feelings, and responsiveness to events.... In telling, the author intervenes authoritatively in order to describe, and often to evaluate, the motives and dispositional qualities of the characters" [Abrams, 33-34].

significance. See *meaning and significance.

silver-fork novel. Same as *fashionable fiction.

simpatico [from Italian *simpatico*, sympathy]. A relative of, and almost synonymous with, the English word 'sympathetic', but yet different from it, the term denoting "an intuitive rapport and understanding" [Ayto, 286]. Also see **Einfuhlung*.

sincerity. The critical term refers to the truthfulness or falsehood of an author as reflected in his work. Sincerity in literature seems to be a simple thing, but in fact it is quite the opposite. Leonel Trilling (1905-75) defined sincerity as "'congruence between avowal and actual feeling'" [Fowler, Roger, 225]. Sincerity has been receiving critical attention only since the 18th century when Rousseau (1712-78) in his *Confessions* very subtly posed as a sincere author. In the Romantic period, the image of the poet was one who sincerely expressed his intense emotions of grief and joy in his poetry. The matter of sincerity was so far simple, but it turned complex when Charles Baudlaire (1821-67), Friedrich Nietzsche (1844-1900), Oscar Wilde (1854-1900), Sigmund Freud (1856-1939) and others doubted the sincerity of the author in his literary works. Baudlaire conceived of the poet as a dandy with a pose or show; Nietzsche perceptively noted that 'every profound spirit needs a mask'; Wilde thought that 'the first duty in life is to be as *artificial* as possible'; and Freud showed that consciousness is always prone to be influenced by the Unconscious that is ever lurking behind it. Therefore, sincerity in literature is always a suspect unless the contrary is proved, and, consequently, the critical term sincerity should be cautiously used.

site. The term has recently been inducted into critical vocabulary. Jeremy Hawthorn writes very clearly about this term: "To describe something as a site has become a favoured way of giving (sometimes exclusive) procedure to external determining forces while playing down or denying the self-initiation of movement or development. "Thus when the subject is described as site, an attack is being made on views of the subject as in control—or even aware—of its own destiny; a subject is, according to such a view, more or merely a site on which extra-subjective forces clash and resolve their differences. Those extra-subjective forces which are given priority can be either language, or history, or ideology, or the class struggle, or whatever. Put simply, the argument thus invoked by the use of *site* denies that the individual is in charge of his or her life, or consciousness, and asserts rather that the subject is constituted by other forces which then proceed either to nest or to fight in it...." The term is sometimes invoked by those deconstructionists arguing for a rejection of any transcendental subject or presence. "In literary criticism the term is often associated with attempts to downgrade the extent to which the author is seen to be in control (conscious or otherwise) of his or her creation" [Hawthorn, 325-26]. Also see *presence.

situation. A critical conditions or circumstances in which the *plot of a *novel begins or develops, or the *action of a play occurs.

sjuzet (pronounced: *syuu-zhet*; and also spelt *suzet* or **syuzhet*) [from Russian *sjuzet*, plot]. The term is especially employed by Russian formalism for finished *plot—'as presented through the formal devices of construction'—as against the raw material or the*events of the *story of the *novel (or *short story) which is called **fabula*. "The *sjuzhet* is the finished arrangement of narrated events as they are presented to the reader rather than the sequence of such events as reconstructed in their 'true' sequence and duration" [Baldick, 206].

skaz [from Russian *skazat*, to tell]. The term refers to a particular set of artificial devices of narrative techniques, especially those of *folk literature. "It usually consists of an eyewitness account of an episode in peasant or provincial life. More specifically it is a narrative related by a fictitious narrator rather than by the author directly. Such a device allows the author considerable scope in the use of speech forms such as dialect, slang, neologism, mispronunciation and so forth, which give a naturalistic vigour and colourfulness which might not be attainable in a more conventional narrative told solely from the author's point of view" [Cuddon, 832]. Nikolai Leskov (1831-95), Mikhail Zoshchenko (1895-1958), Aleksey Remizov (1877-1957) and Isaak Babel (1894-1940), among not many others, successfully exploited *skaz*.

skazka [from Russian *skazat*, to tell]. The term denotes Russian *folk tales. Also see **skaz*.

sketch. The term originally meant an artist's preliminary draught or outline of a finished work. In literary discourse, it is now used to denote a finished short and simple dramatic, narrative or descriptive composition, such as character sketch, descriptive sketch, vaudeville sketch, etc.

skit. A piece of humorous banter, *burlesque or *caricature directed towards a person, *style of writing, *mode of performance, etc.

slang. The term denotes the offensive language or vocabulary of a sub-group of a society. Also see *argot, *cant, *jargon.

slice-of-life novel. A naturalistic type of *novel that presents details of reality without selection or arrangement with a realistic, deterministic and pessimistic view of life. One of its distinctive features (for which it is called a 'slice' of life) is that it "begins apparently at random and ends inconclusively—as if the reader were privileged to observe an ordinary family, for example, going about its routine business... The typical subject matter involves either the defeat of a weak protagonist by nature or society, or the rise to power of a ruthless hero" [Lemon, 9]. Examples are: Theodore Dreiser's (1871-1945) *Sister Carrie* and his 'Cowperwood Trilogy' and Stephane Crane's (1871-1900) *Maggie: A Girl in the Street*.

slow-down. Jeremy Hawthorn explains the term analogically. He writes that it is a novelistic technique that well compares with the slow-motion technique of cinematography: "The narrative equivalent to that slow-motion experience which frequently accompanies moments of great danger or tension. A narrative may suddenly provide what seems (in contrast to that which has gone before or that which comes after) a disproportionate number of pages to what takes place in a (relatively) very short span of time. Precisely because the technique does resemble 'slow-motion-experience' it suggests by analogy that what is narrated is of great subjective importance either to narrator or character or both" [Hawthorn, 327].

socialist realism. Socialist realism is the Marxist view of realism (in literature), i.e. the mode of perception of realism that accords with the politico-economic or historical-materialistic teachings of Karl Marx (1818-81) which emphasizes that: (a) the capitalistic society because of its fragmentation and resulting isolationism, rule of money and gain, and prosaic utilitarianism is 'hostile towards artistic development'; (b) realism, i.e. socialist realism is the only adequate attitude towards literature—socialist realism which demands that "art is a specific 'reflection' of reality"; (c) art is a specific part of the 'superstructure'; (d) social determinations of art do not work mechanically, but only 'in the last analysis', and because of the 'reciprocity' in (this) dialectical pattern of causation, art itself becomes a determining factor, and not merely a determined one." [Thorlby, 518]; and (e) socialist realism does not believe in absolute standard of literature but urges that the standard of literature changes with progressive changes in society. However, at least the last point of socialist realism has been subjected to scathing criticism. Herbert Read writes that "Karl Marx was puzzled to understand why Greek art should 'still constitute with us a source of aesthetic enjoyment and in certain respects prevail as the standard and model beyond attainment'" [Read, 1936, 112].

social novel. A *mode of *novel that "emphasizes the influence of the social and economic conditions of an era on shaping characters and determining events; often it also embodies an implicit or explicit thesis recommending political and social reforms" [Abrams, 193]. Examples of the social novel are: Harriet Beecher Stowe's (1811-96) *Uncle Tom's Cabin*, Upton Sinclair's (1878-1968) *The Jungle*, John Steinbeck's (1902-68) *The Grapes of Wrath* and Nadaine Gordimer's (b. 1923) *Burger's Daughter*. Also see *sociological novel, *thesis novel.

sociolect. The term is formed analogically with *dialect and *idiolect. The term denotes the *parole of a particular social group defined in terms of economic class, caste, age, gender or a permutation of all these. The sociolect of a particular social group frequently carries with it the specific 'values and status of the same group.' Some of the defining elements of a sociolect are its peculiar pronunciation, and lexical, grammatical and syntactical specificities. Many writers convey sociolects by means of idiosyncratic spelling. The sociolect *wimmin*, for instance, means 'women'.

sociological novel. The term is a relative of *social novel and *problem novel. Sociological *novel attempts to realistically portray in detail the social conditions of a particular society of a certain period usually contemporaneous with the author. It frequently stresses on the particular economic and social conditions of a particular class or classes of some society. But if it deals with certain problem or problems of the society, it turns out to be a problem novel. If it overtly or covertly argues for a particular ideological solution to the problems it treats, it should be called a *propaganda novel. And, lastly, if it tries to show how social and economic conditions shape *characters and *events, it verges on the *social novel.

soliloquy. See *interior monologue, *monologue, *stream of consciousness.

solution. The term is loosely synonymous with *denouement that specifically applies to drama, and is sometimes used in the sense of the outcome or disentanglement of the proliferated complications that have been narrated in a *fiction.

soubrette [from French *soubrette* (fem.), coy]. The term denotes 'a pert, coquettish, intriguing maid-servant in comedy' or simply a 'maid-servant' or a 'lady's maid' or the confidante of an *ingénue. Also see *confidant, confidante.

space opera. Lee T. Lemon writes that "A space opera is a science fiction story with minimal verisimilitude, offering chiefly the excitement of interplanetary or intergalactic action" [Lemon, 12].

spatial form. Lee T. Lemon explains the term thus. He writes that it was coined by Joseph Frank in 1945 and that it "is a metaphor intended to suggest one way in which literature—especially literature influenced by Eliot and Joyce—may be read. Ordinarily when we read a narrative we think of it as spread out in time, like music, with one thing happening, then another, and so on. Frank argued that the interlocking patterns of motifs characteristics of much modern literature suggest that we must consider a narrative as we would a picture—that is, we must see that elements that make up the pattern as existing simultaneously, forming patterns that are significant apart from the temporal sequence of the story. (The interlocking motifs in Joyce's *A Portrait of the Artist as a Young Man*, for example, not only help show the development of the protagonist, they also weave their own tapestry, one that contributes significantly to the meaning of the novel)" [Lemon, 95]. Also see *form.

spectacle. Same as *opsis and *scene.

spiel. Same as *story and *yarn.

spoof. Literally, the term means a trick or deception, a hoaxing game, a comedian, or a parody or take-off (a burlesque mimicking). In literary discourse, spoof denotes a light, playful and satirical piece, in prose or verse, that makes fun of a literary convention, an historical event, a literary work, or any other subject merely for entertainment, and not for bitter censuring and connection as in *satire.

spy novel, spy story. Same as *clock-and-dagger novel, clock-and-dagger story.

staircasing. The term denotes a multiplicity of inner or *embedded narratives or *Chinese Box narratives in a single *frame narrative (or outer narrative).

static character. See *developing character.

stereotyped character. See *stock character.

stock character. A *character that represents a particular personality type or a characteristic of human behaviour. The stock character is a *stereotyped character which is easily recognizable for its recurrent appearances in literary or folk tradition. Examples of the stock character are: Velpone (the supreme instance of human cupidity and miserliness) in Ben Jonson's (1572-1637) *Velpone*, the **miles gloriosus*, the absent-minded professor, the nagging wife, the jealous husband, the country bumpkin, the **soubrette*, the wicked stepmother, the damsel in distress, and the whore with a golden heart. Also see *stock response, *stock situation.

stock response. As regards drama, the stock response signifies the conventional audience response to *stock characters. Analogically, in *fiction the term denotes the reader's set, standard, habitual, stereotyped or common but inappropriate or inadequate reaction to a piece of literary work. "The term is sometimes applied to the response of authors themselves to characters, situation, or topic that they set forth in a work" [Abrams, 298]. The term, in both the cases is derogatory. Also see *stock character, *stock situation.

stock situation. Analogous with *stock character and *stock response, the term denotes a conventional *situation that frequently occurs in dramatic or narrative works, for instance, dramatic irony, eternal triangle, deception based on disguise, mistaken identity, etc.

storm and stress. See **Sturm und Drang*.

story. Generally, the term denotes a *tale that contains a series of chronologically arranged *events, but in modern *narratology, according to *The Concise Oxford Dictionary of Literary Terms*, it refers to "the sequence of *imagined events that we reconstruct from the actual arrangement of a narrative (or dramatic) plot*" (emphasis added) [Baldick, 211]. In the sense of modern narratology, therefore, story is synonymous with **fibula* as *plot is with **sjuzet*. However, according to Jeremy Hawthorn story consists of not only *imagined or fictitious* events but may also consist of *real events*. While showing the distinction between story and plot, he writes: "The simple distinction is between, on the one hand, a *series of real or fictitious events, connected by a certain logic or chronology, and involving certain actors*, and on the other hand, the *narration of this* [artificially arranged] *series of events*" [Hawthorn, 337]. Also see *short story.

story line. The imaginary line formed by the scheme of chronological narration of the *events of a *story. *The Oxford Companion to the English Language* explains the term thus: "The sequence or flow of events in a story: the unelaborated routine of the *plot*, as opposed to the *theme* that the plot treats. A common story line is *Boy meets girl—boy loses girl—boy finds girl*, and a twist in such a story line might be *girl meets boy—girl loses boy—girl finds another boy*" [McArthur, 987].

story time and text time. Story time refers to the duration that is actually required by the *events of a *story to occur, or, in other words, the time that is represented in the story, or, simply, the time-in-the-story. On the other hand, the text time refers to the duration that is actually required to relate (the *text of) the story, or in other words, the representational time or the time-it-takes-to-tell-the-story. In only rare cases the two durations are equal; in most cases the one is greater or lesser than the other. For instance, the story time may be three years while the text time, i.e. the time required to tell (or read) the story may be around one hour (for fifty pages).

story within a story. A *story that occurs in another story which is called the *frame story (see *frame narrative, frame story); for instance, in *The Arabian Nights* many stories are enclosed within a frame story. Likewise, in Voltaire's (1694-1778) *Zadig* and Charles Dickens' (1812-70) *Nicholas Nickolby* one frame story comprises other stories. Also see *embedded narrative, *Chinese Box narrative.

stracitta [from Italian *stracitta*, over and across city]. "A form of literary movement in Italy which developed after the First World War. The leader of the movement was Massimo Bontempelli (1878-1960), who elaborated a literary creed known as *novecentismo*. He advocated a break with traditional 19th c. forms and attitudes and sought for what he called 'magic realism'. Yet another attempt to elucidate the essence of reality" [Cuddon, 865]. Also see *magic realism.

strategy. A *jargon referring to either (a) an author's attitude towards his *theme or subject, or (b) his method or technique of dealing with his theme or subject.

stream-of-consciousness novel. The phrase 'stream of consciousness' was coined by the American psychologist and philosopher William James (1842-1910), the elder brother of the novelist Henry James (1843-1916). William James rejected the idea of fragmented, discontinuous, interrupted consciousness. "'The traditional psychology,' James once wrote, 'talks like one who should say a river consists of nothing but pailsful, spoonsful, quart-potsful, bowlsful, and other moulded forms of water. Even were the pails and pots all actually standing in the stream, still between them the free water would continue to flow. It is just this free water of consciousness that psychologists resolutely overlook'" [Flew, 341]. "Experiences, recollections, feelings, aspirations, fancies, etc. seem to the individual to be a 'stream' which, in the last resort, is *independent of him*. James calls this the 'stream of consciousness'" (emphasis added) [Eysenck, 1067].

The term stream of consciousness is sometimes used as synonymous with *interior monologue. But the former is different from the latter in two ways. Firstly, stream of consciousness may be deemed to be a subject-matter (say, for investigation) as well as a technique of *fiction writing while interior monologue is only a technique of presenting a *character's stream of consciousness. Secondly, in interior monologue, as a technique, a character's inner thoughts, feelings, memories, etc. are presented 'directly', as if the author has 'overheard' them, without them being mingled with the author's perceptions and impressions of that character and of anything else related. On the other hand, in stream-of-consciousness technique a character's inner thoughts, feelings, memories, etc. are presented 'indirectly', i.e. these are described by the author adding his own perceptions and impressions of that character and of related things. Some critics take stream-of-consciousness technique to be a sub-category or type of interior monologue but some others think the other way round. However, an example of the stream-of-consciousness technique may be taken from just the beginning of Virginia Woolf's *Mrs Dalloway*: "Mrs Dolloway said she would buy the flowers herself." For Lucy had her work cut out for her. The doors would be taken off their hinges; Rumpelmayer's men were coming. And then, thought Clarissa Dalloway, what a morning—fresh as if issued to children on a beach. "What a lark! What a plunge! For so it had always seemed to her when, with a little squeak of the hinges, which she could hear now, she had burst open the French windows and plunged at Bourton into the open air. How fresh, how calm, stiller than this of course, the air was in the morning; like the flap of a wave; the kiss of a wave; chill and sharp yet (for a girl of eighteen as she then was) solemn, feeling as she did, standing there at the open window, that something awful was about to happen; looking at the flowers, at the trees with the smoke winding off them and the rooks rising, falling; standing and looking until Peter Walsh said, 'Musing among the vegetables?'—was that it?—'I prefer men to cauliflowers'—was that it?"

The stream-of-consciousness novel is a *form of *novel that employs the stream-of-consciousness technique. It describes *blendings* of characters' experiences, recollections, feelings, aspirations, fancies, etc. in the characters' consciousnesses (the process of *blending* being independent of the characters) along with the author's perceptions and impressions. Like the technique of interior monologue does always, the stream-of-consciousness technique, in a stream-of-consciousness novel, sometimes violates the norms of grammar and logic while describing the inner workings of characters' consciousnesses. Though semblances of the stream-of-consciousness technique are to be found as early as in some long self-communing passages in Fyodor Dostoevsky's (1821-81) novels, some believe that the technique was first used by Dorothy Richardson (1873-1957) in her twelve-volume novel *Pilgrimage*. Some other stream-of-consciousness novels are: James Joyce's (1882-1941) *Ulysses*, Virginia Woolf's (1882-1941) *Mrs Dalloway*, William Faulkner's (1897-1962) *The Sound and the Fury*, Anais Nin's (b. 1914) *Ladders to Fire*, etc.

string-of-pearls narrative. Jeremy Hawthorn explains the string-of-pearls *narrative thus: "A narrative that consists of a number of relatively or completely unrelated episodes strung together by a thin thread. The thread may consist of a causal sequence, or the person of an individual character, or whatever. Otherwise known as an *episodic* narrative" [Hawthorn, 338]. Also see *episodic novel.

structuralism. It is a distinctive modern European intellectual approach, originally in linguistics and then in social sciences, that holds, in the field of social sciences, the "view that the key to the understanding of observed phenomena lies in the underlying structures and systems of social organization" [Flew, 341]. Structuralism, or the 'science of signs', was born out of the linguistic theories of Ferdinand de Saussure (1857-1913) and was nourished chiefly by *Russian Formalism, the *narratology of Vladimir Prop, Claud Levi-Strauss's (b. 1908) structuralist analysis of *myth, ritual and kinship and the structuralist theories of Roland Barthes (1915-80) regarding social practices involving food and clothes. Structuralist theories have been applied for interpreting and understanding phenomena in many varied and widely different fields, such as rituals, religions, dresses, buildings, poetry, music, architecture, etc. but, perhaps most influentially, in the field of language which is 'often thought to be the root product of any culture'.

Structuralism (by the bye, a much misused term) believes that to understand any social phenomenon, we must understand the structure that underlies it, because the meaning or significance of it basically depends on that structure. *Structure may be defined as a repeated *pattern* of relations among parts of a whole. "To have structure, an object must have parts united under ordered relations. To say that structure is *the* determinant (rather than *a* determinant) of meaning is to say that it is not the parts themselves but the relations among them that are significant. This does not mean that the meaning remains unchanged when parts are changed, but that it remains invariant with respect to any *systemic* change of parts. Thus a short tone followed by a long tone has a Morse Code meaning. If the short tone becomes long, the signal may retain its meaning, provided the long tone becomes proportionately longer" [Scruton, 451]. Structure may be conceived of as a group of canons or regulations that govern the behaviour of a system, i.e. govern the relations between parts and whole. It should be noted here that the idea of structure is not a sole property of structuralism. "The term is in common use in literary-critical discussion, and, as one might expect, it is used in a number of relatively loose senses. It is usual to make a distinction between a literary work's structure and its plot: whereas a work's plot can be seen as the narrative arrangement of its story, *structure* refers to its total (or total aesthetic) organization" [Hawthorn, 340].

Structuralism has spread its influence over narratology. "Structuralist narratology is especially well advanced. Tzvetan Todorov, Gerard Genette and A.J. Greimas are the key theorists. Greimas developed the theories of the Russian Formalist Vladimir Propp, fitting them more closely to the linguistic model. The basic syntactical functions of subject and predicate have their equivalent functions in narrative actor and action. In *The Morphology of the Folktale* (1968) Propp found 35 'functions' (basic narrative actions) and seven 'spheres of action' in the Russian folktale. Greimas's universal 'grammar' of narrative proposes three binary oppositions which include the six roles (*actants*) he requires: (1) subject/object; (2) sender/receiver; (3) helper/opponent. The parts allow adescription of all the fundamental patterns governing narrative: (1) aiming at something, (2) communicating, (3) helping or hindering. Levi-Strauss developed a phonemic analysis of the Oedipus story; he aimed to establish the structural pattern which gives the myth its meaning. Todorov outlined a comprehensive application of the linguistic model, discovering the rules of agency, adjectival and verbal functions, mood, aspect and so on. Genette divided narrative into three levels: story, discourse and narration. These levels are related to one another through three aspects derived from three verbal qualities: tense, mood and voice" [Ousby, 896]. Besides, Roman Jacobson (1896-1982), Jonathan Culler, Noam Chomsky (b. 1928) and some other structuralists have contributed considerably to structuralism. Special mention may be made of the novelist David Lodge (b. 1935) who, too, has made contributions to structuralist thoughts, laterally though, in such works as *The Language of Fiction*, *Working with Structuralism*, *The Novelist at the Crossroads*, *The British Museum is Falling Down* [contains parodies of modernist writers like James Joyce (1882-1941) and Virginia Woolf (1882-1941)], etc. Also see *poststructuralism, *structuralist criticism.

structuralist criticism. Structuralist criticism is based on the philosophy that the meaning of a literary *text ultimately depends on an underlying or hidden system or *structure of literary conventions and social codes. "As applied to literary studies, structuralist criticism views literature as a second-order signifying system that uses the first-order structural system of language as its medium, and is itself to be analyzed primarily on the model of linguistic theory. Structuralist critics often apply a variety of linguistic concepts to the analysis of a literary text, such as the distinction between *phonemic* and *morphemic* levels of organization, or between *paradigmatic* and *syntagmatic* relationships; and some critics analyze the structure of a literary text on the model of the *syntax* in a well-formed sentence. The undertaking of a thoroughgoing literary structuralism, however, is to explain how it is that a cpmpetent reader is able to make sense of a particular literary text by specifying the underlying system of literary conventions and rules of combination that has been unconsciously mastered by such a reader. The aim of classical literary structuralism, accordingly, is not (as in *New Criticism*) to provide interpretations of an individual text, but to make explicit, in a quasi-scientific way, the tacit *grammar* (the system of rules and codes) that govern the forms and meanings of all literary productions. As Jonathan Culler put it in his lucid exposition, the aim of structuralist criticism is 'to construct a poetics which stands to literature as linguistics stands to language'" [Abrams, 301]. Also see *structuralism, *New Criticism.

structure. See *structuralism.

Stuart period. The period from 1603 (death of Queen Elizabeth) to 1714 (Queen Ann dies and George I ascends the throne) during which the Stuart family ruled England (excepting the duration of the Cromwellean Commonwealth: 1649-1660). The only notable novelist of the period is Daniel Defoe (1660-1731) and the only *novel that came out during the Stuart period was his famous *Robinson Crusoe* (1719).

sturdy indefensibles. The term refers to some wrong expressions in vogue but tolerated. Examples are: 'It's *me*', 'Don't be longer *than you can* help', '*So far from* hating him, I like him', 'The man *of all others* for the job', 'A child *of ten years old*', 'That long nose *of his*', etc.

Sturm und Drang [from German *Sturm*, storm; *und*, and; and *Drang*, stress, pressure]. Literally, the German term or expression means *storm and stress. As a literary-critical term it was actually taken from the title (the full title was: *Der Wirrwarr, oder Sturm und Drang*) of a play by the German dramatist F.M. von Klinger (1752-1831) who was a typical representative of the German literary movement of the last quarter of the 18th century known as *Sturm und Drang*. The movement's "characteristic features were its rejection of the hidebound literary conventions of the past and its glorification of the impulsive hero, the man of genius as opposed to the rational man of the 18th century (all very much of a piece with the emerging Romantic movement in Britain and the rest of Europe)" [Ayto, 294]. The leading figures of *Sturm und Drang* included the poet and novelist Johann Goethe (1749-1832), the theoretician of the movement Johann Herder (1744-1803) and the dramatist and poet Friedrich Schiller (1759-1805). The movement was short-lived but its influence was considerable.

style. A difficult term, indeed, to define, and the French critic Remy de Gourmont (1858-1915) was right when he said that trying to define 'style' was like putting a sack of flour in a thimble. However, style may be roughly defined as a writer's characteristic manner of linguistic expressions (in prose or verse) that comprises his choice of words, figures of speech, syntax, punctuations, rhetorical and otherwise devices, shape of sentences (loose or periodic), shape of paragraph and every such other thing that is peculiar of his linguistic expressions. A writer's style definitely distinguishes his writing from the writings of all other writers as his laugh, walk, handwriting, etc. does and so the French scientist and stylist Buffon (1707-88) in his *Discours sur le style* declared that the style is the (individual) man. If the *structure of a literary work is conceived of as its skeleton, its skin may be imagined to be made of its style (its matter being its sinews). The style not only identifies a writer but also his works; thus, for example, we say Chaucerian, Shakespearean or Miltonic works. Again, the term style may indicate the special features of the literary works in general of a period; and thus we say of works Augustan, Georgean, Elizabethan, Victorian, etc. The term may also refer to the kind or category of language a writer uses, for instance, scientific language, poetic language, journalistic language, official language, etc.; or it may indicate the level or status of a language, for instance, grand style, middle style and low style. This is not all; the term style may indicate many other features of a language. Also see *stylistics.

stylistics. The term is rather a new entrant in the vocabulary of literary studies and criticism, for it began to be used in critical discourses only in the 1950s. Stylistics may be defined as the objective or 'scientific' analytical study of the *styles of literary texts. Jeremy Hawthorn writes: "In the second half of the twentieth century Stylistics grew up as a recognized academic discipline, situated on the borderline between the study of language and of literature (although stylistic analysis can be and is applied to non-literary texts), and concerned to engage in technical study and analysis of what the OED calls 'manners of expression'" [Hawthorn, 344].

stylisation. The literal meaning of the word is the act of conventionalizing of something, or putting something into established usage or fashion. In theatre, the term denotes "The shaping of dramatic material, settings, or costumes in a deliberately nonrealistic manner. For example, a stylization of trees might use triangles and circles on oblongs to suggest trees. The term also refers to an exaggerated manner of moving or speaking that calls attention to itself" [Ayto, 145]. Also see *style.

Subconscious, the. See *Unconscious, the.

sub-culture. An ambiguous term with *plurisignation. Sub-culture refers to the 'culture' of a fairly 'closed' or tightly knit group or community within a society. Culture (another ambiguous term) signifies the general or common civilisation, cultivation and refinement, or the way of life, of a whole society, and includes all the common characteristics of such things of the general people of the whole society as habits, customs, religious, beliefs, food, dress, recreation, tradition, language, literature, etc. The prefix 'sub-' in sub-culture means 'subordinate', 'low', 'below', 'underneath' 'inferior', 'secondary', 'subservient', etc. Therefore, sub-culture refers to the 'culture' of a group or community within a whole society which is deemed by the general people of the whole society to be inferior or subordinate to its general or main-stream culture. A sub-culture distinguishes itself by its peculiar and characteristic language (*jargon, *patois, *slang, etc.), custom, *convention, tradition, ethical value system, literature (folklore, poetry, etc.), recreational activities (dance, song, music, etc.), dress, manners, religious activities, etc.

sub-culture novel. A *novel that portrays the life in a *sub-culture group of society.

sub-genre. See *genre.

sublime, the. The adjectival use of the word 'sublime' literally means 'exalted', 'lofty', 'majestic', 'supreme', 'awe and veneration inducing', etc. and the nominal use of it refers to that which is such or such (one or more of the foregoing). The critical or aesthetic use of the term does not bear significations different from its literal meanings. The difficulty is that the concept of sublimity is hard to grasp completely and harder to express. However, the first written expression of the concept of sublime is to be found in *On the Sublime* supposedly written by the Greek author Cassius Longinus of the 3rd century B.C. But the book "is now ascribed to an unknown author writing in the mid 1st century A.D" [Dudley, 106]. *On the Sublime* "analyses the sublime in literature, tracing 5 sources from which it derives: lofty conceptions, passionate feeling, the correct formation of figures of thought and speech, nobility of diction and dignified composition" [*loc. cit.*]. And the most pithy suggestive definition of the sublime by the author of *On the Sublime* is charmingly correct: "Sublimity is 'the echo of a great soul'" [*ibid*].

The next important book on the sublime is Edmund Burke's (1729-97) *A Philosophical Enquiry into the Origin of our Ideas of the Sublime and the Beautiful* (1757) in which he distinguished between the sublime and the beautiful and said that the former is "associated with the infinite, solitude, emptiness, darkness and terror; the latter with brightness, smoothness and smallness" and further that the sublime is also "associated with powerful emotions, with spiritual and religious awe, with vastness and immensity, with the natural order in its grander manifestations and with the concept of genius" [Cuddon, 875]. Taking the cue from Burke, Immanuel Kant

(1724-1804), the great German philosopher, developed the ideas of the sublime and the beautiful in *Critique of Judgement* (1790), showing that the sublime is infinite while the beautiful is finite. The idea of the sublime, further, is to be found in the works of Homer (?3rd c. B.C.) and John Milton (1608); in the works especially of the three romantic poets P.B. Shelley (1792-1822), Lord Byron (1788-1824) and William Wordsworth (1770-1850); and also in James Macpherson's (1736-96) 'fake translations' in Gaelic of ancient anonymous epic poems: *Fingal: An Ancient Epic Poem*, *Temora: An Ancient Epic Poem*, and *The Works of Ossian* (2 vols.). In the *Romantic period, poets were much inspired by the idea of the sublime.

subliterature, sub-literature. See *literature.

sub-plot. A secondary or subsidiary *plot or coherent sequence of events, that runs alongside the main plot as a variation of, or counterpoint to, it. "Its purpose is usually to contrast with the main story [or plot], complicate or refine the theme, sustain interest, or in general to make up any aesthetic or thematic deficiencies present in the main story [or plot]" [Lemon, 42]. Examples from plays are: the below-stairs plot in Shakespeare's (1564-1616) *Twelfth Night*, the Stefano-Trinculo comic sub-plot in his *The Tempest* and the serious sub-plot involving Gloucester, Edmund and Edgar in his *King Lear*. Though not frequently, sub-plots are also used in *novels, particularly in long ones, like some of Charles Dickens's (1812-70). Sub-plot is also called *underplot. Also see *double plot.

sub-text. The sub-text of a literary work (narrative, dramatic or poetic) refers to those things which are *implied* in the *text but *not explicitly stated*, are not said or done but indicated, suggested—the 'under text' or 'below text' that may be inferred from the text. In the drama, the sub-text is sometimes suggested by pauses, silences and movements, as in the plays of Samuel Beckett (1906-89) and Harold Pinter (b. 1930). As regards the *narrative, "A reader tends to construct a sub-text for herself or himself, imagining or interpreting what is *not* said or *not* done (and *how* it is not said or done), what may be implied, suggested or hinted, what is ambiguous, marginal, ambivalent, evasive, emphasized or not emphasized—and so on. In doing all this the reader exercises insight into 'unconscious' elements in the work itself and thus elicits additional meanings" [Cuddon, 877].

Superconscious, the. See *Unconscious, the.

superfluous man [from Russian *lishnichelovek*, superfluous man]. The term is a distinct type of *character, important and recurrent in the 19th c. Russian literature. "It denotes an idealistic but inactive hero who is aware of and sensitive to moral and social problems but who does not take action; in part because of personal weakness and lassitude, in part because of social and political restraints to freedom of action" [Cuddon, 879]. Such a character type is "a compound of Hamlet and Don Quixote, unable to reconcile the impulses of heart and head, given to over-much introspectiveness, intellectualizing and indecision" [*loc. cit.*]. Examples of the superfluous man are the following characters: Onegin in Alexander Pushkin's (1799-1837) *Eugene Onegin*; Pechorin in Mikhail Lermontov's (1814-41) *A Hero of Our Times*; and Rudin in Ivan Turgenev's (1818-83) *Rudin*, the Hamlet-like character in his *The Diary of a Superfluous Man* and Rakitin in his *A Month in the Country*. Also see *outsider.

supernatural story. A *story in which major roles are played by supernatural or praeternatural beings (such as spirits, poltergeists, ghosts, specters, apparitions, etc.) and in which supernatural or praeternatural situations, actions, witchcraft, magic, marvels, etc. contribute to, or control, the course and events of it. Instances of the supernatural story are: the anonymous *The Arabian Nights*; the Grim Brothers's (Jacob: 1785-1863 and Karl: 1786-1859) *Kinder-und Hausmarchen* or *Fairy Tales*; Daniel Defoe's (1660-1713) *The Relation of Apparition of one Mrs Veal*; Horace Walpole's (1717-97) *The Castle of Otranto*; Fyodor Dostoyevski's (1812-70) *A Christmas Carol*, etc.

superrealism. Same as *surrealism.

surfiction. Same as *metafiction.

surprise. It is the *action, *event or turn at any stage of a *narrative hugely incongruent with the reader's expected course of the narrative (the expectation building up out of his experiencing the course so far). The intellectual or emotional effect the action, event or turn produces on the reader is also called surprise. Also see *suspense.

surprise ending. The ending or conclusion of a *form of *story with an unexpectedly sudden turn or twist that produces a *surprise, amazement or bewilderment in the reader, for instance, in the *short stories of O(liver) Henry (1862-1910). Also called *O. Henry ending.

surrealism [from French *sur*, above, and *realisme*, reality]. A movement in arts and literature that originated in *Dadaism after the holocaust of the First World War but fizzled out in the 1930s, leaving behind its indelible influence on the 20th century plays and *novels. Its synonymous term, *superrealism, was coined by the French poet, prose writer and critic Guillaume Apollinaire (1880-1918) before the official announcement of the movement by the French poet Andre Breton (1896-1966) in his *Manifesto on Surrealism* in 1924. Being horrified and disgusted by the enormous inhumanness and hair-raising destructiveness of the First World War, the propounders of the movement turned away from the hollow bourgeois values with a vengeance and sought to react violently. "The expressed aim of surrealism was a revolt against all restraints on free creativity, including logical reason, standard morality, social and artistic conventions and norms, and all control over the artistic process by forethought and intention. To ensure the unhampered operation of the 'deep mind,' which they regarded as the only source of valid knowledge as well as art, surrealists turned to *automatic writing* (writing delivered over to the promptings of the unconscious mind), and to exploiting the material of dreams, of states of mind between sleep and waking, and of natural or artificially induced hallucinations" [Abrams, 310].

Surrealism rejected formalism in arts—rejected strict adherence to the guidelines for *form or *genre. It wanted to transcend the accepted limitations of the concept of the reality and to broaden it, and with a view to represent that broad idea of the reality it pressed for bringing in dream materials in literature as well as for delving deep into the *Subconscious and the *Unconscious for vital literary source materials. It did not hesitate to frankly expose 'the private chaos and the individual hell'. The ideas of surrealism fast spread like wildfire to different departments: painting, sculpture, poetry, drama, *novels, and even, in some cases, social and political movements (for a short while it was associated with the Communist International). In literature, some of the techniques it emphasised were: free association of images, broken syntax, *stream-of-consciousness, automatic writing, irrational and surprising juxtaposition, induction of hallucinatory state in the writer with drugs, flights of fantasy, dreamlike and nightmarish sequences, etc. Some of the notable practitioners of surrealism (besides Breton and Apollinaire) were: the poet and novelist Louis Aragon (b. 1897); the poets Paul Eluard (1895-1952) and Benjamin Peret (1899-1959); the actor, producer and theorist of the stage Antonin Artaud (1896-1948); the playwright Eugene Ionesco (b. 1912); the novelist and dramatists Jean Genet (b. 1910) and Samuel Beckett (b. 1906); the novelists William Borroughs (b. 1914), Nathalie Sarraute (b. 1902), Anais Nin (1903-77) and Susan Sontag (b. 1933); and the painters Chirico, Max Ernst, Picasso and Salvador Dali.

suspense. Suspense is the incertitude, uncertainty, waiting or irresolution that the novelist or dramatist introduces in his work with the deliberate intention of holding or heightening the interest of the reader or audience. Suspense is a technique in which the author keeps in abeyance for some time the outcome of the *plot at any stage of its progression. For instance, in a detective story a key *character may unexpectedly and suddenly disappear leaving the reader anxiously waiting in anticipation and incertitude but with enhanced curiosity as to whether the character would reappear. Also see *surprise, *detective novel, detective story.

sweetness and light. A phrase perhaps first used by Jonathan Swift (1667-1745) in his *The Battle of the Books*, and then by Matthew Arnold (1822-88) in his *Culture and Anarchy*. In his book, Swift introduced the *fable of 'the spider and the bee'—the spider being the *symbol of the 'modern writers' and the bee that of the ancient writers. Swift said that the spider produced only 'dirt and poison' while the bee produced 'honey and wax' or *sweetness and light*—the two noblest of things to mankind. Arnold in his book equated the light with reason and the sweetness with 'the will of God', and thought that the basic contributions of the artist (the novelist included, we may presume) to mankind are sweetness and light, or 'reason and the will of God'.

switchback. Same as **analepsis*, *cutback, *flashback.

symbol, symbolism [from Greek *sym*, together, and *ballein*, to throw]. Literally, symbol means 'that which by custom or convention represents something else' and, etymologically, 'to throw together, infer, compare'. So in a symbol there is a reference to the existence of two things: two things are thrown together, or one thing is inferred from another, or one thing is compared with another. But in a sign or a metaphor also there are two things. If so, what is the difference, on the one hand, between a sign and a symbol, and, on the other, between a metaphor and a symbol? Sign and symbol are difficult terms and "No satisfactory general definitions exist for these terms although candidates have been presented" [Flew, 327]. A sign is ordinarily understood as something that 'stands for' something else. But this will not do for a definition. Spots are a sign of measles, but spots do not 'stand for' measles. Yet, for a working definition of sign we may say, following the French linguist Ferdinand de Saussure, that a sign is a signifier that *conventionally, rather than naturally*, refers to a signified; for instance, the English word 'horse' (a sign or signifier) refers to the object 'horse' (signified) only conventionally, for we could use any other word for the same object. The sign, i.e. the word 'horse' has *no further significance* or meaning beyond the signified, i.e. the object 'horse'. Likewise the red light of traffic control signifies that vehicles must stop, and beyond this the red light has *no further significance*. But a symbol is a "specially evocative kind of image: that is a word or phrase referring to concrete object, scene or action which *also has some further significance associated with it*" (emphasis added) [Baldick, 218-19]. The national flag of a country, for instance, is a symbol and a rose is a symbol of love.

Again, in the sign the signified is clearly expressed or stated but in the symbol the signified is 'mysteriously indeterminate' and bears 'an unstated suggestion'. This nature of the symbol also distinguishes it from the metaphor which expressly refers to an identifiable, largely definite signified. Thus, "in the sentence *She was a tower of strength*, the metaphor ties a concrete image (the 'vehicle' tower) to an identifiable abstract quality (the tenor: strength).... But the symbolic tower in Robert Browning's poem 'Child Roland to the Dark Tower Came' (1855) or that in W.B. Yeats's collection of poems *Tower* (1928) mysteriously indeterminate in its possible meanings" [*op. cit.*, 219]. The famous albatross in S.T. Coleridge's (1772-1834) 'The Rime of the Ancient Mariner' and Moby Dick or the White Whale (and, in fact, all the *characters) in Herman Melville's (1819-91) *novel *Moby Dick* are good examples of symbol.

The term symbolism refers to three things: (i) a set of symbols, (ii) use of symbols, and (iii) the poetic movement of a group of French poets, such as Paul Verlaine, Arthur Rimbaud, Stephane Mallarme and, of course, Charles Baudlaire—the movement that 'aimed for a poetry of suggestion rather than of direct statement'.

symbolic action. "This jargon term denotes the conscious or unconscious 'ritual' which the writer experiences while creating a work. The work is a 'strategy' for controlling his own problems. The writer disguises his identity and, by doing so, performs a symbolic action. For example, a writer may 'write out of himself' aggressive impulses, guilt complexes, sex complexes, through the symbolic action. These theories were introduced and elaborated by Kenneth Burke in *Attitudes Towards History* (1937) and *The Philosophy of Literary Form: Studies in Symbolic Action* (1941)" [Cuddon, 888]. The idea of symbolic action seems to be commensurate with projection, or with sublimation, of psychoanalysis.

symbolic novel, symbolist novel. A *form of *novel that "emphasizes a meaningful pattern of symbols rather than such conventional novelistic staples as characterisation and story" [Lemon, 7-8]. Hermann Hesse's (1877-1962) *Der Steppenwolf* (which symbolically shows in the instincts of the split personality of an artist the dubious acceptance of life as 'a jumble of images in the "magic theatre" of the imagination') is a good example. Some other writers of the symbolic or symbolist novel are: Elemir Bourges (1852-1925), Paul Bourget (1852-1935), the two Tharaud brothers, Jerome (1874-1953) and Jean (1877-1952), *et. al*.

switchback. Same as *flashback.

sympathy. See *empathy.

syuzhet [from Russian *sjuzet* (pronounced *syuzhet*), plot]. Same as **sjuzet*.

T

tableau. Literally, 'a picture or vivid pictorial impression' or 'a suddenly created situation that takes all aback' or 'a "picture" formed by living persons caught in a static situation'. In literary works (*story, drama, poem), the term denotes "a description of some group of people in more or less static postures" [Baldick, 223].

tain. The term is etymologically related to the term tin-foil but it actually refers to the *language* of a literary work that works as the *silver backing of a speculum or mirror* which reflects the image of an object. In Jacques Derrida's (b. 1930) theory of deconstruction, "the term has the force of undercutting any simple or simplistic versions of realism which assume or argue that representations are *exact copies*" (emphasis added) [Hawthorn, 356]. Deconstruction argues that language cannot completely or perfectly or faithfully reflect the reality, and that how far the language will reflect the reality depends upon the degree of its visibility or prominence. Jeremy Hawthorn quotes from Martin Jay to illustrate the point: "specular or reflective discourses of identity, in which words allegedly mirror thoughts without remainder, have metaphorically forgotten the silver backing, the tain, behind every image. When the tain becomes, as it were visible, the mirror loses its capacity to reflect; *when the materiality of language is foregrounded, signifiers cannot be taken as simple doubles of what they signify*: mere transparent vehicles of signification" (emphasis added) [*loc. cit.*]. Also see *foregrounding.

tale. A simple *narrative, written or spoken, in prose or verse, differing from the *short story in that the latter is more formal and technical than the former, and in that, unlike the latter, the former is more usually 'written in the tone of voice of someone speaking.' Examples of the tale are: Geoffrey Chaucer's (1342-1400) tales in *The Canterbury Tales* and Washington Irving's (1783-1859) 'Rip Van Winkle'. Also see *story, *fable, *yarn.

tall story, tall tale. A humorous, extravagant, outlandish and highly improbable *story that describes impossible feats and *events, such as Geoffrey Chaucer's (1340-1400) 'Miller's Tale' and Francois Rabelais's (1494-1553?) *Pantagruel* and *Gargantua*. Also see *cock-and-bull story.

taste. A term difficult to define, for it has been used in 'a bewildering variety of senses'. S.T. Coleridge (1772-1834) defined it as "the intermediate faculty which connects the active with the passive powers of our nature, the intellect with the senses; and its appointed function is to elevate the *images* of the latter, while it realizes the *ideas* of the former" [Cuddon, 902]. However, taste may be defined as personal preference for, or appreciation of, a work of art or literature; or as the basis of evaluation of a work of art or literature. Taste may be good or bad; the former is appreciable or acceptable, the latter is equivalent to *vulgarity. Taste may vary from person to person as well as from time to time. Even Shakespeare's works, for instance, were once deemed to be lacking in taste (i.e., good taste).

telescoping. Abridging of a really long *event into a desirable length of expression (in speech or writing) in *narratives (cf. telescope word). In his *Ten Novels and Their Authors*, Somerset Maugham (1874-1965) writes: "Of course, in a novel events, whether material or spiritual, have to be telescoped, otherwise it would never end: a long-fought battle must be described in a page or two, and everything but what the author thinks essential has to be omitted; it is the same with a change of heart" [Maugham, 285].

televerite [from a combination of the French word element *tele*, taken from French *television*, and French *verite*, truth, fact]. A reality show on TV screen or "the television of scenes of real life in order to convey a heightened realism" [Macdonald, 1388]. Also see **cinema-verite*.

Telling and showing. Same as *showing and telling.

Tel Quel school. ['Tel Quel' from French *tel*, such, like, similar, and *quell*, what, which]. The term *tel quel* literally means 'such as it is' or 'just as it is'. The Tel Quel school was founded by the French novelist and critic Phillipe Sollers (b. 1936) in 1960 with the view of retrieving the lost or diminished powers of language (as he thought) in literature. In that year, he founded the literary periodical *Tel Quel*, from which this school took its name, and in 1968 published his discourse *Logiques*. Mainly through these two, *Tel Quel* and *Logiques*, Sollers wanted to materialise his aims. "The aims are basically ideological and activist, as well as aesthetic. One of its aims is to restore to language its original revolutionary powers; and it advances the principle that 'literature is language made with language'" [Cuddon, 903]. The school was much influenced by Roland Barthes and such other linguists, and it has concerned itself particularly with the works of such writers as Marquis de Sade (1740-1814), Stephane Mallarme (1842-98), Lautreamont (1846-70) and Antonin Artaud (1896-1948).

ten-year test. A term coined by Cyril Connolly that refers to a rough-hewn devise or test of determining the worth or value of a literary work. According to this test, a work of literature, such as a *novel, should be deemed to have unusual literary value if even ten years after its publication it "is still regarded as being of unusual literary merit, is still being widely read, and is still well thought of in literary and critical circles" [Cuddon, 904]. Instances of literary works which have passed the ten-year test are: William Golding's (b. 1911) *Lord of Flies*, Kinsley Amis's (b. 1922) *Lucky Jim*, V.S. Naipaul's (b. 1932) *A House for Mr Biswas*, J.G. Farrell's (1935-79) *The Siege of Krishnapur*, Malcolm Bradbury's (b. 1932) *The History of Man*, etc. Also see *best-seller.

text and work. Ordinarily, the word 'text' refers to the main body of matter in a book exclusive of notes, glosses, index, appendices, etc. Sometimes the two terms, 'text' and 'work', are used interchangeably, but in critical-theoretical discourse the two are sharply differentiated, though how they are to be separated from one another critics are not unanimous about. However, Roland Barthes suggests that "whereas the work is 'a finished object, something computable, which can occupy a physical space', 'the text is a methodological field', and that '[t] he work is held in the hand, the text in language'" [Hawthorn, 357]. Simply, we may say that *the printed book is a work, the *novel that can be read in the language as printed in the pages of the book is a text.*

text-time and story-time. See *story-time and text-time.

texture. The peripheral or surface qualities of a literary work as opposed to its formal qualities or *structure. The term denotes "those 'concrete' properties of a literary work that cannot be subjected to paraphrase as distinct from its paraphrasable 'structure' or abstract argument" [Baldick, 224]. The term is a *jargon in *new criticism where it refers especially to such elements of a poem as assonance, imagery, sensuousness, etc. as opposed to its idea (which is structural).

Thaw, the. The term was taken from the Russian novelist and poet Grigor'yevich Erenburg's (1891-1967) *novel *Ottepel* (*The Thaw*). It refers to the period of liberalisation of the arts in Soviet Russia, which followed the death of Stalin in 1953, and stands for the view that "a work of art should be judged not by the canons of socialist realism but by the sincerity of the author" [Thorlby, 760]. Some of the writers who represented the attitude of the Thaw were: Konstantin Paustovsky (1892-1968), Boris Slutsky (b. 1919) and Aleksandr Solzhenitsin (b. 1918). The journal *Novyy Mir* ('New World') took a leading part in the Thaw.

theme. Theme is the directly or indirectly expressed *abstract central idea* of a literary work; for instance, the theme of *Othello* is jealousy. It is different from the subject or subject-matter of that work: "While the subject of a work is described concretely in terms of its action (e.g., 'the adventures of a newcomer in the big city') its theme or themes will be described in more abstract terms (e.g., love, war, revenge, betrayal, fate, etc.)" [Baldick, 225]. However, the term also denotes a topic or subject matter that recurs in a number of literary works, for instance, the round table in the stories of King Arthur's court is a theme; and also a *motif or recurring idea in a single work; and, once again, "any meaningful element that is repeated within a work; in *Oedipus Rex* the frequent reference to sight, vision, blindness, etc. constitute a theme" [Lemon, 92]. In any case, the distinguishing mark of the theme is basically its *abstractness*, though it may be expressed through a concrete medium.

Theophrastian character. "The Theophrastian character (after Theophraslus, c. third century B.C.) is a satiric form of the character; it ridicules a vice or folly by depicting an epitome of a more or less obnoxious social type. The form was most popular during the seventeenth century" [Lemon, 48].

thesis novel. Same as *novel of doctrine. Also see *propaganda novel, *proletarian novel.

third-person narrative. See *point of view.

third-person perspective. See *point of view.

Third-person point of view. See *point of view.

thriller. A vague and loose term, it refers to a variety of *fictions, *short stories, plays and films, which relate sensational and exciting *stories of crime and detection, including such fictions as *police procedural, **roman policier*, *cloak-and-dagger story, *ghost story, *horror story, *detective novel or story, *newgate fiction, and, of course, the *Gothic novel or romance. Examples of the thriller are the fictions of Edgar Wallace (1875-1932), Sir Arthur Canon Doyle (1859-1930), Agatha Christie (1890-1976), Dorothy Sayers (1893-1957),

Dashiell Hammett (1894-1961), Raymond Chandler (1888-1959), *et al.*

time novel. "A term used occasionally to denote those novels which employ the stream of consciousness technique and in which the use of time, and time as a theme, is of pre-eminent importance" [Cuddon, 919]. The term is analogous to the term 'time play' which exploits such techniques of altering chronological sequence as *flashback and *flashforward, and of skipping over time as in Shakespeare's *The Winter's Tale* where the Chorus tells us that sixteen years have elapsed since Perdita was 'lost'. Examples of the time *novel are: Marcel Proust's (1871-1922) *A la recherché du temps perdu* (*Remembrance of Things Past*), Dorothy Richardson's (1873-1957) 12-volume sequence of novels *Pilgrimage*, James Joyce's (1882-1941) *Ulysses* and Thomas Mann's (1875-1955) *Der Zauberberg*.

tone. Literally, tone refers to the character or quality of sound or speech, which involves accent, intonation, vocal inflexation, etc. or to a speaker's attitude. As a critical term, tone indicates that a *narrative is a mode of speech which in turn "suggests that there is a speaker who has determinate personal qualities, and who expresses attitudes both toward the characters and materials within the work and toward the audience [or reader] to whom the work is addressed" [Abrams, 217]. I.A. Richards defines tone as "the expression of a literary speaker's 'attitude to his listener'" [*op. cit.*, 218]. The tone may be friendly, intimate, inimical, satiric, comical, detached, somber, morose, pompous, etc. Sometimes in a broader sense the term tone is used to mean *voice. Also see *persona.

topos [from Greek *topos*, a place, commonplace]. The term refers to "certain conventionalized places or settings consisting of a fixed combination of characteristic and stylized objects—a meadow, a tree, a running stream, for example. The term is often used in a broader sense to include conventional collocations of motifs, or themes, in some present-day usages is very close to certain usages of stereotype" [Hawthorn, 364]. Topos (pl. topoi) is "the general basis of an image or idea that recurs in various works" [Lemon, 92]. The poisoned fruit (or an apple, a poisoned dagger, a vicious pet or whatever kills the hero) that recurs in many fairy tales, for example, is a topos, for it suggests the idea that 'one be wary of accepting gifts, that evil is attractive, and so on.'

tour de force [from French *tour*, turn, round, winding; *de*, of; and *force*, force, strength]. The term literally means 'turn of force' or 'a feat, trick or force round something' but as a literary-critical term it means 'a remarkable feat of skill, that fills everyone with admiration', or a writer's show of mastery or a sort of brilliant one-off display. Examples are: Ernest Hemingway's (1898-1961) *The Short and Happy Life of Francis Macomber*, Arthur Koestler's (1905-83) *novel *Darkness at Noon*, Antony Burgess's (b. 1917) *A Clockwork Orange*, etc.

tragedy. A term that applies especially to dramatic works. Any serious dramatic or *narrative work that concludes in a disastrous end of its *protagonist is a tragedy.

transcendentalism. A term with *plurisignation, it refers to "any theory asserting the dependence of the world of experience on the activities of reason" (Kant), "a mode of thought that emphasizes the intuitive and supersensuous" or a "form of religious mysticism" [Flew, 354]. But in literary-critical discourse, the term especially refers to the "particular doctrine adopted by a movement in New England under the leadership of Emerson and his associates, influenced by Platonism and German idealism and reacting against dogmatic rationalism" [*loc. cit.*]. Transcendentalism was also influenced by Henry David Thoreau, the author of *Walden*. Growing out of Christian Unitarianism, transcendentalism flourished in Boston in the mid-19th century. Besides Emerson and Thoreau, some other transcendentalists were: William Ellery Channing, Amos Bronson Alcott, Margaret Fuller, etc. "Transcendentalism was opposed to the idea that man needs an intercessor through whom to reach the divine, and was critical of formalized religion. Like the physical universe itself, all constructive practical activity, all great literature, all forms of spiritual awareness were viewed as an expression of the divine spirit" [Ousby, 936]. The transcendentalists exerted a strong influence on the American literature of the mid-19th century, particularly on the works of the novelists Nathaniel Hawthorn (1804-64) and Herman Melville (1819-91) and on the poetry of Walt Whitman (1819-92).

transposition. "Transposition occurs when an event is thrown out of its natural place in the chronological sequence. The beginning in medias res [sic.] (Lat. 'in the middle of the action') is a type of transposition characteristic of the classical epic; the first event narrated in the plot is actually an event which would in reality have occurred somewhere near the middle of the story" [Lemon, 43]. *Flashback and *flashforward are two other sorts of transposition.

travelogue. A talk, lecture, article, film, account, or *narrative on travel.

travesty. Usually used as synonymous with *parody. A travesty is a slighting, trivialising, trifling, mocking, subversive mimicry of a dignified literary work. Examples are: Saavedra Cervantes's (1547-1616) *Don Quixote* (which is a travesty of chivalric romances), Alexander Pope's (1688-1744) *The Dunciad* (in which Pope hits back at Lewis Theobald who severely criticised his edition of Shakespeare), Jane Austen's (1775-1817) *Northanger Abbey* (in which she mocks at the *Gothic novel) and James Joyce's (1882-1941) *Ulysses* (which is partly a mimicry of Homer's *Odyssey*). Travesty is to be sharply distinguished from *burlesque, for while the latter mocks a *non-serious* but dignified literary work gravely, seriously, solemnly, the former mimics a *serious*, solemn and dignified literary work frivolously.

trick ending. The ending or conclusion of a story or narrative where there is a sudden and unexpected deceptive device that renders the reader astonished, amused or puzzled, as in the *O. Henry ending. Also called *twist ending.

trilogy. A group of three interconnected *novels or plays, each of which is a complete unit in itself. Shakespeare's *King Henry VI* (which comprises Parts 1, 2 and 3) is an example of dramatic trilogy. In the *narrative category, J.R.R. Tolkein's (1892-1973) *The Lord of the Rings* (which consists of *The Fellowship of the Ring*, *The Two Towers* and *The Return of the King*) and Jean-Paul Sartre's (b. 1905) *L'age de raison* or *The Age of Reason* (which comprises *The Age of Reason*, *The Reprieve* and *La mort dans l'ame*) are two examples.

tropism. "A term popularized by the French novelist Nathalie Sarraute (b.1902) which refers to mental and imaginative life as perceived by her. Thus perceived, it comprises millions of tiny little responses to innumerable stimuli" [Cuddon, 948]. "For her the biological tropism, a reaction to a stimulus, describes the almost imperceptible movements concealed behind the social façade of gestures, actions and language, the authentic, constantly moving realm of instinctive reactions" [Thorlby, 696]. Sarraute illustrated her concept of tropism in her *novels *Tropism and the Age of Suspicion* and *Portrait of a Man Unknown*.

truth. See *fiction and truth,*sincerity.

Tudor period. The period from 1485 (accession of King Henry VII) to 1603 (death of Queen Elizabeth) during which the Tudor family ruled England. The period was noticeably fecund as regards productions of plays and poetry, but not even a single *novel was produced.

turning point. A conspicuous moment, stage or point in a *narrative or play when or where there is a definite and final change in its course or direction towards conclusion. The turning point is the crucial point or *climax where **peripeteia* or *anagnorisis occurs.

twist ending. See *trick ending.

twopence coloured. H.W. Fowler, in his *A Dictionary of Modern English Usage*, writes about this entry: "The insertion of irrelevant details,resort to needless rhetoric, and such devices for the heightening of effect, move the reader (...) to exclaim in more modern phrase 'twopence coloured!'" [Fowler, H.W., 1996, 668].

type character. See *developing character.

typicality. A term floated into literary criticism by the Hungarian Marxist critic Georg Lukacs (b. 1885) who laid the foundation of Marxist criticism of literature. Being influenced by the aesthetics of Hegel, Lukacs "has used the idea of 'typicality' to indicate the process whereby, in classical realist literature, events and individuals are at once uniquely particularized, and representative of broader, deeper trends in history itself. A George Eliot character, for example, is neither an isolated 'personality' nor a mere emblem of some underlying reality; the peculiar complexity of such a character lies in its dialectical unity of the individual and the representative" [Fowler, Roger, 254-55].

U

ubi sunt, ubi sunt? [from the Latin phrase *ubi sunt*, 'where are they?']. The phrase occurs in the opening line of many medieval songs and other works, and hints at a sense of regret for the transience of human life, loss of youth or loved ones, etc. and at a wistful nostalgia, at the same time. Though it is an especial poetic element, it may be found in *narratives as well.

Ultima Thule [from Latin *ultima*, farthest, and the name of a Thule, place or region in northern Europe in ancient times]. The term literally means 'farthest Thule', but figuratively it suggests a sense of a remote goal, a mysterious country or region, or an (unachievable) ideal.

ultraism. "A radical attitude whose quest and objective in literature (and art) is for a kind of *reduction ad absurdum* [i.e., to reduce to absurdity], or for an expression of experience which seeks to go beyond the limits of the medium. Hence phenomena like 'happenings', the use of different coloured pages in a novel to suggest tone and mood, gimmick books in which the pages can be rearranged as the reader wishes" [Cuddon, 953]. Linguistic ultraism is to be found, for instance, in James Joyce's (1882-1941) *Finnegans Wake*, George Orwell's (1903-50) *Nineteen Eighty-Four* and Anthony Burgess's (b. 1917) *A Clockwork Orange*. In all of these three *novels the writers have employed very much 'private' languages—'ultra languages', so to say. *Dadaism, *expressionism, *surrealism, the theatre of the absurd, etc. are instances of literary ultraism.

uncanny, the. The uncanny in literature is the weird, supernatural or very strange and horrific in a *story or *fiction. "In Tzvetan Todorov's theory of the fantastic, the uncanny is an effect produced by stories in which the incredible events can be explained as the products of the narrator's or protagonist's dream, hallucination, or delusion" [Baldick, 233]. Edgar Allan Poe's (1809-49) story 'The Tell-Tale Heart' is an example of the uncanny. Also see *fantastic, the; marvelous, the.

Unconscious, the. The term refers to "the totality of psychic processes, acts and states conditioned by realities which the individual is unaware of" [Petrovsky, 322]. In psychoanalysis, the Unconscious is also called System Unconscious. "The *Unconscious* or the *System Unconscious* is that part of the mind in which mental processes are dynamically unconscious; in contrast to the conscious [i.e., the conscious part of the mind].... 'To sum up: exemption from mutual contradiction, primary process (mobility of cathexes), timelessness, and replacement of external by psychical reality—these are the characteristics which we expect to find in processes belonging to the System Unconscious'—Freud (1915)" [Rycroft, 173]. In modern literary critical jargon, such terms are not infrequently being used as the Unconscious, the Superconscious ('a level of individual mental *activity* in solving creative *tasks*, uncontrollable by the individual conscious volition'), the Subconscious ('Synonym for Unconscious never used in psychoanalytic writings) as well as such terms which are not used in scientific psychology as 'preconscious', 'co-conscious', 'extra-conscious' and 'creative unconscious'.

underplot. Same as *sub-plot.

undramatised narrator. See *dramatised narrator.

uninvolved narrator. The term denotes the *narrator who is the objective teller of the *narrative and does not take part in the *actions of the narrative at all, or if he at all takes part he does so only minimally. The term is synonymous with *detached narrator.

unity. A classical concept in drama (especially in tragedy), it implies three obligatory 'unities' in drama: unity (or oneness) of time (i.e., the *action must span not more than a single day); unity of place (i.e., the action must take place at a single place or area); and unity of action (i.e., there must be only a single action, having none or minimal extraneous actions).

universality. The quality of a literary work that appeals to all readers (or spectators) of all times.

ur-text [from the combination of German prefix *ur-*, original, first, and English 'text']. Literally, the term means 'original text' or 'first text'. As a critical term it refers the first or original version of a later-day altered text; for instance, James Joyce's (1882-1941) earlier work 'Stephen Hero' is the ur-text of his *A Portrait of the Artist as a Young Man* (the former was done in c. 1904, the latter was published in *The Egoist* in instalments from February 1914 to September 1915). Shakespeare's (1564-1616) *Hamlet* is believed to have had a ur-text in German.

utopia [from a pun on two Greek words *eutopos* (*eu*, well, and *topos*, place) and *outopos* (*ou*, no, not, and *topos*, place)]. Literally, 'utopia' means 'a place, or a no place, where all is well'. The term 'utopia' was coined by Sir Thomas More (1477-1535) in his book *Utopia* (written in Latin). Utopia denotes an imagined ideal place, or the idea of such a place, where the most superior or perfect human society is supposed to exist—a place like the island of Utopia in More's *Utopia* where 'the best state of commonwealth' exists. The antonym of utopia is *dystopia, i.e. a most bad place.

V

vapours. In old medical treatises, the word referred to 'exhalations supposed to arise in the stomach or elsewhere in the body, affecting the health' and was supposed to lower the level of spirits and induce depression, melancholy, hysteria, faintness, etc. as well as eccentric behaviour. Heroines of the 18th century *fictions are rather frequently found to have undergone the effects of vapours.

verbocrap [from Latin *verbum*, word, and Middle English *crappe*, chaff, excrement]. A type of crude *officialese heavily marked by 'polysyllabic circumlocutions, crude syntax, faulty grammar and a self-important, orotund tone' dear to bureaucrats and semi-literate officials. Also see *journalese.

verisimilitude [from Latin *veritas*, true, and *similes*, like]. Literally, the term means 'Likeness to the truth'. Verisimilitude in a fictional work (narrative or dramatic) denotes the presence in it of the impression or appearance of the reality (when read or viewed by someone) that it deals with. It refers to the work's intrinsic authenticity or probability within the terms of the logic of *fiction. It is in this sense that such works as Francois Rabelais's (?1494-1553) *Gangantua* and *Pantagruel*, Jonathan Swift's (1667-1745) *Gulliver's Travels*, Voltaire's (1694-1778) *Candide* and H.G. Wells's (1866-1946) *The First Man in the Moon* have verisimilitude like the realistic novels of Jane Austen (1775-1817), Thomas Hardy (1840-1928), Henry James (1843-1916), Arnold Bennett (1867-1931), *et al*. However, "In the end, verisimilitude will depend as much on the reader's knowledge, intelligence and experience (and his capacity for make-believe) as upon the writer's use of those same sources" [Cuddon, 964]. Also see *verism, **verismo*.

verism. The literary theory according to which a work of literature should represent the truth or reality as much faithfully as possible, however immoral or disagreeable that truth or reality may be. Also see *verisimilitude, **verismo*, *neo-realism, *naturalism.

verismo [from Italian *vero*, true].The term denotes an Italian form of *naturalism best exemplified by the *novels and *stories of the Sicilian novelist and dramatist Giovanni Verga (1840-1922), which depict the harsh lives of the Sicilian poor. *Verismo* lays its main emphasis on 'truthfulness', particularly in representing "the more squalid aspects of life: poverty, despair and violence, among other things" [Cuddon, 964]. Also see *verisimilitude, *verism, *neo-realism, *naturalism.

veritism. "This term was used by Hamlin Garland in his *Crumbling Idols* (1894) to assert a more scientific standpoint, in part a reaction against Howells' [William Dean Howells (1837-1920)] moralism and his emphasis on the 'smiling' aspects of life (which to Howells were the 'typically American' aspects). Garland, drawing on Darwin and social determinism, stressed that literature was democratic when it was scientific and engaged with social problems; this meant that realism had no inherent optimism or ethics" [Mottram, 216]. Also see *verism, **verismo*, *naturalism.

vernacular [from Latin *vernaculus*, domestic, indigenous, native, which is from *verna*, a home-born slave]. An everyday mainly oral language of a rural lower social class (contrastive to urban upper social class) people.

verse novel. Same as *novel-in-verse.

Victorianism. In its value-neutral sense, the term refers to the identifying psychological and social features of the remarkable historical period during which Queen Victoria reigned England: the period from 1837 to 1901. Among the features are: (i) unsurpassed visionary optimism, (ii) ideal of absolute moral rectitude, (iii) sexual priggishness, particularly 'determination to maintain feminine 'innocence' (i.e., sexual ignorance)', (iv) narrow-mindedness in all sorts of beliefs and opinions, (v) unconfirmed and unstable skepticism about religion (under the influence of Darwinism and positivism), (vi) shameless hypocrisy, (vii) struggle between liberal ideas and orthodox bigotry, (viii) feminist agitation for equal rights with men, (ix) conflict between penumbrous poverty and sunshine affluence, etc. Also see *Victorian period.

Victorian period. The period during which Queen Victoria reigned: 1837-1901 (the period is sometimes dated from 1832 in which year the first Reform Bill was passed). Few dramas were turned out during the period, but the period saw phenomenal output of *novels and poetic works. Some of the famous British novelists of the period were: William Thackeray (1811-63), Anthony Trollope (1815-82), Charlotte Bronte (1816-55), Emily Bronte (1818-48), Anne Bronte (1820-49), Charles Kingsley (1819-75), George Eliot (1819-80), Wilkie Collins (1824-89), Aldous Huxley (1894-1963), George Meredith (1828-1909), Thomas Hardy (1840-1928) and R.L. Stevenson (1850-94). And some of the famous American novelists of the period were: Nathaniel Hawthorne (1804-64), Herman Melville (1819-91), Mark Twain (1835-1910) and Henry James (1843-1916).

view point. Same as *point of view.

vignette [from French *vigne*, a vine]. Literally, the term means 'a little vine'. Earlier, vignette only meant a small ornamental design, usually a design of vine-leaves and tendrils, on a blank page in a book, but now it also denotes a written *sketch or short composition that shows considerable literary skill. A vignette in the second sense may be an independent literary piece, like Virginia Woolf's (1882-1941) short story *Kew Garden*, or a part of a long literary work, like William Faulkner's (1897-1962) memorable description of the wild-spotted horses in his *The Hamlet*.

villain. The principal wicked *character, or the main *antagonist of the *hero or heroine, of a play or *narrative.

virtual reality. "Electronically simulated physical spaces and objects, for example those generated by computer games or the simulators used to train pilots" [Hawthorn, 373].

voice. An important modern literary-critical term, it is same as *implied author. M.H. Abrams very clearly explains the term 'voice': "The term in literary criticism points to the fact that we are aware of a voice beyond the fictitious voices that speak in a work and a persona behind all the dramatic personae, and behind even the first-person narrator. We have the sense, that is, of a pervasive authorial presence, a determinate intelligence and moral sensibility, who has invented, ordered, and rendered all these literary characters and materials in just this way" [Abrams, 219]. The (imagined or suggested) tone, timber, pitch, etc. of the voice approximately match the writer's or author's true persona or personality, attitude (toward the material he deals with), standpoint, *viewpoint, etc. In short, through the voice we may meet the author himself *tete-a-tete*. Also see *narrator.

voice-over. The term denotes "the background voice of an unseen narrator in a film, etc." [Davidson, 1118].

Volksmarchen [from German *Volk*, people, nation, and *Marchen*, fairy tale]. Literally, the term means *folk tale. *Volksmarchen* is a *tale that is continuing to exist down generations through oral transmission and has not been written down, and so it is different from **Kunstmarchen* which, though earlier had been being transmitted through oral tradition, has been rendered into characters.

Vorurteil [from German *Vorurteil*, prejudice]. The term is sometimes used in the sense of 'pre-judgement' (following the German philosopher Martin Heidegger's hermeneutic philosophy) and sometimes in the sense of 'prejudice' (following the philosopher Hans-George Gadamer). However, in literary-critical discourse it is generally employed "referring to the reader's predisposition to interpret in one way rather than another" [Hawthorn, 373].

Vraisemblance [from French *Vrai*, truth, and *sembler*, to seem]. The French term is synonymous with the English term *verisimilitude, and is increasingly being used in the pejorative or dismissive sense 'the more the status of realism has been brought into question.'

vulgarity. See *taste.

W

Waldeinsamkeit [from German *Wald*, forest, and *einsamkeit*, loneliness (*ein*, one; *einsam*, lonely; *einsamkeit*, loneliness)]. The term was perhaps coined by the German romantic poet, novelist and dramatist Ludwig Tieck (1773-1853) and it was frequently used during the German romantic period. "It implies a turning away from reality into dream world, a yearning for distant countries (of the mind as well as of actuality), a yearning for remoteness of time and place. The concept of the forest is important because forests are remote, wild, dark, lonely places where the spirit may commune with Nature. A good deal of poetry and fiction of the period dwells on this quasi-mystical longing.... Goethe's poem *Wanderers Nachtlied* is a well-known example of the expression of the feelings involved [in the term]" [Cuddon, 979].

Wardour Street English ['Wardour Street' from the 'name of a street in London mainly occupied by dealers in antique & imitation-antique furniture']. The term refers to a style of writing in English that is rather heavily encumbered with archaic words, out-of-mode phrases, and insince and artificial expressions, as in William Morris's (1834-96) translation of *The Odyssey*.

Waverley novels. The *novels of Sir Walter Scott (1771-1832) are generally collectively called Waverley novels because all the novels of Scott published after his first novel *Waverley* "were described as being 'by the author of *Waverley*'" [Ousby, 984]. Also see *Leatherstocking Tales, *Wessex novels.

well-made novel. The term is analogous to the French dramatist Eugene Scribe's (1791-1861) term 'well-made play' that "refers to a neatly and economically constructed play which works with mechanical efficiency." The well-made novel, likewise, progresses following a strictly schematic programme quite artificially. "The well-made novel begins with a definite problem set for the protagonist (in Austen's *Pride and Prejudice*, will Elizabeth Bennet marry Darcy?), develops through a series of complications or trials (Elizabeth's prejudice and Darcy's pride), and ends when all of the difficulties that have developed along the way are resolved. As a pejorative, 'well-made' describes novels and plays in which the problem and the resolution are too pat" [Lemon, 8].

Weltanschauung [from German *Welt*, world, and *anschauen*, to look at, to watch, or *anschauung*, perception]. Literally, the German word means ideology or philosophy (of life). As a literary term it is used to denote a writer's world outlook, or his attitude to the world or life in general, or his attitude to 'the prevailing spirit or vision of a period', or, lastly, 'the more general outlook shared by people in a given period'. For instance, Thomas Hardy's (1840-1928) *Weltanschauung* was that human life is absolutely controlled by an irrational and cruel fate or that of the poets of the 1930s, such as W.H. Auden, Stephen Spender,

Cecil Day Lewis and William Empson, was that life perforce makes us disillusioned and cynical.

Weltliteratur [from German *Welt*, world, and *literatur*, literature]. The term literally means 'world literature'. It was coined by the German poet and novelist J.W. von Goethe (1749-1832) but was not clearly defined by him. However, the term is generally understood as meaning that literature which "is of all nations and peoples, and which, by a reciprocal exchange of ideas, mediates between nations and helps to enrich the spirit of man" [Cuddon, 981]. In short, *Weltliteratur* or world literature is that literature which is enjoyed and appreciated by the peoples of all times and all climes. Interestingly, Thomas Carlyle (1795-1881) also spoke of 'World literature'.

Weltschmerz [from German *Welt*, world, and *schmerz*, pain]. The term literally means 'world pain', i.e. pain begotten from the perception of evils in the world. "*Weltschmerz* is a feeling of ineffable sadness and depression brought about by contemplation of the state of the world and its evils. The term connotes in particular a sort of fashionable apathetic pessimism" [Ayto, 323]. It is a sort of feeling ill-at-ease in the world inspite of everything.

Wendepunkt [from German *Wende*, turning, and *Punkt*, point, spot]. The term literally means 'turning point'. *Wendepunkt* denotes "An important element in the theory and practice of the *Novelle*" [Cuddon, 982]. Also see **Novelle*.

Wertherism. The term was taken from the *sentimental novel of J.W. Goethe (1749-1832)—*Die Leiden des jungen Werthers* (*The Sorrows of Young Werther*). The sorrows of the young hero of the novel, Werther, are due to his hopeless love for a young married woman, and the sorrows are exotically disproportionate to his lost love, so much so that they seem 'a fashion for morbid and self-indulgent melancholy' which Wertherism denotes.

Wessex novels. The novels of Thomas Hardy (1840-1928) are collectively generally called Wessex novels, because the setting of all of them is the imaginary vast region Wessex in the southern most part of England between Bristol in the north and Southampton in the south. Also see *Yoknapatawpha.

West. The word is used in various meanings; for instance, 'the West' signifies 'Europe or Europe and America', 'West End' denotes 'the fashionable quarter in the west of London', 'Wild West' signifies 'the western United States in the days of the first settlers, chiefly cattlemen and goldminers, before the establishment of law and order.' But, in his *A Glossary of Contemporary Literary Theory*, Jeremy Hawthorn writes about West: "We use this term to define not just a specific geographical area, but to refer to a covert, half-conscious fashion to a range of assumed values: 'the West' thus *excludes* both communism and post-communist eastern Europe, the 'third world', Islam, and so on. 'The West' sounds like a geographical description, but it often seems to include a strange mix of countries and areas: western Europe, the United States and Canada, Israel, Australia and New Zealand—states and areas that are clearly being yoked together for ideological and political rather than geographical reasons" [Hawthorn, 374]. Also see *Western, *Westerners.

Western. Ordinarily, the adjectival word means situated in the west, i.e. in countries or regions like the western part of Europe, the U.S., Canada, etc. But the term also refers to a genre of fiction (usually *novels and *short stories) which is associated with the western states of the United States (sometimes called the Wild West), more particularly the border states of Arizona, New Mexico, Western Texas and some other adjacent regions. This genre of fiction—the Western—is especially distinguished for its descriptions of the American Indians's and the White pioneer settlers's romantic, outlandish, extravagant and fascinating life and activities—their accoutrement, cuisine, hunting, trapping, ranching, brigandage, conflicts, etc. James Fenimore Cooper (1789-1851), the author of *Letherstocking Tales, was the first novelist to write Westerns. Some other writers of this genre of fiction (many of whom were cowboys) were: Davy Crockett (1786-1836), A.B. Longstreet (1790-1870), Sol Smith (1801-69), J.M. Field (1810-56), G.W. Harris (1814-69), Francis Bret Harte (1836-1902), Andy Adams (1859-1935) and, of course, Zane Grey (1875-1939). The early writers of Westerns left their influence on Mark Twain (1835-1910) and William Faulkner (1825-79).

Westerners. The term referred to the Russian intellectuals who in the 1840s opposed the ideology of the Czar and the Russian Slavophiles and pleaded for closeness of Russia to the open, liberal and progressive culture of the *West. Some of the 'Westernist' writers were: Ivan Turgenev (1818-1883), Nikolai Ogaryov (1813-77) and Alexander Druzhinin (1824-64).

who-dun-it, whodunit. Both the terms are colloquial and are illiterate abbreviations or forms of 'who did it?' Both refer to a *story of mysterious crime and crime detection. The terms are synonymous with *thriller, *detective novel, detective story and **roman policier*.

wild zone. "A specifically female area of culture, often presented in a utopian or idealized manner for polemical effect" [Hawthorn, 374].

willing suspension of disbelief. The term was coined by S.T. Coleridge (1772-1834) in chapter XIV of his *Biographia Literaria* "to describe that state of receptivity and credulity desirable in a reader or member of an audience (in current jargon, 'the receptor'). The reader must 'grant' that he or she is *about to read a story*; a person in the audience is 'asked' to *accept the dramatic conventions of the theatre and stage*" (emphases added) [Cuddon, 984]. Without the minimum acquiescence to the fictitiousness of a literary work (fictional, dramatic or poetic) nobody can enjoy and appreciate it. Holding in disbelief any literary work, which of necessity is imaginary and therefore full of falsity, will stand in the way of its enjoyment and appreciation, and so disbelief in it must be held in suspension willingly. Also see **als ob*.

writerly text. See **lisible*.

X

Xanaduism. The term is coined from the name of the mysterious, imaginary, transcendental and oneiric place, Xanadu, in S.T. Coleridge's (1772-1834) poem 'Kubla Khan'. It now denotes "A form of academic research which entails the quest for sources behind works of imagination" [Cuddon, 987].

Y

yarn. Specifically, an incredible *story spun out by a sailor, but commonly or generally simply a *tale or *tall story.

yellow-backs. "Cheap editions of novels bound in yellow boards, including the 'railway novels' of the later years of the 19th c" [Cuddon, 988].

Yoknapatawpha. The imaginary Mississippi county which is the setting of many of William Faulkner's (1897-1962) best-known works as the fictional region Wessex was that of all the novels of Thomas Hardy (1840-1928). Also see *Wessex Novels.

Z

zanni, zany [from Italian *zani* or *zanni* which are from Gianni or Giovanni, a name]. Originally and generally the terms denote the proper name of a servant-clown *character of comedy, or any kind of jester. Recently, the terms are also being used occasionally "to describe an idea (or person) which is off-beat, odd, crazily funny" [Cuddon, 990].

zaum [from Russian *zaun*, 'trans-sense']. The term is a short form of Russian *zaummy yazyk* which means "a language [*yazyk*] which would be 'beyond sense'. For example, neologisms, onomatopoeic effects, arbitrary combinations of sounds, a play with the morphological components of ordinary words. It is a notable feature of work produced by Russian Futurist [see *futurism] poets, especially Khlebnikov [Viktor Khlebnikov (1885-1922)] and Kruchenykh" [Cuddon, 990].

Zeitgeist [from German *Zeit*, time, and *Geist*, mind, spirit]. The term literally means 'time spirit' or 'mind or spirit of the time or age', but it refers to the prevailing trend, fashion, taste, mood, attitude of a given time, age, or period. The term was first given currency by the German philosopher G.W.F. Hegel (1770-1831) who argued that one and only one universal *Geist* or Spirit reveals itself through successive higher stages of history. Also see **Giestesgeschichte*.

Zeitroman [from German *Zeit*, time, and *Roman*, novel]. Literally, the term means 'time novel' or 'period novel'. In literary-critical discourse, the term denotes the *novel which describes its author's critical analysis and evaluation of the philosophico-social-spiritual aspects of contemporary period, such as Thomas Mann's (1875-1955) *Der Zauberberg* (*The Magic Mountain*), which diagnoses the sick mind of contemporary civilisation.

Zhdanovshchina [from Zhdanov, the surname of Andrei Zhdanov, the Secretary of the Central Committee of the U.S.S.R. in control of the revolutionary ideology, and Russian *shchina*, time]. Literally, the term means 'the Zhdanov time'. It refers to the time of Andrei Zhdanov who "brought heavy pressure to bear on prominent Soviet writers who were deemed not to be following Party doctrine. Among the most prominent were Anna Akhmatova [1889-1967: poetess], Mikhail Zoshchenko [1895-1958: short story writer and humorous writer] and Boris Pasternak [1890-1960: poet and novelist]. Later, comparable pressures were put on Alexander Solzhenitsyn [b. 1918: novelist], who in 1969 was expelled from the Union of Soviet Writers and in 1974 was deported to West Germany" [Cuddon, 991]. Also see *dissident writers, **degage*, **engage* writer.

BIBLIOGRAPHY

A. DICTIONARIES, GLOSSARIES, ENCYCLOPAEDIAS, COMPANIONS, ETC.

Abrams, M.H., *A Glossary of Literary Terms* (7th edn), 1999, Harcourt Asia PTE Ltd and Harcourt College Publishers, Texas, USA.

Ayto, John, *The Wordsworth Dictionary of Foreign Words in English*, 1995, Wordsworth Reference, Hertfordshire, England.

Baldick, Chris, *The Concise Oxford Dictionary of Literary Terms*, 1996, Oxford University Press, Oxford, New York, Delhi, Calcutta, etc.

Bradbury, Malcolm and Jean Franco (eds), *The Penguin Companion to Literature*, vol. 3 (USA and Latin America), 1971, Penguin Books, England and Australia.

Brown, Calvin S. (ed), *The Reader's Companion to World Literature*, 1964, A Mentor Book, Published by The New American Library of World Literature, United States.

Cuddon, J.A., *The Penguin Dictionary of Literary Terms and Literary Theory*, 1999, Penguin Books, London and New York.

Daiches, David (ed), *The Penguin Companion to Literature*, vol. 1 (Britain and Commonwealth), 1971, Penguin Reference Books, England and Australia.

Davidson, G.W., M.A. Seaton and J. Simpson, *The Wordsworth Concise English Dictionary*, 1995, Wordsworth Reference, Hertfordshire, England.

Dubois, Marguerite-Marie, *et al*, *Larousse's French-English English-French Dictionary* (2 vols in One), 1976, Pocket Books, New York.

Dudley, D.R. and D.M. Lang, *The Penguin Companion to Literature*, vol. 4 (Classical and Byzantine, ed: Dudley; Oriental and African, ed: Lang), 1969, Penguin Books, England and Australia.

Eysenck, H.J., *et al* (eds), *Encyclopedia of Psychology* (2 vols), 1975, Fontana/Collins (copy right with K.G. Herder, 1972, West Germany).

Flew, Antony, *A Dictionary of Philosophy*, 1983, Pan Books, Great Britain.

Fowler, H.W., *A Dictionary of Modern English Usage*, 1996, Wordsworth Reference, Hertfordshire, England.

Fowler, H.W. and F.G. Fowler, *The King's English*, 1993, Wordsworth Reference, England.

Fowler, Roger, *A Dictionary of Modern Critical Terms*, 2001, Routledge & Kegan Paul, London and New York.

Frolov, I. (ed) *Dictionary of Philosophy*, 1984, Progress Publishers, Moscow.

Henry, Sir Paul (ed), *The Oxford Companion to Classical Literature*, 1969, Clarendon Press, Oxford.

Hawthorn, Jeremy, *A Glossary of Contemporary Literary Theory*, 2003, Arnold (of the Hodder Headline Group), New York.

Lass, Abraham H., *et al*, *The Wordsworth Dictionary of Classical and Literary Allusions*, 1987, Wordsworth Reference, England.

Lemon, Lee T., *A Glossary for the Study of English*, 1988, Oxford University Press (Indian 3rd impression), New Delhi.

Macdonald, A.M., *Chambers Twentieth Century Dictionary*, 1981, Allied Publishers, Bombay, Delhi.

McArthur, Tom, *The Oxford Companion to the English Language*, 1992, Oxford University Press, Oxford and New York.

Mobley, Jonnie Patricia, *Dictionary of Theatre and Drama Terms*, 1998, N.T.C. Publishing Group, Illionis, U.S.A. (South Asian edn published by Viva Books, New Delhi, Mumbai, Chennai).

Mottram, Eric, Malcolm Bradbury and Jean Franco (eds), *The Penguin Companion to Literature*, vol. 3 (U.S.A. and Latin America), 1971, Penguin Reference Books, England and Australia.

Nataf, Andre, *The Wordsworth Dictionary of the Occult*, 1994, Wordsworth Reference, England.

Ousby, Ian (ed), *The Wordsworth Companion to Literature in English*, 1994, Wordsworth Reference, Hertfordshire, England.

Petrovsky, A.V. and M.G. Yaroshevsky, *A Concise Psychological Dictionary*, 1987, Progress Publishers, Moscow.

Richards, Jack; John Platt and Heidi Weber, *Longman Dictionary of Applied Linguistics*, 1985, Longman Group Ltd., England.

Rodway, Allan, 'Glossary' in *The Craft of Criticism*, 1984, Cambridge University Press, Cambridge, London, etc.

Runes, Dagobert D. (ed), *The Dictionary of Philosophy*, 1957, Jaico Publishing House, Bombay.

Rycroft, Charles, *A Critical Dictionary of Psychoanalysis*, 1972, Penguin Books, England, U.S.A., Australia, etc.

Sawyers, Robin, *The Wordsworth English-German German-English Dictionary*, 1995, Wordsworth Reference, England.

Scruton, Roger, *A Dictionary of Political Thought*, 1983, Pan Books, London, in association with The Macmillan Press, London.

Seturaman, V.S., 'Glossary' in *Contemporary Criticism*, 1998, Macmillan India Ltd, Chennai.

Skeat, Walter W., *The Concise Dictionary of English Etymology*, 1993, Wordsworth Reference, Hertfordshire, England.

Taylor, John Russell, *The Penguin Dictionary of the Theatre*, 1966, Penguin Books, England and Australia.

Thorlby, Anthony (ed), *The Penguin Companion to Literature*, vol. 2 (Europe), 1969, Penguin Reference Books, England and Australia.

Tylor, E.B., *Dictionary of Anthropology*, 1988 (first Indian edn), Goyalsaab, Delhi-110007.

B. OTHER WORKS

Allott, Miriam (ed), *Novelists on the Novel*, 1962, Routledge and Kegan Paul, London and New York.

Atkinson, J., *et al*, *Dictionary of Psychology*, 1988, Goyalsaab Publishers, New Delhi, by arrangement with Drysdale Publishers, U.S.A.

Baker, Ernest A., *The History of the English Novel* (10 vols), 1957, Barnes & Noble, New York.

Booth, Wayne C., *The Rhetoric of Fiction*, 1983, The University of Chicago Press, Chicago Press, Chicago and London.

Bradbury, Malcolm and McFarlane, James, *Modernism* (1890-1930), 1978, Penguin Books, England, New York, etc.

Cary, M. and Haarhoff, T.J., *Life and Thought in the Greek & Roman World*, 1961, University Paperbacks, Methuen, London, and Barnes & Noble, New York.

Cazamian, L., *A History of French Literature*, 1966, Oxford University Press, Glasgow, New York, Bombay, Dacca, etc.

Cecil, David, *Hardy, the Novelist*, 1997, Kalyani Publishers, Ludhiana, New Delhi, Madras, Calcutta, etc.

Daiches, David, *Critical Approaches to Literature*, 1993, Orient Longman, Hyderabad.

Dudley, D.R. and D.M. Lang (eds), *The Penguin Companion to Literature*, vol. 4 (Classical and Byzantine, and Oriental and African), 1969, Penguin Books, England and Australia.

Ellmann, Richard and Charles Feidelson (eds), *The Modern Tradition* (*Background of Modern Literature*), 1965, Oxford University Press, New York.

Forster, E.M., *Aspects of the Novel*, 1966, Penguin Books, England and Australia.

Friedman, Alan, *The Turn of the Novel*, 1970, Oxford University Press, London, Oxford and New York.

Frye, Northrop, *Anatomy of Criticism*, 1973, Princeton University Press, Princeton, New Jersey, U.S.A.

Hockett, Charles F., *A Course in Modern Linguistics*, 1970, Oxford & IBH (by arrangement with Macmillan Company), New Delhi, Calcutta and Bombay.

Kettle, Arnold, *An Introduction to the English Novel*, vol. 1, reprint 1993, Universal Book Stall, New Delhi (by arrangement with Unwin Hyman, London).

——, *An Introduction to the English Novel*, vol. 2, reprint 1999, Universal Book Stall, New Delhi (by arrangement with Unwin Hyman, London).

Koch, Stephen, *A Guide to the Craft of Fiction*, 2003, The Modern Library, New York.

Kumar, Shiv K. and McKean, Keith, *Critical Approaches to Fiction*, 2003, Atlantic Publishers and Distributors, New Delhi.

Lefebure, Molly, *Samuel Taylor Coleridge: A Bondage of Opium*, 1977, Quartet Books, London.

Long William J., *English Literature : Its History and Its Significance* ,1989, Kalyani Publishers (with permission of Ginn and Company, Boston), New Dellhi and Ludhiana.

Lubbock, Percy, *The Craft of Fiction*, 1993, B.I. Publications, Bombay, Calcutta, Delhi, etc.

Maugham, Somerset, *Ten Novels and Their Authors*, 1954, William Heinemann, Melbourne, London and Toronto.

Mottram, Eric and Malcolm Bradbury (eds for U.S.A.) and Jean France (ed for Latin America), *The Penguin Companion to Literature*,vol. 3,1971, Penguin Books, England, U.S.A., etc.

Muir, Edwin, *The Structure of the Novel*, 1957, The Hogarth Press, London.

Neill, S. Diana, *A Short History of the English Novel*, 2002, Kalyani Publishers, Ludhiana and New Delhi.

Nicholls, Peter, *Modernisms*, 1995, Macmillan, London.

Norris, Christopher, *Derrida*,1987, Fontana Press, London.

Powell, Jim, *Derrida for Beginners*,2000, Orient Longman, Hyderabad.

——, *Postmodernism for Beginners*, 2006, Orient Longman, Hyderabad.

Raduga Publishers, *History of Russian Literature: 11-17 Centuries*, 1989, Moscow.

Read, Herbert, *Art and Society*, MCMXXXVI, Faber and Faber, London.

——, *The Meaning of Art*, 1984, Faber and Faber, London and Boston.

Rice, Philip and Patricia Waugh (eds), *Modern Literary Theory*, 2001, Hodder Arnold, New York.

Rose, H.J., *A Handbook of Greek Literature*, 1964, University Paperbacks, Methuen, London.

Russell, Stella Pandell, *Art in the World*, 1975, Rinehart Press, San Francisco.

Sarker, Sunil Kumar, *A Companion to E.M. Forster* (3 vols.), 2007, Atlantic Publishers and Distributors, New Delhi.

Scholes, Robert, *Elements of Fiction,* 1968, Oxford University Press, London and Toronto.

Simons, Jon, *Contemporary Critical Theorists: From Lacan to Said*, 2005, Atlantic Publishers and Distributors (in association with Edinburg University Press, U.K.), New Delhi.

Vassily, Novokov, *Artistic Truth and Dialectics of Creative Work* (*trans.* Evgeni Filippov),1981, Progress Publishers, Moscow.

Wilson, Colin, *Mysteries*, 1979, Grafton Books (a Division of Harper Collins Publishers), London.